D0889687

HIGH-FLYING

ADVENTURES

IN THE

STOCK

MARKET

HIGH-FLYING
ADVENTURES
IN THE
STOCK
MARKET

MOLLY BAKER

JOHN WILEY & SONS, INC.

New York • Chichester • Weinheim • Brisbane • Singapore • Toronto

Published by John Wiley & Sons, Inc.
Published simultaneously in Canada.

This publication is designed to provide accurate and authoritative information in regard to the subject matter covered. It is sold with the understanding that the publisher is not engaged in rendering professional services. If professional advice or other expert assistance is required, the services of a competent professional person should be sought.

Band-Aid is a registered trademark of Johnson & Johnson.

Library of Congress Cataloging-in-Publication Data:

ISBN 0-471-35936-X

Printed in the United States of America.

10 9 8 7 6 5 4 3 2 1

For Slim, of course.

PREFACE

Before I knew any investment professionals, I was familiar with only a few facts regarding the species. They wear suits, they carry briefcases, they attend conferences, and they bring research reports home to read before they go to sleep at night.

Since I have met and worked with investment professionals over the past seven years, I know much more. They are bright, they are funny, and they often have poor diets and difficulty sleeping. And they have a passion for what they do. They love looking at companies, watching the stock market, and talking about what makes it all go round.

It was just this passion that made me want to observe and write about investment professionals and their world. Jerry Frey and his team at Delaware Investments allowed me to do just that. For over a year, I followed the team and the progress of the mutual funds they run, particularly the Delaware Aggressive Growth Fund, which has subsequently been renamed the Delaware Select Growth Fund. This book is the result of that immersion. My goal was to give the reading and investing public a flavor for what their dollars in the stock market and mutual funds do all day. I discovered that managing a mutual fund, leading a team of intelligent and idiosyncratic people, and operating in the U.S. stock market is exciting, challenging, and rewarding. Any failure of these pages to render those emotions and that reality is entirely my responsibility.

This book is a work of nonfiction. All of the characters and events described are real. All meetings detailed are those during which I was present and taking notes; the participants knew that I was not an investment professional, but a writer doing research.

Phone conversations consist of the half I listened to and the details that were told to me later by either or both parties. I have included some conversations in which all parties related the details, and their own words, to me. Although the cooperation of Delaware was essential to my research, neither the firm nor the Aggressive Growth team has endorsed this telling of their story.

Names have been changed in five instances where someone receives a mere mention by the book's main characters. "Mike Garrison," "Paul Sutton," "Dave Adams," "Peter Allmen," and the company "Quick Zone" are pseudonyms. I have changed no other names. If I had, I would've been more creative than to have a Stew and a Stu, a John and a Jon, and a Geri and a Jerry.

MOLLY BAKER

Malvern, Pennsylvania
March 2000

ACKNOWLEDGMENTS

This book could not have been possible without the cooperation of several key individuals on the Delaware Growth team. I would especially like to thank Jerry Frey, who (although he may have regretted doing so at various times), when asked if a former *Wall Street Journal* reporter could follow him around for a year, replied, "Where would you like to sit?" The team was giving of their time and patience, and to them my thanks: Marshall Bassett, Jeff Hynoski, Steve Lampe, Lori Wachs, Geri Grzegorski, Leandra Bowie, Stuart George, and Vincent Brancaccio. Several other people at Delaware assisted me in my research of the funds and the market in general: Dinah Huntoon, Gretchen Ebert, Helen Merichko, and Linda Finnerty, former head of Delaware's media relations. Wayne Stork and Dick Unruh were also instrumental in allowing me to spend a year at Delaware Investments.

Several research sources were helpful in tracking down facts, numbers, and historical information on stocks and mutual funds: Zacks Investment Service, The Investment Company Institute, Lipper Inc., Morningstar Inc., Securities Data Corporation, and *The Wall Street Journal.*

When it came time to transform my months, notebooks, and files of research into a book, four people were incomparable in the suggestions and encouragement they offered. My thanks to them: Elisheva Urbas; Philip Gerard; my editor, Pamela van Giessen; and my agent, Sloan Harris. The entire crew at John Wiley & Sons was enthusiastic and helpful throughout the bookmaking process.

Editors' suggestions helped me get from chapter to chapter and draft to draft, but friends and family got me from page to page. Ann

Baker, Anne Sclater, Shoshana and Len Feiner, and Peter Brodsky all gave freely of their time and opinions when faced with a final draft. Special thanks to Elizabeth and Linda Dieveney, who were attentive readers as well as sources of support and dinner during the final stages. Elizabeth Leik, Karin Round, Laura Wexler, and Lois Baron were a constant and much-needed well of encouragement and procrastination.

A final thanks goes to my family for always being supportive and not touching my piles.

M. B.

CONTENTS

HIGH-FLYING

FLYING

ADVENTURES

IN THE

STOCK

MARKET

PROLOGUE

SCALING
MOUNTAINS

Jerry Frey settles down into the high-backed black upholstered seat near the center of the theater. The domed movie screen, rising four-and-a-half stories from the floodlights at the base of the theater, washes over his head and surrounds the seating area on both sides. The crowd is encased in a whiteness of possibility. They face the possibility of being thrilled or frightened, and certainly the promise of being entertained. For the mere forty-four minutes of the film, they will be transported to another world, another experience, and another reality.

Tonight, the crowd is here to see the much-anticipated movie *Everest*. There'd been buzz about the movie ever since the team of climbers and a film crew ventured to Nepal in 1996 to attempt to scale the indomitable peak. While the crew was on the mountain, climbing teams ahead of them were nearing the summit of the so-called "roof of the world" just as fierce storms were settling in below. As the climbers trudged on, slowly and ever closer to the goal that had eluded so many, they were unaware of the tragedy the gathering storm clouds would bring. The determined struggled on, pulled toward their goal by so much inner physical and mental strength, only to be trapped in the success of their achievement by uncontrollable outside forces. But that was the nature of mountain climbing—especially at the sport's highest altitudes.

While many who set out to scale Everest that day didn't make it to the top, eight climbers who attempted the feat didn't make it to the bottom. At least four of those eight had reached the peak, stood

1

there briefly, and surveyed their accomplishment from the roof of the world. They had reached the summit. And now, they had to get down. As with so many climbs, the descent is often most treacherous, most fraught with dangers. The body has been pushed to its limit, the mind has slowed, and the thin air takes its toll. All of the focus is directed toward reaching the top, while mere survival gets little attention. The question is, "Will I make it to the top?" not, "Will I make it to the bottom?" The tragic Everest climb had been the subject of several books, a made-for-TV movie, and, now, this larger-than-life Imax rendition of the ascent.

Many in the crowd settling in to watch the drama knew what the risks of those dizzying heights felt like. While they weren't mountain climbers themselves, they were adventurers of another sort. They had all surely spent hours, if not days, wondering whether they should continue to climb higher. They had wondered, "Should I take the risk of slipping, losing any ground for just a few extra steps?" Every step brought them closer to the top. But the higher they climbed, the trickier those steps were. The air thinned; it was difficult to see, and harder to think straight. But, ahead, there were always the flags others had planted—inviting them, challenging them to take those extra steps, to risk it. Those victory flags waving in the wind always look so many steps closer than they really are. The silence of their flapping is like the inverse of a car's rear-view-mirror warning: objects viewed ahead are *further* away than they appear. Or, simply, this is not as easy as it looks. But others had made it. It would be so nice to stand victorious and plant *your* flag at the top, to see your own colors flapping in the wind, for all to see and admire. If others had done it, why not me? Or, should they be satisfied with the accomplishment of the moment? Should they be pleased with the opportunity to simply be on the mountain and have the chance to compete, with no realistic sights set on reaching the top?

Goldman Sachs, perhaps the most prestigious firm on Wall Street, had invited the group to watch the Imax movie with their families. The seats were filled with some of the firm's most treasured clients: money managers. The nearly 150 men and women who had brought wives, husbands, friends, and a few children, were the

individuals who controlled many of the dollars invested in Philadel-
phia-area mutual funds and pension funds. The crowds that now
nestled in upholstered seats and would later laugh and mingle
among blue-raspberry water ice and puff pastries were some of the
area's top decision makers on what to do with more than $400 bil-
lion. It was a healthy slice of the $12 trillion pie of assets in U.S. in-
vestment companies. And they were the men and women who said
buy it, sell it, save it, spend it. They controlled the wallets for some
of the biggest investment companies in the nation, and, at $400 bil-
lion, those were pretty big wallets.

Jerry Frey watched over just about $2.5 billion that coursed in
and out of Philadelphia—across trading desks, over phone lines,
through wire transfers, and by way of mutual fund purchases and
sales. Jerry's was not the largest mutual fund in the area, nor was he
a dominating personality like so many who capture the mutual fund
and stock market spotlight. But Jerry's performance, his stock market savvy, and his decisive buying power had definitely made him
one of a handful of "go-to" guys in Philadelphia. When investment
bankers and salespeople made their roadshow stops and touted the
new, young, and aggressive companies across the country that were
looking for investors, Jerry's name was always on the Philadelphia
"must-see" list. If Jerry showed no interest in meeting with the company and its executives, the salespeople would often call, pleading
for a meeting. If they didn't get the company in front of Jerry, the
executives might wonder about the quality of the investment bank
or the salesperson.

Especially this summer. The performance of Jerry's aggressive
growth mutual fund made him not only the number-one growth
guy in Philadelphia; it made him the reigning number-one growth
guy in the country for the past twelve months. It was not a good sign
for a growth company if he had no interest in seeing its roadshow. As
of midyear, Jerry's fund was up over 20 percent—twice as much as
most financial planners tell investors to expect for an entire year.
And it was only July. The numbers had caught the eye of *Barron's*,
which, earlier in the year, had run a full-page article on the fund,
and personal finance publications like *Mutual Funds* magazine had

begun to swoon over his performance. Jerry ignores the publicity and refuses interviews as a matter of course. He knows that being number one halfway through the year means nothing. It's a little like having to tell people that no, you didn't make it to the top of Everest, but you made it halfway—and the view from there is really beautiful. It's difficult to be satisfied with almosts and best efforts in a game where someone will win, in a climb where someone will have a better view.

Secretly, Jerry wondered to himself if this could be his year.

He had had some great years in his nearly twenty on Wall Street. There was 1987, when he was up almost 100 percent heading into October. But then came the Crash, and he lost every penny of those profits and then some. In 1995, he was up more than 70 percent while the overall market gained 37 percent. He felt he had one standout year left in him somewhere. He knew his career numbers were admirable, but he felt he had the talent and luck to post one knockout season for the record books. He was like a star athlete trying to predict the peak, wanting to savor the high point before starting the slide down into pulled muscles and "remember whens." Sometimes, on his drive into work or on his noontime walk to the train station for a slice of pizza, he would wonder if 1998 might be the year. It was one of those things he never talked about with anyone he worked with or anyone who might call him on it later. But, on his best days and in his finest summer moods, he would give in to himself just a little and think, "Yep, this could be it."

Jerry needed a year to be "it." He was fifty-two years old and in charge of an investment team. His name was on top of three mutual funds for the first time in his career. Wall Street certainly doesn't have a retirement age, and old back or shoulder injuries don't hinder investment performance, but most top mutual fund managers don't do it forever. Just as so many actors dream of directing when they've "made it," money managers hope to "open their own shops." They call them "shops," as though they were casual places that sold paper doilies along with screwdrivers and chicken salad. But really, they hope to log in some great performance numbers that can help them raise a few hundred million dollars, which they will manage from some ranch in Jackson Hole, Wyoming, or a mountain cottage in Pennsylvania, and collect a few million dollars every year as their fee and take 20 percent of the profits. Whether Jerry actually does it or not, he needs to know that he's good enough that he could if he wanted to. He needs to know that he'd strategized, done his research, followed his gut, and, at the end of the year, been declared the winner; that he'd made it to the top and could plant a flag for all to see waving in the wind.

In climbing, there's a window of opportunity. You've got to time your ascent between the monsoon season and the winter snowstorms. The winds need to be just right, and the final assault on the peak must begin in the middle of the night, in order to leave enough daylight hours for a successful descent. You've got to understand how and when to use the right equipment, when to spend the time to take extra precautions, and when to forge ahead toward the top. You often need to wait for the right permissions from governments, and in some cases you spin the prayer wheel and hope for a celestial okay.

The stock market is no different. There are seasons and cycles, booms and busts. To reach the top, you need to be positioned in the right industries and the right companies at just the right time. You've got to be ready to ride them on their ascent and be out before their descent. An investor needs to understand how and when to use some protection—when to be cautious and when to go for it. The economy needs to be rolling, and you often need a little help from the government to keep interest rates and inflation in check. And, of course, it doesn't hurt if you give a prayer wheel a spin and get that celestial nod.

For the past few years, Jerry's been on a streak—along with the stock market. But how long would things hold out? How many more years would the stock market keep climbing and helping him achieve chart-topping returns? And if he reached the top, how long would the circle of investors he knows have millions to pledge to him before being replaced by a circle of new, younger investors he hasn't met?

When he thinks honestly about his goals and the invisible calendar that passing time continues to blow pages from, he figures that he has about two or three years to make it happen. If it happens, he can live the Wall Street dream—start his own firm, make some *real* money, and be responsible for building something; essentially, be elected to a de facto investment hall of fame. He has spent his entire life competing, measuring himself against others with a silent confidence. That public nod is all he has ever wanted.

He'd been this close once before. As a high school football player, Jerry was said to have had one of the most accomplished sophomore season in the history of his school—itself a football powerhouse in the gridiron haven of rural Pennsylvania. He was following in his older brother's footsteps, but was quickly expected to outpace his brother's successful cleats. Jerry's and the team's playing would attract recruiters from Notre Dame and Dartmouth, and he would even enroll in the University of Alabama with plans to play football for the Crimson Tide. He was small for the sport, but Jerry was tenacious, aggressive, and competitive. In his junior year, the team and the town of 2,200 fans had their sights set on an undefeated season and were hoping Jerry would help lead them there. In an early-season scrimmage, Jerry was hit after a play and went down hard. The coaches pulled him off the field and the game went on without him. But Jerry wasn't giving up. At sixteen, he'd found what he was good at. It was something that made everyone around him happy. It made everyone who watched say, "Wow, look at Jerry Frey." Being good at football was the thing he was most passionate about as a teenager. Being good at football meant winning. And you couldn't win if you weren't playing. While the coaches weren't watching, Jerry ran out onto the field and sent his replacement back to the sidelines. Jerry Frey was no sideline player. This was his sport, this was his year, this was his chance. On the very next play, he was hit again. This hit incapacitated him for much of the next two seasons and brought an end to his dreams of football glory. At sixteen, in a small American town in the 1960s, the cheers and hopes and dreams could be intoxicating. At fifty-two, in the world of the American stock market in the 1990s, the cheers and hopes and dreams beckoned again.

After the crowd makes it up the aisles and into the rows of seats in the theater, a strawberry-blond man in a blue and white seersucker suit stands up to address them. With a young woman in a black pantsuit, a banking colleague, he is co-host of the evening. He has his sleepy two-year-old son perched on his hip, as if to say that investment banking is for families—or at least Goldman Sachs is the family-friendly investment bank. He is the firm's salesman assigned to cover clients in the Philadelphia area, so he starts his welcome off with a sales pitch. He lets the crowd know that, along with creating the movie they will soon view, Imax, the company, is a worthy stock—research analysts at Goldman Sachs had declared it so—and it had closed right around $12 on the Nasdaq Stock Market that afternoon.

Like a speech that opens with a joke, this bit of information immediately puts the crowd at ease. Some even take it as a joke, and laughter courses through a few rows of the theater. The crowd had mingled a bit in the foyer of the museum during the buffet of crab cakes, fettuccine, and cheesesteak sandwiches, but most guests stuck with the families or colleagues with whom they had come. Social skills are not necessarily high on the list of traits required of successful money managers. Instead, the profession demands proficiency in eighth-grade math; basic understanding of business; a dogged patience in front of a computer screen of numbers, charts, and reports; and an untiring ear for a sales pitch. Ah, and now this salesman was giving them exactly what they needed to relax. They are perfectly at ease listening to his pitch for shares of Imax stock, the Goldman Sachs research expertise, and the firm's trading desk. Listening, most often, is a passive act. But these men and women know that listening to a sales pitch—whether over the phone, across a conference table, or in front of a four-and-a-half-story movie screen—puts them in charge. It is the money manager who makes the decision. "Yes, I'll take it . . . buy me everything you've got . . . I want 10,000 shares . . . I have to own it . . . I'm putting the order in right now . . . I want every share known to man." But, just as often, the answer is, "I'll pass . . . No thanks . . . Don't you have anything better to do? . . . You're actually trying to sell that piece of dogshit company? . . . Don't ever try selling me that thing again."

So, as good salespeople do, the Goldman Sachs host lets those in the crowd at least *feel* like they are in control. They can decide to climb a little higher and buy, they can decide to be less aggressive and sell, or they can bide their time and hold. Should they go for the extra ten points here, or sell a stock off a dollar or two there, before it goes down further? They all eye the same goal—to beat the market and be the top performers at the end of the year. At times, it's easy to think the outcome is something they can control—to believe that they can maneuver in and out of stocks ahead of the market, outsmart the competition, or predict the sure things. But, like the mountain, the market has outside forces. Sometimes they are forces as powerful, anonymous, and unwieldy as global economics, war, or political impeachment; at other times, a mere missed number, a phone call gone awry, or a misleading report in a newspaper brings investors down. They are all forces that can swell and heave and torture. Often, the punishment is delivered indiscriminately. At other times, it seems that it is handed out to those who strive to go too high or who appear to be greedy.

As the lights dim, a woman's voice comes over the sound system and introduces the spectators to the theater and its monstrous specifications for sound and sight. She notes where the exits are, but forewarns the audience, "Just keep in mind that once you leave, the doors will lock behind you and you will not be able to return." There are no second chances in this show. Her voice rises as she nears the end of the introduction, "Finally, the images you are about to see on the dome are very large and very realistic. Should you experience any dizziness or motion sickness, simply close your eyes and the feeling should pass." This show is not for the weak. Really, you either have it or you don't. You can make it to the top, or learn to enjoy the scenery from the bottom.

A few in the crowd look around at each other and smile, as if to say, "You don't know who you're dealing with." They have set their sights on the peak, and they are primed.

Her voice continues as the theater goes black. "Now you are prepared for an experience like no other as we proudly present our feature presentation."

The next day, the stock market drops nearly 200 points.

CHAPTER 1

DON'T YOU
JUST LOVE IT?

Just before 8:30, Jerry Frey walks into his office building and heads toward the Au Bon Pain bakery in a corner of the foyer. He is one of hundreds of professionals who walk through the lobby's heavy glass doors every morning. At a little under six feet tall, with neatly trimmed brown hair, and clad in a navy suit, Jerry does not exactly stand out in a major metropolitan corporate tower. Like thousands of other office plazas across the country, this is a building of anonymous dark suits, law and accounting firm doors littered with a mosaic of surnames, and the requisite coffee-and-bagel franchise.

Jerry walks alongside the elevator bank that services floors ten through sixteen. To his left stands a sixteen-foot-high copper-coated disk, pieced with hundreds of small hexagons that make the circle look like a monochromatic jigsaw puzzle. The disk, the stack of bronze books hanging on the wall above it, and the charred-wood globe next to it are half of a sculpture that graces the lobby at One Commerce Square, the tower Jerry has worked in since moving to Philadelphia two years ago. The other half of the sculpture backs up against the elevator bank to floors two through nine. There, suspended from the ceiling, is a green hoop of oxidized copper. The green ring matches the disk in size and color, and if placed on top of one another, the disk would fill the blank space in the ring, and the two would form a complete and solid circle. Separated, as they are, the pieces form "The Diaxiom," which, according to its creators, represents the known and the unknown. The tangible and the intangible. Light and dark. Knowledge and ignorance.

Every day, Jerry enters the building by way of the known, passing the puzzle pieces that are in place and interlocked to form a circle. He stands between the two halves of the sculpture while he waits for the elevator that will carry him to his office. The known is to his right, the unknown is to his left, and the stock market is waiting to open on his computer screen nearly forty stories above. At the end of the day, Jerry leaves his building by way of the north side, passing the empty green ring. He finishes every day with the certainty of the unknown following him. It is a fitting, if not entirely obvious, reminder to a professional investor in the stock market: at the end of the day, there is often more that is unknown than known. To Jerry, the suspended ring issues a silent taunt or challenge every day, as if to say, "Let's see if you can jump through this hoop."

On this morning, and nearly every weekday morning, the known for Jerry is that he will order a cup of coffee, a small fresh-squeezed orange juice, and a corn muffin. Or, if the weekend's run-to-the-end-of-the-driveway race with his nine-year-old son had a closer-than-usual finish, he will order a blueberry muffin. "I figure it's better for me," he says. He stands quietly in line behind other businessmen, maintenance men already taking their first break, and women wearing tennis shoes and toting their pumps in plastic grocery-store bags. One would never guess that he is a man who, after eating his muffin and drinking his coffee and juice, will oversee more than $2 billion of stock market investments.

He stands in line, wearing an off-the-rack suit and a tie and shoes his wife bought for him. They are all high quality and attractive, but they do not ostentatiously announce power or wealth. His beeper, cellular phone, and calculator are all zipped inside his black canvas briefcase, and he is minus a *Wall Street Journal* tucked under his arm—the telltale sign of investors or those with an interest in their investments. But if you happened to be standing behind him on the random weekday morning when he says to one of the food servers staring blankly back at him, "You raised your prices, didn't you?"—well, then you would know that Jerry is a man who takes note of a twelve- or fourteen-penny change in the economy. And it would not surprise you that he manages over $2 billion and moves millions of that lode around every day. On his way to the elevator, Jerry catches one last glimpse of the copper disk, the known. He will leave the known behind and ride the thirty-nine floors to his office, his spreadsheets, his research, his telephone, and his computer screen—all reminding him of what is unknown.

On this July day, there is so much that is unknown.

The year is half over, and yet Jerry is no closer to knowing how 1998 will end for him than he was on the first day of January. Every January, with just a turn of the calendar page, the financial race begins anew. In some sense, all mutual funds and even many companies get to start over on January 1. Mutual fund managers, stock analysts, and company executives spend twelve months working toward one number: year-end performance. "Where did you end up on December 31?" You would never ask a manager, "Where did you end down?" Someone who ends down doesn't need someone else pointing it out. Asking might even jinx your own market performance in the next year. Besides, it's just plain rude.

At the start of January, everyone's year-to-date performance is exactly the same. Zero percent. That's how much you've made for your shareholders that year. And that's exactly how much the stock market is up or down for the year. Zero percent. Everyone is standing at the bottom of the mountain together. Anything is possible, nothing is predictable.

It is possible that all of the stocks Jerry owns will go up; that he will find the next Microsoft, the next Home Depot, and the next McDonald's before anyone else does; and that he will have the best performance of any mutual fund at the end of the year. Unfortunately, it is also possible that many of Jerry's stocks will go down and that he will misjudge the opportunity to buy into what everyone will later anoint as the next Dell Computer. It is possible that he will end up somewhere in the middle of the pack of the more than 7,000 mutual funds offered in 1998.

Sitting off to the side on Jerry's L-shaped desk is a forest-green canvas portfolio, zippered shut. In it, he keeps a collection of papers he deems important: his performance record at his previous job, the compensation agreement he worked out for himself and the people working under him, and a list of his annual accomplishments and goals. The three-sheet memo to the chairman of the company, describing Jerry's progress and his outlook for the new year, is his own sort of report card on what he has done and what remains to be done. It is simple, straightforward, and slightly modest. Like Jerry.

Looking ahead to 1998, he listed his top goals for the new year: "Finish building a quality investment shop . . ." and "Continue to build on the investment performance and marketing skills necessary to sell."

So it would be a year of building. A year of creating something that would last. There was no mention of money, assets, or even cash in Jerry's goals. He simply wanted to help build. Build a reliable and talented team that would help him manage the funds; build strong portfolios of consistent, high-quality stocks; and ultimately, build wealth for his shareholders and employees by doing his job well.

These are terms with which Jerry is most comfortable. Words that deal with building. Words like *concrete, I-beams, steel struts,* and *ISO drawings.* Before embarking on a career as a Wall Street professional, Jerry helped build things. He worked for engineering firms and contracting firms and on construction crews. He can talk at length on the properties of various cement mixes and the difficulties in working with the compounds. One of his first summer jobs as a teenager was mixing mortar for the stone mason who lived across the street from his house. And, at his last job before moving to New York and the world of investments, he helped to oversee the building of a new 100,000-square-foot warehouse at a Procter & Gamble diaper and tissue plant.

And now, on a warm July morning in Philadelphia, Jerry is again thinking about building. He is busy structuring, rebalancing, and rethinking his portfolios. Jerry is strategizing about the precise mix of technology, health care, and retail stocks to hold in his mutual funds. Should he buy more restaurant stocks and sell computers? Pull back in financial services and load up on the Internet? Every day, with nearly every trade, he weighs his options and his choices, trying to find just the right mix. And, like the mixing of cement to build a foundation, every decision Jerry makes will affect future decisions. Certain choices will open more doors in the future; others will rule out particular options. With every move he makes, Jerry has to consider that future and what might be behind those closed doors and available options. He cannot see into the future, but he must try.

When Jerry contemplates the future, he is not seeing his retirement years or his three children going off to college. The future is more immediate.

The end of the year. December 31.

Jerry and a team of five stock analysts who work with him run three mutual funds for Delaware Investments. They shuffle stocks in and out of the Trend Fund, the DelCap Fund, and the Aggressive Growth Fund. The funds invest in some of the fastest growing, highest flying companies in the economy; thus, they are aptly dubbed the firm's "growth group." Most simply, the Trend Fund invests in small companies with hopes of growing bigger; the DelCap Fund invests in medium-size companies poised to grow bigger; and the Aggressive Growth Fund invests in companies of any size that are focused on growing. And growing very aggressively. These are usually the newest companies to enter corporate America. They offer the nimblest technologies or approaches to products and problems. They are also the companies that move the most and the quickest in the stock market—in both directions. Aggressive growth stocks and mutual funds are often those that can disappoint and please more swiftly than any others.

On the conference table in his office, a stack of papers had greeted Jerry when he came back from his Fourth of July holiday. On top of the stack was a single page with a bold heading in black ink: "Dateline Delaware. July 1, 1998." Under the headline was a photocopied cutout of a chart in *The Wall Street Journal*. The text above the chart read: "The Delaware Aggressive Growth Fund continues to hold first place in Lipper rankings with 60.62 percent total return for the 52-week period ending June 25." Of all 860 mutual funds that invest in growth stocks, Delaware's fund was number one over the past twelve months. Of all the men and women who do what Jerry and his team do, they had done it the very best. For twelve months running. Jerry hardly glanced at the chart.

It was the kind of inner-office rah-rah memo that marketing or public relations or corporate communications sent around when the firm was mentioned positively somewhere. To the professionals in these cheerleading departments, it was a sort of corporate pat on the back. To Jerry, it was an affront and a challenge. It meant that the other people at the firm hadn't been aware of his performance until *The Wall Street Journal* pointed it out. But more importantly, it reinforced his knowledge that this was not a business that got by on pats on the back in July. It was a business of "What have you done for me lately?" Late December, in particular.

On every piece of fund advertising and promotional material, Delaware, like every other investment firm, was required to print: "Past performance is no guarantee of future results." It was the industry's reminder to shareholders that great numbers in the past had no bearing on success in the future. This summer, Jerry needed no reminder.

It was a season of record-breaking temperatures across the country. Houston companies were declaring a dress-down summer to deal with the 100-plus degree days. New York City's hospital emergency rooms were filling up with heatstroke victims, and Philadelphia, where Jerry worked in an air-conditioned office on the thirty-ninth floor, had issued an extreme heat warning.

And it was no different in the stock market. The Dow was up, the S&P was up, and the Nasdaq was up. These indicators led people to make such pronouncements as "The market's on fire," "The bull marches on," and "Stocks are only going up." The statements are often made with more conviction than belies the shaky understanding behind them. When people—from professional investors to the media to the general public—speak about "the market," they are most often referring to one of the major indexes: the Dow Jones Industrial Average, the Standard & Poor's 500 Index, or the Nasdaq Composite Index.

At its simplest, the Dow, the longest standing "market" substitute, is a daily average of the prices of thirty stocks. The biggies. The strong and steady. The captains of corporate America across all industries. Names like Exxon, Coca-Cola, Boeing, McDonald's, General Electric, and Procter & Gamble. They are companies that have grown, adapted, and endured. With only thirty companies, the Dow is the most elite and exclusive of all the indexes used to stand for "the market." It is the revered Senate of the American stock market. The Dow stocks have the most pull—up or down—to affect the market.

The S&P 500, an average of 500 stocks, acts more like the House of Representatives—a little broader constituency, with more room for days or weeks of ups and downs to average out. The 500 stocks that make up the index are some of the largest and most successful companies in the country, and they are chosen for their strength to endure and their depth to represent the American economy—or at least the American stock market. The thinking goes that 500 strong companies, watched as one basket, should be a reasonable indication of the health of U.S. companies overall. These are the companies that are elected to stand in front of the markets and let investors and economists know how the rest of corporate America is doing. If the S&P 500 struggles, a tough battle must be going on out there on the assembly lines and in office-park cubicles. If the S&P 500 climbs, things are right with the world. Americans are earning it and spending it.

The Nasdaq is the most recent addition to the list of must-follow indexes of the stock market. The index is made up of all of the stocks that trade on the Nasdaq Stock Market, a trading market that companies can choose as an alternative to the New York Stock Exchange. The Nasdaq Stock Market has come to be known as the market for technology companies, so, despite the index's roster of over 5,000 stocks, it tends to move in the direction of tech companies.

During the summer of 1998, the three indexes were setting records—seemingly daily. The Dow was up 15 percent, the S&P 500 was up 19 percent, and the Nasdaq had gained 22 percent for the year—and it was only the start of July. It seemed the bull market had been raging for over a decade—since the Crash of 1987—and the past three years had been host to annual gains of more than 20 percent in all three indexes. The long accepted and admired investment goal of a 10 percent return per year was tossed out the window, along with such concepts as value investing, buy and hold, and understanding a company's business. Investors had gotten used to getting more out of the market, and now they were demanding it. And the challenge to Jerry's team, and every other mutual fund out there, was to try to be the ones who could meet those demands.

After his morning ritual of muffin and coffee, sports pages and silence, Jerry retreats to his desk to get his bearings on his stocks and their place in the world before the market opens at 9:30. Until trading begins, the numbers and letters that fill the computer screen sit immobile. The first column is filled with ticker symbols, the three- and four-letter shortcuts by which stocks are identified. These are followed by columns that show the latest price and whether, on that most recent trade, someone paid more or less for the stock. This pattern is repeated three times across and dozens of rows down, fitting hundreds of stocks and billions of dollars on the screen's 17-inch span. At 9:00 in the morning, the screen looks like an average spreadsheet, or any other computer-created data sheet waiting for someone to act upon it.

When the stock market's opening bell rings at 9:30, the screen jumps to life. The ceremonial opening happens when some executive from the New York Stock Exchange, or some celebrity, or a chairman of a new company going public that day, rings a brass bell, like a schoolteacher, from the balcony above the stock exchange floor. But, given the activity that explodes on Jerry's computer screen, it would be more apt if a gun was fired into the air from the balcony instead. Thousands of investors and traders have been pent up at the gates since early morning; their hooves are stomping and they want to get running. Immediately, the ticker symbols begin flashing red, green, and white, indicating if the most recent trade was up, down, or even, and the numbers alongside them jump up and jump down as fast as Jerry's eyes can scan from column to column. Jerry has been staring at letters and numbers just like these every working day for nearly twenty years.

In his office, Jerry takes a bottle of aspirin out of his desk drawer and shakes one tablet into his hand. "Only two things have been clinically proven to be good for your heart: regular exercise and taking an aspirin every day." Jerry often repeats this advice to himself with the same tone of authority as a proclamation from the Surgeon General. Of course, in addition to keeping the blood flowing smoothly into the atria and out the ventricles, that single white aspirin tablet can help prevent any headaches the stock market might serve up throughout the day. With the pill in his mouth, he gulps down the nine ounces of fresh-squeezed orange juice in one long draught. He snaps the plastic lid back on the cup and drops it into the nearest of his four trashbins. It is just the first deposit of the day. When the stock market closes, the bins will be bulging with the day's debris.

Every day, Lea, one of the assistants to the growth group, opens and sorts the incoming mail into six piles, one for each member. Many days, Jerry's stack measures as high as two feet. Often, it is divided into two piles, or bound with rubber bands, to keep from toppling and littering his desk.

Most of the mail is research reports from Wall Street analysts who cover companies and industries, write out their opinions and predictions, and send them to Jerry and thousands of other investors across the country. There are also magazines and invitations to conferences and upcoming meetings with analysts, strategists, or company executives. In addition to the mail, there are the faxes. They add several more vertical inches of reading material to Jerry's stack. It seems the group's fax machine is rarely silent; new research, new numbers, and new ideas pour in from all over the country. The group goes through 600 reams of paper—3,300 pounds a year—for faxes alone. Jerry's mail for the year, if stacked, would rise fifty stories— eleven floors higher than the entire distance from the tower's plaza fountain to Jerry's office on the thirty-ninth floor.

Jerry gets around to looking at his mail every two or three days. Even then, he does little more than glance at each piece. He lines up two or three trash bins behind his desk and stands above them holding a stack of mail. Sometimes he lets the stack rest in his arm while he peels each piece off and drops it into the bin; the rare exceptions flutter into a small pile on the floor. More often, Jerry uses his thumb to fan through an entire stack, treating several inches (and several weeks or months of someone else's work) as one piece of mail. After only thumbing through the stack once or twice, he lets the pile drop with a thud into one of the bins. He doesn't believe in keeping or filing reports, and he maintains that if something is known long enough to be written on a piece of paper—especially paper that was likely printed at least a week ago—that information is already in the stock price. Don't take up space on my desk, don't clutter my mind, and don't waste my time.

Mail and faxes are only a part of the data, information, rumor, opinion, and prognostication that arrive in Jerry's office daily. This morning, his secretary, Geri, brings in a stack of printouts of voice-mails and e-mails he had received while he was away. She has typed out all of his messages, organized them according to date, and high-lighted in yellow the important elements: appointments, meetings, names, and numbers.

"Don't you just love it?" he reads the five-word e-mail message silently to himself. The subject of the e-mail: Amazon.com. He lets out a laugh, leans back in his chair, and reads the message again, this time out loud. "Don't you just love it?"

Jerry is not prone to giving out stock tips, and he even shies away from talking about his job or the stock market with his family and friends. But this was one he did give away. Jerry knew that the woman who sent the e-mail would take the tip as exactly that—not a sure thing, not an investment strategy, but merely a tip, an idea, a hint. He knew that the woman's bank account and her emotions could handle a loss in the stock market, and that she wouldn't take a big gain as a sign of her, or Jerry's, market genius. To those with the money—and even many of those without it—the stock market can be a game, and she was looking for the next play. Perhaps most importantly, she simply caught Jerry on the right day. When she called last fall, Jerry had already spent a few months buying and selling shares of the Internet bookseller for his mutual funds. He knew the company, he'd met the executives, and he un-derstood the business model. Most of all, he understood the hype—he knew the story around the stock, he listened to why peo-ple were buying it, he watched who was buying it, and he watched how the stock behaved.

So, this old friend listened to Jerry's advice and bought in when the shares were trading around $15. When it comes to story stocks like Amazon, Jerry never gets caught up in exact numbers or who bought what when. Instead, he says things like, "She bought a pile of the stuff," like it was half-price Halloween candy in the bargain bin.

When Jerry received the e-mail, Amazon.com's shares had just hit $139.50 a share.

Just minutes later, Jerry is chatting on one of his regular calls with an institutional salesman. It sounds pretty formal, but institutional salespeople are really just brokers who call on professionals during the day, rather than baby boomers during the dinner hour. Jerry speaks with about half a dozen salespeople throughout the day, and receives calls, messages, and faxes from countless others who would like to bend his ear and open his wallet.

"Amazon—I told you this thing was gonna work, didn't I? It's about time you guys got on board . . . I don't know, it's up eight points again today. These things are basically being bought retail—I don't know that a bunch of institutions are buying it up here."

Jerry has bought and sold shares of Amazon.com several times in the past, but this summer he has been mostly a spectator in a sport he thinks is being played mainly by individuals: "retail." Retail is for those baby boomers who get the broker calls during dinner, and for those retirees and Gen-X computer junkies who log onto their E*Trade or Charles Schwab Internet accounts and buy 50 or 100 shares at a time. He doesn't see many of his colleagues playing the game—salespeople and others on Wall Street have told him so. This combination—Jerry's theory that Amazon is a game being played by amateurs, and the company's record-setting stock price—is starting to pique his interest again.

He chides himself for selling out too early, the last time he owned Amazon shares. "I left a lot of money on the table." And now he's thinking of heading back to the table for another helping.

"If there's ever been a stock that fits into the Peter Lynch camp—you know it, you use it, you like it, you buy it—this is it. These people buy a book, and then they go and buy the stock right behind the book." It is another in a long line of Wall Street maxims. Chalk one up to Fidelity Investments' legendary mutual fund manager, Peter Lynch, for telling all individuals they could *Beat the Street* and get *One Up on Wall Street* in his bestsellers of the same names.

The salesman on the phone moves on to the sale at hand.

"Are you guys taking this thing public?" Jerry asks. "Goldman is? And how much did you guys piss away in a day on this thing? . . .

Antique ink stands? Oh brother . . . I have an Odyssey putter and it doesn't do me any good. . . . Yeah, we did the Inktomi deal. I paid up for more afterward. It was just recommended and the stock was up $40. It's up another $8 today."

Sure, the stock is up 90 percent in three days. But initial public offerings (IPOs) were like that. Weren't they? Such jumps had become so common this summer that Jerry and the salesman didn't even pause to gasp over the numbers. Instead, the salesman moved right into a pitch for his next Internet–IPO sure thing. He was calling to offer Jerry a spot on the dance card of eBay, an online auction company that was initially started as a way to locate collectible PEZ candy dispensers. Sure, any number of Donald Duck, Mickey Mouse, or Superman heads spitting lemon and cherry sugar pellets could be found in grocery stores today for $1.39. But, to find the classic ones—well, surely a Web site would help. An Internet site seemed to be the solution and cure-all for every corporate and personal ailment as the last decade of the twentieth century was coming to a close. And now, investors were going to be given a chance to own a small piece of this wonder Web site that offered customers the chance to bid on not only PEZ dispensers, but antique inkwells and used golf clubs. It was something Jerry would have to think about.

*   *   *

At eleven o'clock, Jerry gathers the members of the growth group in his office for their weekly meeting. The group has held such meetings since Jerry took over last year. Besides giving an opportunity to exchange ideas and information, the meetings give Jerry a chance to check in with the team, to take the pulse of his workers. Are they too optimistic? Are they down? Do they need to be bucked up? And like any tight-knit office group, the team enjoys the chance to exchange banter, tease one another, catch up with each other, and catch their breath.

The meetings begin with Jerry's discussing the overall market and the group's funds. It's like Jay Leno's opening monologue—it puts everyone at ease and updates the team on what's gone on and where things stand as of today. Then the exchange starts—sometimes in such rapid-fire market lingo that the language sounds foreign to all but the participants. They speak in a string of stock symbols and precise decimals rather than company names and whole numbers. Their speech is peppered more with nicknames of Wall Street analysts and arcane industry data and lore than with simple pronouns and adjectives. After Jerry's warm-up stretch, the meetings build steadily to a high-speed sprint of information exchange. Eventually, there is a requisite cooldown of bashing the competition across or down the street in Philadelphia, or delivering a healthy ribbing of the guy in the next chair over.

They have all settled into the beat of the gatherings. Each of the group's members brings something unique to the table every week. Jerry brings with him a stack of research and charts and the hope that others will take these when they leave. Marshall brings color, energy, and enthusiasm to share, while Jeff brings an endless supply of technospeak, market data, and strategic opinions from far and wide. John brings a pronounced level of conservatism and skepticism that comes with the territory of following financial stocks—those that can swing most violently with the merest shifting of economic winds. Steve's contribution is a fresh combination of the eagerness and confidence found in newly minted Ivy League MBAs ready to make their mark and their millions on Wall Street. The only member missing today is Lori, who is out on maternity leave until after Labor Day.

Jerry has put the group together in much the same way he builds portfolios. He looked for personalities that would complement each other, and he wanted strengths to compensate for weaknesses. Broken down most simply, Jerry and Jeff invest in technology, Marshall and Lori cover retail and consumer, and John and Steve do the financials and business service stocks.

Jerry starts today's meeting by pushing to the center of the table the chart ranking the Delaware Aggressive Growth Fund number one. "A little publicity, courtesy of *The Wall Street Journal.*" The others sitting around the table lean in a bit to see the chart, but no one rests on the numbers for long. Jerry's group has moved on to a new day, a new week, a new month.

"As for performance, one place we got nicked was Advanced Fibre. We got run down by a truck there. We lost one to one-and-a-half percent on that one transaction." Jerry scans the printout that details the daily performance of the three mutual funds. "We'll figure out a way to get it back. We've got to see where we can push it and get it back."

To Jerry and the men sitting with him at the blond-wood conference table, that 1.5 percent comes out to just under $1.5 million in the Delaware Aggressive Growth Fund. They lost it last Tuesday, and now they've got to find it somewhere else. They lost it when Advanced Fibre, one of the 65 companies they held in the mutual fund, announced it might have some difficulty meeting expectations. When companies make such an announcement—usually a few weeks before revealing their actual results, which would no doubt come as a disappointment to investors—everyone knows the expectations of which the companies speak. They are not the expectations of the company executives, whose projections may have been laid out in corporate strategy meetings. They are the expectations of Wall Street. They are the estimates and predictions proclaimed by the hundreds of Wall Street stock analysts on whom professional money managers have come to rely.

It's a bit like a parent sending out the family Christmas letter to let all the aunts and uncles and old neighbors know that little Johnny is getting straight As and will be going to Harvard next year. The problem is that the letter was written with exuberance in November, before final exam grades were tallied, and long before college acceptance letters were in the mail. Across the country, 175 holiday missives arrive, singing Johnny's praises in advance of his achievements. Like Johnny, corporate America—and, very often, executives of companies that are newly public and have very little experience with Wall Street analysts, quarterly estimates, and an unforgiving investment community—must sheepishly come forward. They are forced to admit that they won't be wearing Crimson Hs across their chests next fall, and no, the company won't be earning $148 million this quarter, like everyone has come to expect. Instead, it'll be a little closer to $75 million—but please don't sell our stock. Sure; and community college is a fine substitute for the Ivy League.

"We haven't used any deals yet, so we've got a lot of dry powder," Jerry says.

The others nod.

"But, that doesn't mean you can run around and throw a bunch of deals that are working in the funds," he adds. Most mutual funds, especially those investing in small companies, like Jerry and his gang do, have the chance to buy into "deals," or IPOs. But often, the deal with "deals" is that some investment banker, or some stock analyst, or some stockbroker, or some institutional salesperson has got to owe you a favor. If you're owed a big favor, you get signed up for 10 percent of the deal. You get your shares—maybe 100,000 of them—when the deal is "priced" by the bankers on Thursday night. Then, on Friday morning, your trader takes those shares that you got for $12 last night and sells them for $14 to some Wall Street brokerage house that can resell them to someone else for $14.50. It's a quick $200,000 and a shot in the arm to the fund. If it's a popular IPO—a really hot deal—the shares can jump from $12 to $60 or more in one day. That 400 percent increase could add nearly $5 million to a lucky mutual fund's bank account. In one day. Actually, in one trade.

"We're about 41 percent in technology right now, so the performance of the fund is going to be driven by where tech goes. But, that's where we want to be. We want to be in the more aggressively oriented names. We can own bigger names—if they're aggressive. Go where the growth is." Like a coach with a clipboard, kneeling on a locker room floor, Jerry looks around the table as he speaks these words and meets the eyes of the men who will help him—who must help him—win this game.

Marshall takes the pause as an opening to congratulate Jerry on his latest winner from the world of Internet stocks. "Inktomi. That one played even more than I thought the band would allow." Jerry bought into the IPO of the Internet software company just four weeks ago, and the stock has already tripled.

Marshall leans his chair against the sill under the windows that fill half a wall of Jerry's office. The smokestacks in the rail yard of Philadelphia's train station spew silently in the background, as they have for nearly 70 years. Marshall holds a fat-free pretzel rod between his middle and index fingers and wags it like a smokeless cigar.

The others nod in agreement over Inktomi's stunning performance and let out a few "Yeahs," as is customary when any new technology stock cruises in on some fiber-optic cable, spins your head on your hard drive, doubles your Internet caching abilities, or puts just under a million dollars in your wallet—or, in this case, your mutual fund.

Steve, the newest and most eager addition to the team, lets out a "Whew" in praise of the boss.

In hopes of putting a quick end to the glory moment, Jerry brings the conversation back to the numbers on the page—what Jerry calls "the scorecard." It's a weekly printout that compares the performance of each of the group's three funds to that of 99 of its peers. It ranks Jerry and his peers—or, in this case, his competition—according to their performance for the latest week, month, and twelve months, and for the current year. The columns and rows are constant reminders that every move has an effect, and every dollar adds up to the only number that counts: where you stand at the end of the year.

For Jerry's group—and for much of Wall Street—the numbers that appear on their annual bonus checks are closely tied to the numbers on those six sheets of paper. This year, the six members of the growth team are working toward a pot totaling about $3.3 million in salary and bonus. If the group performs better than 75 percent of its peers in all three of its funds, Delaware will pay them the whole package. As performance slips below that line of achievement in any of the funds, the company keeps more of the pot, and Jerry and his team get less and less. Every Monday morning, the printouts stare back at the group, from their desks and conference table, like a $3 million carrot. In those weeks when the carrot dangles within reach, it seems to be yanked up just as their arms stretch out to grab it. The numbers on the page sit silently in black ink, and the $3 million carrot swings slowly, alluringly, hypnotically taunting, "It's not December 31, and you can't have it."

"The month-to-date numbers, it's probably as much my fault as it is anyone else's," Jerry says. Indeed, it's been a rough few days, thanks to Advanced Fibre, and the group has plummeted in the rankings.

Jeff, the only player who missed out on the last round of praise, offers, "I'll step up to the bar on that one."

With his hopes of shouldering the blame dashed again, Jerry tries, "Well, don't take it as the end of the world. Ninety-seventh, month-to-date. We've been there before."

"And it's only three trading days in," Jeff pushes his round glasses back on the bridge of his nose and runs his hand through his dark brown hair—never disturbing his perfect side part. "And yesterday we smoked 'em."

Finished with old business, Jerry opens the meeting up to anything the rest of the players have planned for the coming weeks.

"Earnings begin Thursday. But the onslaught won't really start till next week," Jeff says. "Earnings" occurs just after the end of every quarter. It's the roughly two-week period when companies announce to Wall Street, their investors, and the public how business was during the previous three months. If business hasn't been so great, a company will often preannounce the quarter, as was the case with Advanced Fibre. Letting investors know before the actual results come out is an effort to soften the blow—to the stock price and possibly to the company's reputation—by giving investors advance warning. Most often, the effort fails. Investors, an unforgiving lot, are quick to move from one stock into any of 11,000 others that maybe haven't announced that they're going to miss the quarter. The stock price usually craters when institutional investors who care nothing about advance warnings sell millions of shares, and it will take the company at least several quarters of very good news to earn back most investors' trust.

If a company's quarterly business has been good, on the other hand, it announces its results a week or two *after* the close of the quarter. Then companies watch their stock prices to see just how good investors thought the quarter was. In most cases, if a quarter has been very good, and if Wall Street research analysts are confident that their expectations and estimates will be met and exceeded, a "whisper number" will start to be heard through the investment world before actual results are announced. It's like an unpublished, updated earnings estimate by analysts: "Well, we're telling all of our clients the company is going to make 60 cents a share this quarter, but I'm telling you I actually think they're going to do much better and make 66 cents." It's the inside track in a community that is made up of people already on the inside. But, just like anything else that has been around long enough, "whisper numbers" are easy enough to come by now that there's a Whispernumber.com Web site for dispensing just such information. Of course, actually logging on to Whispernumber.com is an admission that you didn't get the word first, so you're not really on the inside. Insiders—professionals, that is—do not log on to Whispernumber.com.

Never wanting the conversation to get mired in work or the intricate details of earnings season when it doesn't have to, Marshall lobs from across the conference table, "I'm gonna be on holiday."

The word whips Jerry's head to the right to face Marshall. "Where you from, London? That's what they say over there." He says this as if the group may not know. As if most people still save the trip to Europe for retirement. He can't accept that most of the people in his industry are the kind who spent high school summers in Europe, or arranged semesters abroad in Madrid, Paris, or Beijing. Jerry spent his summers in high school mixing cement and playing baseball.

"I'm from the South. It's practically the same language down there," says Marshall. Indeed, Marshall's Kentucky lilt and the collection of colorful phrases he exported with him when he moved north are the most distinct and recognizable of the group. He inquires after your "kinfolk," and if he's busy, he'll be with you in "two shakes." The picnic-blanket casualness that echoes through the halls when Marshall says, "I reckon so," is countered in formality and gentility when required. Although he may call someone Jim a dozen times a day, Marshall won't send out a correspondence until he tracks down a middle initial and can address the envelope to a "Mr. James T. _____." "There is a proper way to do things," he says.

Then it is Jeff's turn to log in his own plans with the group. "Robbie has a semi conference the last week of July. Then there's an Internet conference the first two days of the next week. And the networking industry has something the last three days of that week." Jeff uses more technology, investment banking, and business school ("tech," "I-banking," and "b-school") lingo than anyone else in the office. He calls Robertson Stephens, the San Francisco investment bank, "Robbie," and the semiconductor stocks are "semis." Microsoft is "Microsofty," and, if Jeff is standing, he will often genuflect as he says it. He talks about having kids as "going long," as in "you have to keep them."

Marshall withdraws his pretzel rod, "I'm gonna blow out my CDNOW at some point. My target is 30."

"I'd lower your target on that. Let's try 29⅝." Jerry is in mentor mode, with his forearms framing the performance sheets in front of him. His back is straight when he surveys the faces of his team looking for an opening. Finding somewhere he might impart a little knowledge or experience. Trying to pass something on from the past to an industry that worships the future. "I've told you not to think in round numbers. You don't all want to get to the door at the same time as everyone else." It's a lesson he repeats often—trying to get Marshall and the others in his group to think a little differently than the rest of Wall Street—but then again, not too differently. If $30 seems like a reasonable price for Marshall to sell the shares of the Internet music retailer CDNOW, which he bought for $16 a share, who's to say that a hundred other mutual fund managers haven't also said to themselves, "I'll sell when it hits $30." On the other side of those trades, there may not be a hundred buyers willing to pay $30 for a share of CDNOW. So, how about giving up a few pennies a share and getting in position at the head of the line rather than the end?

"Tandy had good comps today," Jeff offers.

"Circuit City had very good numbers."

"You may be the only living analyst that still follows Tandy."

The computer world and the world of investing have changed drastically in the nearly twenty years since Tandy's TRS-80 line of computers made it the number one personal computer company in the world, followed by Apple and then by Commodore, with its PET and Commodore 64 machines. The early models plugged into television sets instead of monitors and didn't have hard drives. When hard drives were invented, they sold for $1,700 and stored five megabytes of data. Average home computers today cost about that for the entire system, and they come with hard drives that can store 8,000 megabytes of data.

Jeff was studying computers and their components long before Tandy topped the charts in sales. He remembers "the day I saw my first D-RAM," when he was twelve years old, like others might recall seeing their first *Playboy*. Jeff did his seventh-grade science project in 1975 on microelectronics and brought a chip to show the class. Now, almost 25 years later, he has hanging on his wall a faded poster from a 1990 Museum of Modern Art exhibit titled "Information Art—Diagramming Microchips." Jeff can look at the print and confidently declare it to be the architecture of an Intel 386 chip. It is exactly this all-consuming enthusiasm for his job and his industry that a colleague says is both Jeff's best and worst quality.

The meeting continues to tour technologies and products and prices and performance and people: "DVD . . . it's been dribbling and drabbing for a while . . . Palm Pilot . . . all of a sudden you turn around and it's a million dollars . . . early adapters . . . price points . . . Legato . . . servers . . . saving the analysts' asses this quarter . . . storage is absolutely exploding."

The utility of this information has waned for Jerry. He shuffles the papers in front of him into a neat stack and taps the edge lightly against the table. "Lori's gonna stop by Friday to say hello."

Lori has been out of the office since having her second child two months ago. She still checks in almost daily with Marshall, getting and giving updates on stocks and companies. After a summer excursion to the shopping mall, she called in to tell Marshall to sell out of one of the group's retail stocks. "There's way too much merchandise on the sale tables. The quarter can't be going well," she warned him. Marshall put the sell order in, and, before long, Lori's assessment proved correct. The company preannounced a weaker-than-expected quarter.

"Yeah, she's gonna bring the baby with her when she comes," Marshall says.

"You think we should get together and have Geri get her a gift?" Jerry asks as he looks around.

"We already got her a gift. Or at least we all gave you money to get her a gift—but if you haven't, then can I have my forty dollars back?" John asks, and tosses into the air the baseball he's been holding.

The group feels very comfortable with its boss. They ride and tease Jerry as much as they do one another, and they take advantage of his open door to relay the latest joke from the Internet or the trading desk just as often as they stop in to run an investment idea by him. Even though the group's hierarchy positions Jerry with the final say on trades, to him they are a team. In presentations, he lists all six members as both portfolio managers and analysts. They share the top rung as well as the bottom. Jerry is quick to point out that there would be no rungs for any of the six to stand on if it weren't for Geri and Lea, the two assistants holding the whole ladder up for the group.

Jerry is on his way back to his desk, a de facto adjournment of today's meeting. The numbers and letters on his screen continue blinking red, green, and white, like the minilights on a Christmas tree. The market has taken no note of Jerry's weekly meeting, and now it is nearly an hour ahead of him and he has to catch up. From 9:30 in the morning to 4:00 in the afternoon, the Dow, the S&P 500, the Nasdaq, and all of Jerry's stocks are constantly moving up or down. Like an amorphous giant inhaling and exhaling billions of dollars. Up and down, up and down.

* * *

Even to professionals like Jerry and his team, the market remains an anonymous, intangible, and unpredictable being. The market is no one place, and it is no particular group of traders or companies or investors. "The market" doesn't mean the floor of the New York Stock Exchange, or Merrill Lynch's trading room, or the mutual fund performance tables in the newspapers. It is always an undefined "out there" or "they." "You'll have to move fast out there. . . . They're really marking 'em up today. . . . They're gonna take that stock out and shoot it. . . . I got hammered out in the market yesterday." Many would say that the market is the sum of all available information and all parties playing in it. But it is likely even more than that. As all of these elements combine and interact in unknown and unpredictable ways, the market produces its own force, its own volatility, and its own mystery.

No longer does the term "Wall Street" refer to the several-blocks-long locale in Manhattan, where the New York Stock Exchange and many brokerage firms are housed. "Wall Street" is now a virtual Wall Street that encompasses financial firms, mutual funds, and discount brokers from coast to coast and all points in between, including downtown Philadelphia. Telecommuting, the Internet, and red-eye flights that traverse the country while the sun and the market rest, have made it possible for Wall Street to be wherever investments and the stock market are followed or discussed. Today, it happens to be a conference room down the hall from Jerry's office.

Come lunch hour, Jerry and Jeff are meeting with a Wall Street analyst who covers the software industry. Jerry will have more than 170 such meetings with research analysts this year.

Next to the platter of turkey, tuna, and roast beef sandwiches laid out on a shelf lining one of the walls, the analyst has set up the equipment he takes on the road. He has a laptop computer plugged in, a telephone plugged in, an additional battery plugged in, and he is wearing a beeper. (For those who can't reach him by any of these almost conventional means of communication, the analyst has his own 1-800 number.) In the barter system of Wall Street, the analyst's firm has paid to have the sandwiches, chips, cookies, and assortment of sodas delivered from the Au Bon Pain in the building's lobby. In exchange, the firm gets to put its analyst in front of Jerry and Jeff, gets its research ideas heard, and possibly gets some buy orders from Jerry's trading desk. The voltage recharge for the array of micro machines is a bonus.

"Yeah, they're a little like Oracle," Jeff has already launched into stock talk while Jerry inspects the sandwich wedges. "When everyone else hit the wall, they just said, 'Okay, Oracle's gonna win it.'"

The analyst had just returned from a trip out west, where he had visited Oracle's colorful chief executive officer. The group isn't even all seated yet, and he's already able to offer them something the other 84 software analysts on Wall Street can't. "Yeah, you've got to pass six sports cars to get to his house. And the house is very Japanese. He has Samurai warriors—real ones—lined up and down the hall, ponds in the living room, rice-paper walls. He's a real risk taker."

Jerry has settled into the chair across from the analyst. "I tell you, you come to my house, it doesn't look anything like that." No, in place of sports cars, you'd find a Ford Ranger pickup with a few dents in it from hauling trees on the weekends. No rice-paper walls, and furniture from L.L.Bean fills the children's bedrooms.

"Would you buy Oracle now?" Jerry asks.

The analyst launches into his endorsement of the company's shares and the information he learned on his trip west. The meeting continues as part question–answer session and part seventh-grade lunchroom gossip—a game of "You tell me something, I'll tell you something."

The analyst runs down the list of companies he covers and knows something about, and Jerry or Jeff interrupts when something interests them.

"Compuware . . . Manugistics. They just shot themselves. Ego and bravado. They blew everything into the March quarter so they could say they had a better quarter than I-2. . . . Network Associates. I'm very positive on the stock, but we're restricted, so I can't say anything."

With that, the analyst has doled out at least his third or fourth useful bit of information to Jerry in exchange for his lunch hour. Wall Street analysts are paid to write and talk about companies that their firms trade stock in and do investment banking work for— stock offerings to the public, acquisitions of smaller companies, and sales to larger companies. When the firm is hired to perform one of these tasks, the company shows up on the "restricted list," and the analyst is prohibited from speaking or writing about the stock until the business at hand is completed to avoid any conflict of interest or accusations of inside information. Saying "I'm restricted" is little different from "I can't tell you about the party because it's a surprise."

Jerry does not pursue the point, nor does he act on this bit of information. He simply logs the data into his constantly turning Rolodex of facts, rumors, observations, research, and conversations.

Now it is Jerry's turn to offer something useful. "Compuware. We should see a big bulge in their revenue some time, in the testing software . . . I asked Ceridian what they were spending on Year 2000 . . . I asked about next year, he said it's all going into testing. Platinum? Yeah, right after they came out, he was up there with his ponytail and leather jacket with 'Platinum' across the back . . . I was in a breakout session and the guy I'm sitting with says to me, 'It's like having your company run by Bon Jovi.'"

"There's a rumor today that IBM was gonna buy Gateway," Jeff offers.

"Tell you what, that makes a hell of a lot of sense."

"Yeah, 'cause IBM's proved for ten years that they don't know a damn thing about PCs and that Ted Waitt and Gateway know everything," Jeff says with satisfaction.

When the meeting ends, the analyst packs up his recharged equipment, and Jerry puts another sandwich on his plate to take down to his office. They both leave the meeting with more than they brought to it.

In his office, Jerry is back on the phone with another salesman, getting an alternate view of the world and the stock market. "How come I don't own more of this deal? It's the only thing I own that's up . . . Manugistics is up. This analyst was just telling me about a contract Manugistics just got with Nokia. I think he's out there on the road talking it up, so that's what gave Manugistics the pop. That's what happens when you get a lunch with a guy and not a breakfast—somebody else got there first."

On Wall Street, there's inside information and then there's insight information. Inside information is known to those directly involved with the company—officers and directors—and usually pertains to facts about earnings, possible mergers, or new offerings. Trading on such information is strictly forbidden and monitored by the Securities and Exchange Commission (SEC), the regulatory agency that governs the securities industry.

Insight information is known to those on the inside track—professional investors like Jerry, traders, analysts, and brokers who live and breathe the market every day. Insight information is word that a positive research report is in the mail, or it is an early demo of a whizbang new product. Much of Wall Street and many of Jerry's and his team's decisions are fueled by just this type of information.

"There's a seller of a big block of shares out there . . . the company might drop their prices this week . . . the new software launch is running behind schedule . . . Fidelity is going to put a pile of cash to work in tech stocks. . . ." They may turn out to be facts, or they may prove to be rumors; either way, such savory market tidbits will move stocks. More often than not, they will move stocks before any individual investor hears or reads about them in the papers. And by that time, those on the inside track will have moved on to a new tidbit of information and a new chase.

* * *

Steve steps into Jerry's office bearing a few pages of a spreadsheet printout and announces himself as Captain Data. "A couple of people around here . . ."—he sweeps his arm to indicate the offices surrounding Jerry's—"meaning everyone, have been asking about this, so I thought I'd xerox it and pass it out."

"Oh really? Does it mean anything?"

"Yeah, it shows relative performance of the funds, and it shows it by individuals," Steve explains while Jerry's eyes quickly scan the chart.

"Huh, looks good," Jerry says, as he places the papers on his desk, not giving them much attention or import.

Steve quickly grabs the papers. "Yeah, I knew *you'd* like it. You look great." And indeed he does. The chart breaks down the stellar performance the group's funds have had in the first six months of the year. They can each see what industry sectors contributed the most, which stocks contributed the most, and, next to those stocks, the initials of the group member who contributed the most. It has been a strong run for technology stocks, and the highest numbers stand in black ink against the initials GSF: Gerald Shaw Frey.

"But you know, if you're gonna give that out, I'd give it with the caveat that this is just one data point," Jerry warns. "It's not something to bank on as an absolute. You can get bogged down by looking at these numbers, and we shouldn't."

Again, he's concerned more about pointing out who's on the bottom than he is about pointing out who's on top. Ego is a natural by-product of the investment industry. Why feed it unnecessarily? In any competition, game, or team where keeping score is worthwhile, someone is always going to be last. When your stocks aren't doing well and you aren't contributing as much as the others, you feel it before you step out of bed in the morning and while you lie awake at night thinking about your performance. So why put it down on paper and pass it around? "You know everybody wants to be contributing, so you don't want somebody else—no matter where they are—to think that someone else is dragging them down," Jerry says.

*   *   *

On the second Monday in July, the sun streams into Jerry's corner office. The market has been open for a little more than an hour, and much of his screen is green. It is the kind of pause in his day and his world that prompts him to call his best friend from childhood, Stew. Growing up in Tunkhannock, a rural town of 2,200 just west of Wilkes-Barre and Scranton in northeast Pennsylvania, it would have been difficult not to know each other. But their fathers worked as salesmen at the same Ford dealership. When Jerry's father died, the year Jerry turned twelve, Stew's family took him with them on a fishing trip to Canada, and the two have been close ever since. They played sports together, spent afternoons and weekends at each other's homes, and eventually shared a house together before Jerry moved to New York and Stew married. Stew lives in the town where the two spent their boyhood and is the athletic director of the high school where they had their storied careers in multiple sports. Jerry calls him several times a week—"to check in." The only mention of Wall Street or the stock market is Stew's usual response when he first hears Jerry's voice on the other end of the line: "Must be a slow day in the stock market."

"How 'bout them Yankees?" Jerry starts off today's call. "Aren't they unbelievable? They are on such a roll. What do you think of the Bronx Bombers?" The two have a standing annual bet on their favorite baseball teams. Jerry sides with the New York Yankees, Stew with the Cleveland Indians. Five dollars rides on the team that finishes the season with a better record. In his athletic director's office, which is tucked inside the door labeled "AudioVisual Room," Stew has a framed painting of a baseball diamond hanging on the wall. Resting in the bottom panel of the frame are three five-dollar bills signed with messages of woe and revenge from Jerry Frey.

Jerry continues, "We are gonna kick your ass in the fall . . . wanna make a side bet on it? . . . My fear is that we're the best regular-season team in baseball and we're gonna blow it in the Series. Wells is gonna get gout in his toe or something. . . . Yeah, the papers said he hit his toe on the stairs. Yeah—have you ever in your life hit your toe coming *down* the stairs? He probably has gout from drinking beer or doing something stupid like that. . . ."

In the weeks to come, Jerry will spend many more calls distressed over the Yankees' summer standing. Will they be cursed by their midseason success? Of course, this may just be Jerry projecting his fears about his own group and funds onto the Yankees. Will they blow it when it counts? Then again, it could just be one more piece of evidence that Jerry is much better at making bets on the market than on the baseball season.

"Jeez, I just broke my computer. . . . Hey, I ran into Hazel the other day. . . . Sheesh, isn't she a bird." The conversation takes a familiar turn into the common territory of old friends, the old hometown, and the old days. It is a stream of names deferred to as "Mrs." This and "Mr." That and "Coach" So-and-So. They are again the twelve-year-old boys with their fishing poles hanging over the riverbank.

"How's your golf game going? . . . Me? Well, you know, change your grip on every hole, mumble, talk to yourself, change your stance on every hole. . . ."

Jerry's calls to Stew, and his weekend trips back home to visit his mother and old friends, are his dose of reality. They are what ground him while he spends his weekdays watching the market climb, chasing the high fliers, and riding it when it's going up. It is a reminder to himself that he can compete in this game with the Harvard MBAs, the 28-year-old millionaire portfolio managers, and the egos that ate Manhattan, but he is not one of them. He is the boy who grew up chasing balls fouled into the woods behind the school, for a dollar a game; the 28-year-old who spent weeks learning about the properties of steel beams on construction sites; and the reserved money manager whose most common utterance at the market or a stock is "Oh brother." And that is exactly who he wants to be.

Last week, Jerry was out buying trading cards with his two oldest boys. They spent their allowance on baseball and football cards, and even Jerry found one he wanted to own. He paid a dollar for a card of the former Phillies first baseman, John Kruk. "You watch him and you think, 'He is a really disgusting human being.' He's really like a softball player playing baseball."

Most fans of Kruk and the Phillies would agree. He was a grace-less player in a graceful game. Reporters said he batted best when he was fat. The fans said they liked it when he drank. He was well known for what the Phillies' team office called his "country person-ality," an exception in a game of political owners, fast money, and savvy free-agents. Before turning pro, he played for Allegheny Com-munity College, not far from where he grew up in Keyser, West Virginia—population: 5,900.

It isn't likely that John Kruk will be inducted into the Hall of Fame anytime soon, although he did help lead the Phillies to the World Series in 1993. They lost in game six, the closest the team and the city had been in thirteen years. He still holds the Phillies' team record for on-base percentage. The stat means that John Kruk could get on base more consistently than any other player. He may not have hit a home run, and he may have walked to first. But he got on base and kept his team in the game.

As one fan posted to one of the numerous Web sites devoted to Kruk, "More than anything, though, it's just that he's so NORMAL. He looks like that guy from the machine shop you always see in the neighborhood bar."

No longer having a card collection of his own to expand with the Kruk acquisition, Jerry put the card in the visor of his car. Passengers have commented on the card, and questioned him why in the world he would have "that guy" up there. Jerry just smiles and cocks his head slightly, "I kind of like it."

CHAPTER 2

DOLLAR
DAYS

On the bookshelf under the wall of windows in Jerry's office sit two stacks of documents. From the door of his office, they look like stacks of paperwork you might find in nearly any office cubicle in corporate America. But if you are inside Jerry's office and have the opportunity to look at the stacks up close, you see that they are not mere collections of random papers and pamphlets.

In the stacks are dozens of printed booklets with slick glossy covers, filled with numbers, text, and colorful company logos. The spines of the stapled booklets are aligned neatly, as though they are a treasured collection of decades' worth of *National Geographic*. Instead, they are initial public offering (IPO) prospectuses. And they have all been sent to Jerry's office in just the past two weeks. They are from companies and investment banks hoping to catch a bit of Jerry's attention and time—a breakfast, a lunch, an afternoon. And they are looking for a bit of his fund's money—one or two million dollars here, several hundred thousand dollars there.

There's a dietary supplement company, Natrol; a biotechnology enterprise, Dyax; Hanger Orthopedic Group; Golden State Vintners; Family Golf Centers; U.S. OnLine; Microstrategy; I-Cube; Presidio Golf Trust; Global Vacation Group; and Cyberian Outpost. They offer the chance to own a piece of companies representing nearly all industries—from railroads to computer technology to book publishing. The companies are big and small, old and new. Elder-Beerman is hoping to splash onto the scene of public companies and the American stock market this summer, after being run as a department store out of Dayton, Ohio, since 1883. By contrast, Broadcast.com officially became Broadcast.com the company, in May—just two months prior.

The prospectuses serve as the official invitation to Wall Street's IPO party. Open one up and learn all the details. And, just maybe, inside one—or even inside several—is the winning stub, the lucky number, the golden ticket from Willy Wonka's chocolate bar wrapper.

* * *

Just after lunch, Jerry gathers his group for their weekly meeting. It is the second Monday in July.

"So, everyone see the numbers? Aggressive Growth, pay attention there, because new money's coming in and it's making the position sizes smaller . . . ," Jerry reminds the group. The fund's strong performance has attracted more attention and more dollars, but as the cash piece grows bigger, every piece of the pie doled out to a stock gets smaller and smaller. They've got to remember to spend the new cash to keep all of the equity portions up and earning money in the market. Of course, the more money that comes in, the harder it is to stay nimble and trade in and out of stocks quickly. Ah, the burden of success.

Jerry's opening remarks continue with the issues on his mind, the stock market of the moment, and some directives for the funds. "Semiconductors. You got me. They like Intel again, so now they're running. They knocked the numbers back so far that now they're gonna beat the numbers. . . . You know, it's amazing . . . I'm surprised Applied Materials isn't down more than it is today. . . . The Internet—you see the money coming out of those and trying to get parked somewhere else."

"I don't try to be a student of semis," says Marshall, who follows Landry's Seafood and Borders Bookstores a lot more closely than he does the semiconductor industry. "But it seems like they get a jump in July."

"Yeah, there's a tendency in July to do some summer stocking."

"TI—2x orders from Compaq." The group has been with Jeff long enough to understand that his code means that Texas Instruments is getting twice as many orders from Compaq as Wall Street once expected.

"So, do you wanna back the truck up on Texas today? Are we concerned with volatility, or are we trying to get to 40 percent for the year?" John asks. Should we be conservative, or do we go for it and try to jack up our numbers from here?

"Aggressive Growth is a fund for performance," Jerry reminds them. "This isn't a fund we're going to have to play a lot of defense in. We need to take a look at it today. We need to keep pushing on the upside of things. We can continue to use some deals, but not a whole bunch." He wants the group to think aggressively. Buy what's going up, get positioned in the better names. Know your companies, know what's going to make it happen for them. Read the market as well as you read research reports. Hot deals and IPOs—some are fine, but boosting the funds that way is likely to attract an accusation of using steroids: "Oh, that fund is up just because they got in a bunch of hot deals." We want to win, and we want to have played clean and fair. Dietary supplements are okay, but illegal drug use is unseemly.

Like a parent overseeing the progress and constantly changing character of three children, Jerry is not supposed to have a favorite fund. He is supposed to treat them all equally and express praise, criticism, and pride across the board. Professionally, as a manager of the three funds, Jerry treats them all the same. They each receive the same attention and analysis. Privately, he has a particular affinity for the Aggressive Growth Fund. The fund was handed over to Jerry and his team to manage last spring, when the fund was tiny—a mere few million dollars—and garnered little interest from anyone. So, having managed and grown the fund from close to nothing to nearly $100 million, the growth team doesn't have to make excuses for any other manager's useless baggage on the downside, nor share any credit for its success. In the industry's grand game of musical chairs, mutual funds and managers are shuffled around so frequently that it's rare for a manager and a fund's performance to align perfectly. Someone always seems to have been there before, or someone else has taken over midstream. Jerry and the Aggressive Growth Fund are the rare pairing where performance numbers generally match up: the 61 percent performance of the fund since last summer can be listed next to his name with no asterisk nor special caveats.

"Treat it as an aggressive performance fund," Jerry continues. "Let's keep the number of names down. It may raise our turnover, but I'm not worried about turnover . . . I don't have much else to say, except I missed my lunch. I didn't bring it in and I'm hungry."

John leaves to get on a conference call, and Marshall drinks water from a plastic cup with glitter that sloshes around in a plastic base—one of Wall Street's summer giveaways. The cup had come courtesy of Wheat First Union and served as an invitation to the firm's stock conference on Nantucket. The growth group's offices were also bouncing with colorful inflatable beach balls, courtesy of Goldman Sachs, and bright blue Frisbees from SunTrust Banks. "Summer is for sun, fun, games, and the stock market," Wall Street's trinkets seemed to say.

"As for the year, we've got the reporting period now and the reporting period in September. So, we've only really got two more to go," Jerry says. "If we stay in the way the world is going and out of the way the world is not going, we should be all right. Unless we have another October '87."

"Or '95, or '97, or '93," adds Jeff, the group's self-appointed market historian.

"Yeah, October every year is awful. You just don't want to own them in October. And don't forget that it's usually September that comes out and pukes all over everybody before we even get to October," Jerry responds. "And now we've got Japan . . . political problems . . . they're struggling with the government, which is gonna take a lot longer to get through than just a financial crisis."

"Yeah, and tech sales are gonna be down in France today," Jeff says. "They're still drunk from winning the World Cup."

"I'm going to France in September, so I was kind of glad they won," Steve joins in. "I thought they were gonna be in a bad mood."

"You're going to France?" Jerry asks.

"We're paying this guy too much," Jeff interjects.

"I've never been to France. How old are you?" Jerry quickly retorts.

"Twenty-nine."

"You're not going to Paris, are you? I've always wanted to go to Paris."

"You should go," Steve encourages.

"You're not taking the Concorde, are you?" Jerry asks, still incredulous.

"No."

"Okay. Well, bring some champagne back," Jerry says, satisfied that the group will at least get something out of his analyst vacationing in France. The closest Jerry has gotten to "the Continent" is a business trip to London.

"Then, for deals, there's this Broadcast.com," Jerry says.

"It's supposedly white hot," Jeff reports.

"If the market pulls in, we've got to have higher, more aggressive, growth names. Looking at the numbers—twelve months, and year-to-date—number one, number one. I can tell you right now which direction those numbers are trending. Down." He laughs out loud.

It's the middle of July and the Dow has been hovering around 9000 for the past two weeks. The index has been flirting with setting new records, but has failed to climb back to the 9200 mark it saw in May. "It wants to break through. . . . It's bumping up against it. . . . The market's just taking a breather," say many market watchers, strategists, and financial reporters, as though the stock market is a star pitcher giving his arm a rest. Jerry, an optimist about his stocks, is a realist about the market: he figures that, like an athlete (no matter how good), the market can't keep up forever. And, when the market falters, they've got to take advantage of it. They'll do so in the manner that millions of individual investors learned during the decade since the last major stock market crash: buy the dips.

"Morgan Stanley said this is a normal pause in an extremely long five-to-ten-year bull market," says Steve, who is second to Jeff in market prognosticating.

Jerry laughs, "Take that to the bank."

Conversation mires and the group disperses. Jerry has called the play. Get out there, be aggressive, push on the upside. Go for it.

* * *

As members of Jerry's team, they are all looking to contribute. They want to see their own initials next to the big performance numbers. Each of them wants to bring the winning ticket to the boss. Each is looking for the stock, the idea, or the trade that will make the difference. They have been absorbing Jerry's lessons since they arrived in the group. Know the market, know your companies, and, perhaps most importantly, know yourself. If you don't know what you're looking for, at least know it when you find it.

Each of the team members makes regular visits to Jerry's office, trying out ideas like they are modeling dresses for the prom. They each have the authority to make decisions and trades without Jerry's approval, but he is often sought out for guidance or concensus. The auditioning of a new stock starts modestly, with the company mentioned as an aside or brought up merely as a piece of trivia until Jerry's interest can be gauged. If Jerry actually puts his pen down or looks up from his desk or computer, the visitor continues strutting the idea down the catwalk. More information comes out as confidence builds. There is always the hope that Jerry will say it's the best idea he's heard all year. Or the hope that he will inquire in awe as to how you figured all of this out so quickly. But Jerry won't. He is as modest in his praise as he is in his criticism. Jerry begins by laying out an opposing argument, and then, just as you change your mind and agree with his sound reasoning, he turns to offer the strengths of your original position. Jerry's analysts often walk out of his office with no more direction on whether to buy or sell as when they walked in.

An hour after the group meeting, Marshall is back in Jerry's office. "Did you see Cendant down 10 percent all of a sudden?"

"Yeah, somebody printed a million shares of it," Jerry says, looking up from his screen. A "print" is just more Wall Street lingo for a trade. You can phone the order in to the trading desk, you can walk it over to the trading desk, or you can send a trade request by e-mail. But the trade is official when the firm gets a printed confirmation that it has occurred, which it will keep scrupulously filed in case the Securities and Exchange Commission or the National Association of Securities Dealers wishes to inspect it.

On Wall Street, "Print it" delivers the same sort of conviction and bravado as "Book 'em, Danno."

"Yeah, it was on CNN about Cendant and their accounting issues, and none of the analysts know diddly-squat about what's going on," Marshall says.

"Looks like it may have been a pretty good idea to sell some of this the other day—sometimes it's better to be lucky than smart."

"Yeah, it was a pretty good idea to sell some," Marshall nods. "Now might be a good buying opportunity." He is looking for the edge and waiting for an okay from Jerry. He's judging the stock and its place in the market to see if this one might give him just enough room, just enough upside, to pass the guy in front. And now he's asking Jerry to lean his head out the window into oncoming traffic and let him know if this stock is the one.

Jerry leans in to look at his computer screen. He glances at Cendant and at the overall market, and he looks at all of the other stocks that populate his screen. "Sounds like maybe we oughta find out what's going on."

"Yeah, I've got calls out, trying to see what's going on," Marshall says, walking out the door, as if his phone may be ringing at this very moment.

Twenty minutes later, Marshall is eating popcorn in the hall. He is leaning up against Geri's desk and wearing only one shoe, a mode he calls "business casual." His black sock contrasts sharply against the pale green carpet that covers the floors of Delaware's offices. The official custom-dyed color is Aegean Mist, but the color is precisely the same shade green as that used on the back of a dollar bill.

While he snacks, Marshall trades stock names and prices with Jeff. "Cendant is sort of in this range—where it's not cheap enough to buy and it's not cheap enough to sell." The stock's not yet a bargain for a small investment that could pay off big, nor are the shares down enough for Marshall to take a loss and sell out all together.

Another fifteen minutes and he is back in Jerry's office.

"I just put in a call to a salesman to see if they knew anything, so the analyst got on the squawk box and asked if anyone knew anything about Cendant," Marshall says incredulously.

"That oughta bring it down about ten points," Jerry scoffs and leans back in his chair. Indeed, announcing a troubled stock over a trading floor's speaker system is akin to shouting "Fire!" in a theater, with the exception that the former is not an arrestible offense.

"Yeah, he told me he was just so embarrassed that they're so far out of the loop on this one. So, I put in an order to sell another 100,000 shares."

"You sure you don't want to buy?" Jerry asks. It is as if he has just reached behind his ear and produced Marshall's card. The two have reversed roles in the thirty-five minutes since they last discussed action they should take on Cendant. It is just the kind of debate Jerry wants his group to play in their own minds. Two sides to every issue, two sides to every trade. If everyone is selling, should we consider buying? Each individual trade is a battle in the war. Someone will buy and someone will sell. And someone will win.

"Yeah, I'm sure," Marshall quickly replies.

"I think you might want to buy. I bet there's a big buy out there. You check your screen, I bet there's a big block out there." His lesson dispensed, Jerry picks up the phone to make a call. It is a common tactic he uses to freeze the discussion. It precludes any formal conclusion to the conversation. Instead, it forces the issue to hang in the air like a department store perfume ambush. He's hit you with it, now it's up to you to deal with it.

A few phone calls later, Jerry is battling the same issue with one of the stocks he's been following. "Vinny? Yeah, I want to buy another 77,000 Pacific Gateway . . . shit . . . it's flopping around like a dead carp with prickly heat . . . shit. . . . There's a rumor that some Japanese holder wants to sell a two-million-share piece at about $40, then the stock went to $38 and they said, 'I don't want to sell at that price.' So now everybody on Wall Street is working to get the stock, but nobody has the shares yet. And the stock's just flopping around 'cause everybody knows there's two million shares out there."

After official trading has stopped at four o'clock, Marshall comes in for his daily postgame analysis with Jerry. Marshall and Jeff alternate checking in during the day—giving their own take on things, and delivering the latest news and rumors they have heard. They offer a diversion in Jerry's day, and, most times, some humor. When both are out of the office, their visits are decidedly missed, and Jerry finds himself making the rounds to other offices instead. Initially, he may be in search of some market information or news on a specific stock, but really he is just looking for someone to talk to—a break from looking at his screen.

But the close of the market belongs to Marshall. When he is out, Jeff stands in. When both are away from the office, Steve usually takes up the mantle.

"All our funds beat every index I've got on my screen except one," Marshall says. The performance of the indexes is known as soon as the market closes, so that's the earliest competitive gauge. The results of other funds aren't released and won't show up on the computer screen until after five o'clock. So, for the hour after trading ends, the group must be satisfied with beating the anonymous market, a number generated by a computer.

Much more than mere satisfaction is at stake in the race to beat the market. Beating the indexes, or at least those your fund closely resembles in strategy, is of tantamount importance to a manager. For one, most Wall Street pay packages are calculated, in part, according to how a manager performs versus the relative indexes. But, more importantly, for many managers, the competition to beat the market pits intellect against an index or man against monkey, or thinking against dart throwing. Whatever the metaphor, the competition is the same. If you're not a good enough manager to beat a fixed group of stocks over an entire year, maybe you shouldn't be playing the game.

Jerry and his team have been beating their benchmarks—the indexes the funds are measured against—since he took over. But he is not willing to settle for beating merely the benchmarks. As Jerry often says when he looks over his performance sheets, sprinkled with his own and a smattering of index returns, "I want to beat them all. I don't want to see one in there I'm not ahead of." He wants his thinking to count for something—to count for those percentage points that will put him ahead of the competition and the rest of the market.

Now, as of mid-July, the Delaware Aggressive Growth Fund is a full seven percentage points ahead of the Dow, and two points ahead of the S&P 500. He has the biggies beat—to most people, he is beating the market. But it's not enough for Jerry. There's still the Nasdaq, the technology-heavy market index that people have been slower to claim as "the market." It doesn't matter to Jerry how slow other people might be, or how they may not even notice how well the Nasdaq has done lately. It is a major index, and Jerry's not beating it. And he wants to be.

"It's been very tough to beat the Nasdaq lately," Jerry agrees with Marshall. The Nasdaq was up another 1.1 percent today, and the Aggressive Growth Fund climbed 1 percent.

"Yeah, that's because it has two stocks."

"It has four stocks." It's a common argument that has become more vociferous in the past few years: The top few stocks in the Nasdaq carry so much weight in moving the index that what the rest of the market has been doing is often obscured. Jerry cites a former colleague in New York when he points out to people that the Nasdaq was up a remarkable 21 percent for the first half of the year. But when the four largest companies in the index—Microsoft, Dell, Cisco, and MCI Worldcom—are removed, the Nasdaq is only up 5 percent for the six months.

It's like having your grades in English and Physics count for half of your grade point average because they were the biggies, while all those As you earned in dozens of other subjects—History, Calculus, Music Appreciation (Clapping for Credit), and so on—are hardly counted.

"So overall we had a pretty good day. That Cendant cost us 14 beeps."

Beeps. Prints. Pieces. It's all part of the lingo that stock market professionals adopt like a regional accent. A beep is a basis point—a b.p.—or a hundredth of a percentage point. Cendant's decline for the day cost the group 14 beeps, or .14 percent in performance. Even Jerry, who is loath to speak in most Wall Street lingo, has picked up "beeps." "I heard Marshall saying it, and I just thought it sounded cool," he says.

"Maybe we can make it up tomorrow, maybe we'll just punt it," Jerry says. The debate continues. First you wanted to buy and I said no, then you wanted to sell and I said buy. We've gone through the mental exercise; maybe we'll just get out of it tomorrow and end the discussion there.

"I'm kinda sick of having it around anyway," Marshall says and leans up against a wall of Jerry's office, while Jerry types in a few other tickers. "Trend. Sweet. Up 52 beeps."

"Nasdaq. Up a percent and change," Jerry says, reminding him that, yes, we did well, but the Nasdaq Index did twice as well.

Jerry has been returning calls since the market opened. Eight minutes into the trading day, it is time for a break. He dials up his friend Stew at home. "Did you hear they're gonna send Jaret Wright back to Little League? . . . Yeah, they say he's not old enough to play in the majors." The market is up and Jerry could use

July 10, 1998	Year-to-Date Performance	Rank
Aggressive Growth	20.9%	28
Trend	13.5%	31
Delcap	16.3%	48
Dow	15.1%	
S&P 500	20.9%	
Nasdaq	23.7%	

some good banter with his buddy. No, the Cleveland Indians are not trading one of their ace pitchers nor are they sending him back to Little League. It's just that Wright is 22 years old, a rookie, and very good at the game. The kind of guy that impresses, and secretly makes envious two men in their fifties who have numerous injuries between them and who fancy themselves athletes with once-great potential. Besides, Wright's an Indian, and Jerry goes after Stew and his favorite team any chance he gets.

When the Indians were playing in the 1995 World Series, Jerry took out a series of advertisements in his hometown's local paper that Stew and everyone else received twice a week. Like hopes for a pennant, Jerry's series started small. It was an ad about the size of a playing card with a cartoon drawing of the Indians' mascot, Chief Wahoo. The grinning Chief and his head-feather were circled and then crossed out like a no-smoking sign. The ads got successively larger, displaying the same cartoon and adding tag lines as the drawing took up more of the page. The questions and mystery surrounding the unsigned ads also grew. Everyone knew the ads were intended for Stew, with the kind of certainty that is possible in a town of 2,200 people where the biggest Cleveland Indians fan writes a sports column for the local paper. Just before the World Series was to begin, the Chief's face was splayed across an entire page of *The New Age Examiner,* along with the question, "They Lost in Four in '54,

Will they take a Dive in '95?" At the bottom of the ad, in small print, were the words, "This is a paid advertisement." That's when Stew and the whole town knew it had to be Jerry Frey. For, as many of them would remember later, "Jerry was the only one who had the money to take out a full-page ad." Calling for a full-page ad in *The New Age Examiner* in 1995 bounced a patron from dealing with the "personals" department to the advertising department, and the ads went for $387.

When he is off the phone, Jerry stares at the numbers on his computer screen. He puts his right index finger above his lips like a mustache and flutters it up and down. He is concentrating on the numbers and the changes and what they all mean.

"You know, baseball's changed," he starts in. "It's sad, but it's changed. Take Cleveland, they want to buy Randy Johnson, then they'll have three dominant pitchers. They buy Randy Johnson and they'll buy themselves a pennant. It's like the Marlins. They went out and bought everything they needed. They won the Series and then went and sold them all—decided they were too expensive, not enough ROI."

Like young boys trading cards and amassing the best collections, professional team owners swap players and options and draft picks. Truly, they buy and sell men. And they are doing it for increasingly astounding amounts of money. And that is what it's about, return on investment, ROI. What do I get out of you? Will you help me win the race for the pennant? Will I be able to sell more tickets at higher prices next season? Will you be the winner I am paying you to be?

The world of mutual funds and investment managers had transformed itself to be a not too dissimilar environment. Shareholders were increasingly focused on performance, and mutual fund companies were increasingly focused on shareholder dollars. Will you help me win the race to December? Will you help attract more shareholders and more dollars to the firm? Will you be the winner I am paying you to be?

The competition to win over those shareholders and dollars has intensified as individuals have gained more knowledge and control of their own retirement money. One company has been incomparable in pointing out to American investors just who the winners in this game are: Morningstar Inc. The company began in 1984 when there were just 1,200 funds with $370 billion invested in them. Morningstar tracked funds and published data that were intended to help individual investors and professionals alike choose among mutual funds. The company developed a "star" system to help investors navigate mutual funds' promises and their records at keeping those promises. By 1990, the stars were ubiquitous and had become a standard selling point in the industry.

Morningstar's star ratings have become as imperative to mutual funds as the Associated Press and *New York Times* rankings are to college football, or as the *Consumer Reports* endorsement is to marketing cars. Morningstar's professionals review a fund's performance, its processes, and what it promises to do, and consider these in relation to all other funds making the same promises. They then give the fund a star rating—one through five. A fund might prefer to be passed over rather than receive just one or two stars. A middle-of-the-road three stars is exactly that, mediocre. But four or five stars, that is a ticket to the show. With four, and especially five, Morningstar stars attached to a fund, a firm can bank on it. A mutual fund company can turn to its marketing department, its advertising agency, and its sales staff, and say, "Print it."

This year, Delaware has had only one five-star rating among its stock funds. It has a handful of threes and fours, and some funds and managers have been lauded in the press, but the funds have claimed only one blue ribbon. The sixty-nine-year-old firm was a premier name in the industry decades ago, when the business was focused on pension fund dollars. But, as more attention and assets flowed into mutual funds, Delaware, like so many firms, was left behind. Three years ago, Delaware was bought by Lincoln National Corporation, a midwestern insurance company with hopes of winning big in the competition for mutual fund dollars. Now, with new money and a new focus, the company has hired expertise in the mutual fund field, and has created new task forces dedicated to updating its strategy. Delaware not only wants to stay in the game, it hopes to become a major player in the mutual fund business—a business imperative to many financial institutions in the 1990s. The firm has committed to a new advertising campaign and has plans to put its sales force behind a few select funds to try to get some momentum going.

It has the money, the people, and the funds; now what it really needs are a few more little stars.

*   *   *

Throughout the trading day, Jerry makes several trips up the circular flight of stairs to the fortieth floor, where his two traders, seated in front of multiple computer screens, watch the market and keep score for Jerry. He likes to check in at the extremes—when things are going very well and when things are going not so well. He wants to boost people up when things are down, and bring them down a notch when things are flying high.

"How's Yahoo!? Still moving?" he asks, and leans back against the file cabinets behind the traders' chairs. It's his way of letting them know he's relaxed about the trade—just give me the truth.

"Yeah," Stu says as he looks at the screen, "it's getting away from us." He sighs and starts shifting papers on his desk, looking for the right answer for Jerry, or, better yet, hoping to miraculously find a few thousand shares hiding somewhere under his printouts. Jerry had asked Stu to start buying Yahoo! last week, but Stu decided that it was too expensive and he'd buy it when it came back down—as surely it would. The stock had gone from $42 to $50 since Jerry put the order in with Stu, and they hadn't bought a share.

"Well, it's like sex, we'll just keep trying 'til we get it right," Jerry says.

"Yeah, Stu's still trying," adds Vinny, the other trader.

"Yeah—thanks, Vin."

Some stocks you own, some you simply rent. For an investment, you buy a stock, put it in your portfolio, and leave it there. You add to it at times and you sell from it at times. But it's a member of the family and you build a relationship. You learn about the company, you know the products, and you understand the factors that move the shares. Most of Jerry's and the group's funds are made up of core holdings that they have owned for several months and followed even longer. They are usually neither the flashiest nor the fastest movers in the portfolio. They are companies like CVS, the drugstore chain; Profit Recovery Group, which helps retailers manage their prices; Home Depot; and Gemstar, a consumer electronics and technology company. These investments provide most of the profit in the funds and command the most research from the team.

Long-term investments make up the bulk of the portfolios, but there are also companies that are trades. With stocks that are trades, you buy when you think they're going to go up, you sell when you think they're going to go down. There's little concern for the company and its products. The only investment factors to be concerned with are that the stock is going up and it will come down—usually, very quickly. One of the risks with a lot of stocks that are trades is that most everyone else sees them as trades. There's a story behind the stock—a new fad, a hot IPO, or the toy of the season—and everyone likes what they're hearing. Take Planet Hollywood. People love going to the theme restaurants and seeing movie stars and the real props from movies, and they like putting their hand inside the imprint of Arnold Schwarzenegger's on the buildings' outside walls. Sure, the company also sells food and collects revenue, but IBM it is not.

Jerry likes to save a little room to try to boost the funds in the margins—the edges—with stocks he views as trades. Amazon.com is just such a stock.

He sold out of the Amazon.com shares he bought last summer after the stock climbed more than 150 percent. But lately, he's been thinking it's a stock he'd like to play with again. He's watched the stock climb $13 in one day, slip $21 another day, and bounce back up $11. He wants to get in. But playing with a stock like this is like gauging the jump rope on the playground. For the past few weeks, he's been watching the trades on his screen, moving his arms and hands in time with the jump rope. He's in sync now, and just needs to get his confidence up to jump in and join the game. It seems the stock is setting new records daily, and every casual investor and hot-stock junkie wants to own a few shares.

That's precisely why Jerry wants to buy it: because everyone else is. But he doesn't want to own it because everyone else wants to own it. He wants to *trade* it because everyone else wants to own it. Nearly twenty years in the stock market and another fifteen watching and working with people every day have taught him to differentiate between an investment and a trade.

When he's looking for more affirmation of his strategy than can be found in a midyear return number of plus 20 percent, Jerry likes to turn his thoughts and words to one of the great economists of all time: John Maynard Keynes. "People think John Maynard Keynes was just an economist, but he was a heck of an investor," he will say, opening up one of his familiar stories like a family patriarch inviting all to the hearth. "Yep, and he was a momentum investor before it was called momentum investing." As a British economist writing during the Great Depression, Keynes was certainly decades ahead of the trend of chasing growth stocks on the way up—now known as momentum investing, or "The Big Mo." "He believed that you didn't have to chase the prettiest girl, just the one everyone else thought was the prettiest." Then Jerry leans back in his black leather and stainless steel ergonomic desk chair, waiting for the listener to nod at the profundity of the observation. "Yep, if ol' Keynes were investing today," he pauses for dramatic effect, "he'd be in Amazon, Yahoo!, Excite, CNET. He'd be in all of 'em."

A few weeks ago, Amazon.com had announced that the company would be holding its first conference for Wall Street research analysts. Much of the investment world that followed technology companies would be in the neighborhood anyway. Microsoft would be hosting its annual conference the day before in Redmond, and Amazon.com was in nearby Seattle.

Jerry figured the company wouldn't go to the trouble of inviting everyone to Washington and then announce bad news. Would they? But then again, if he'd been invited to the meeting, and he'd figured out that good news must be coming, who hadn't? This was the sort of game that story stocks required an investor to play—especially an investor more interested in trading the stock than owning the stock. In the past decade or so, professional investors seemed to have perfected the practice of "Buy on the rumor, sell on the news." Buy when the buzz is starting, and dump the stock when the good news is actually announced. It was a game that often rewarded the aggressive investor and punished the company with good news to share. Just as often, those who got burned were individual investors who read the good news in the morning paper or heard it on CNBC, and decided they were the only ones who'd picked up on its implications. Confident of this sure-win idea, they called their broker, or logged onto their online trading account, and bought those shares the mutual fund was willing to sell for full price, only to watch the shares go tumbling down as the days wore on and investors' interest wore off.

Jerry decided he'd watched Amazon's stock price long enough. He decided he could judge just how far it might fall on an off day, and where it would turn around as it was starting to take off. He was ready to jump in.

"Stu? Vinny?" Most calls to the trading desk start out this way, as if the two traders share one name. Jerry punches in the four-digit extension of the trading desk, and whoever is available—or has the quicker hand—picks up. Jerry's professional life has revolved around numbers and speaking with people over the telephone, but the trading desk extension is one of the only telephone numbers he has memorized. When he's leaving a message for someone to call him back, he stalls the conversation while he frantically searches his desk drawer for one of his business cards so that he can look up his own telephone number. He could transfer the call to his assistant and let her leave the message, but this man who invests billions of dollars in technology companies has no interest in learning how to transfer a call.

"I got a little project for you. I want to buy 10,000 shares of Amazon. They've got an analyst meeting coming up next week. See if you can work it at these levels." Trading desks have their own language, and Jerry speaks it fluently. The translation of Jerry's instructions to Vinny would go something like this: "There's something I'm gonna try out here; it may not work exactly as planned, but I could make a boatload of money. I'm gonna step up and buy a large block of this hugely volatile stock that everybody else is afraid to buy and no one really expects to go higher. I know what I'm doing; I have a plan. Trust me on this one. Don't try to outsmart me or second-guess me. Do what I ask you to. Oh yeah, and don't go out there and advertise what I'm doing and drive the price up. Be discreet. Get me a good price."

Vinny is Jerry's trader of choice for projects that require a gut instinct of when to buy and sell, and for trades that need to be made with no emotion. Vinny is more of a hired gun trader. Jerry goes to him with directives he doesn't want questioned.

Stu, the senior trader of the two at thirty years old, had spent years trading derivatives and things that are complex enough to be called financial instruments rather than simply stocks or bonds. Although no one says as much, it is accepted that Stu tries to be smart about trades—he tries to game them. As in any professional relationship balanced squarely on respect and admiration, Stu wants to be able to call Jerry and tell him he has executed a trade better than Jerry had asked. He wants to be able to go to the boss and say, "Oh, that mistake you made on that trade you regretted making—well, I figured out the situation ahead of time and put the trade on hold." For trades that need a little more massaging or detective work, or those that need to be approached with more trepidation of the wallet, Jerry is more likely to call Stu.

Stu lacks the bragging swagger of a Wall Street trader but carries with him the quiet reverence for education and hard work of a self-made success. The youngest of four siblings, Stu is the most financially accomplished member of his family, and cousins and uncles call upon him when they are short of cash. The calls are a vivid reminder to Stu of the world he grew up in and the world of Wall Street that swirls and rings with cash-register dollar signs and bells all around him. Stu fell in love with the fast-paced world of deals and trading and, admittedly, "so much money," when he was in high school and saw the movie *Wall Street* for the first of several times.

But the world of Wall Street has changed in the decade since Michael Douglas, as the movie's lead, Gordon Gecko, blared loudly across the movie screens of America, "Greed is good." In the stock market, greed still rules, but no longer is it found among only the investment bankers and the leveraged buyout kings and corporate raiders who rule the financial world. Hundreds of other players now wield power over the markets and hold out their hands for a payout.

Today's stock market seems to be ruled by technology entrepreneurs, venture capital firms, Internet start-ups, and mutual funds. More than 7,000 mutual funds are now investing the savings and salaries and dreams of Americans who hope to cash in on the greatest stock market boom in history.

This summer, Jerry is trying to position himself and his funds to take advantage of every one of these powerful dynamics—and to keep each one in balance. It's a little like juggling several balls while looking straight ahead, but knowing where they all are and sensing when one is straying and needs attention. Some days, he focuses on investments the fund already owns. What's going right? What could go wrong? Other days, he asks the same questions of companies he doesn't own. There are days when his phone rings to schedule meetings with companies where "everything is going right . . . you gotta see them . . . this deal is white-hot." They are companies passing through town, getting the story out there for their IPO, or telling their story a second or third time, hoping to sell even more stock. Other days, Delaware's own marketing team calls Jerry to set up meetings. Essentially, these callers are saying, "Wow, your numbers are terrific. We've got to get out there and sell and collect some fees while we've got something good to say." Or, more generously: "You're really making your shareholders happy. Let's give more individuals out there a chance to get in on some of these returns."

For now, Jerry's numbers are exceptional, there are countless Internet and high-tech companies wanting to go public, and marketing seems to have his extension on speed-dial. His arms are moving quickly and the balls are circling in a fluid course dictated by Jerry and gravity. Up, down, up, down. It is the same course that investors have come to expect from the stock market for decades. Yet, for years, it seems to have only gone up as more investors have scrambled to get in. Will this be the year, or even the summer, when the market succumbs to the pull of gravity?

* * *

Marshall marches into Jerry's office, nodding smugly with his lips pursed tightly. "We should short Quick Zone." With his hands on his hips, it is a confident call.

There are investments and there are trades, and then there are shorts. Rather than believing in Quick Zone the company—buying the stock and making an investment—Marshall wants to cry foul. He wants to short the stock—a little like reverse investing. He's certain the stock will go down, and he wants to be able to profit from that conviction by betting against the stock. "Shorting" a stock is exactly that—betting it will go down. When investors short a stock, they actually sell shares they don't have (trading desks allow this) and then buy the shares to "cover" the "short" when the stock does indeed go down. That's a winning bet. When the stock doesn't go down, the investors will have to buy the shares at a higher price—the trading desk is not about to let them off the hook. That's a losing bet.

It's like being able to go to the toy supplier and borrow a few hundred Beanie Babies or Furbies or Cabbage Patch dolls while they are the must-have fad. And you get to borrow them on credit. You sell them to salivating buyers who are convinced this is the fad that will last. And you sell them for a screaming profit. Once the craze has passed and the prices have plunged, you go back to the toy supplier to pay your debt at the now rock-bottom prices. Alternatively, the sure fad may turn out to be a sure thing, and the toy supplier may call to let you know she needs her inventory back. You're stuck buying up those toys with those salivating buyers. And you're paying screaming prices. Then you know what getting squeezed in the market feels like.

Most mutual funds, Jerry's included, aren't allowed to short stocks on the theory that the practice carries a little more risk than an average fund holder should be exposed to. But that doesn't stop the group from talking about shorting as if it's allowed. It gives them a whole other arena in which they can prove themselves right. Not only can I pick investments on the way up, I can also call 'em on the way down.

"They're going into these little local service businesses, putting in networks. I think that's an indication that they're throwing in the towel on their base business," Marshall continues his assessment of Quick Zone. "I think the network infrastructure in this country is pretty well installed. . . . And, they're not making their numbers."

Jerry laughs, "That'd do it right there." One of the most punishing rules of the game has become "You miss your numbers, you lose."

"Quick Zone? Well, that one's basically behind us. We're out of that one now." Jerry looks to Marshall for confirmation.

"Oh yeah, we're completely out. And we got a good price. We didn't make a lot of money, but we made a little money."

"Sometimes you make a lot of money, sometimes you make a little money. And sometimes you make a little money just by not losing a *lot* of money," Jerry decrees with a smile. Sure, sometimes the smart move is to buy the right stock and hold on; other times the best decision is to sell the wrong stock down a little instead of holding on long enough to watch it plummet beyond recovery.

It's one of the recurring lessons in the lecture series that Jerry's team unwittingly signed up for when they joined his group. They each know how to build a spreadsheet, analyze a balance sheet, build complex discounted cash flow models, and talk about present value like it was the lunch menu. But Jerry often finds the need to remind them that these functions are merely tools of their job. Analysis is not what shareholders have hired them to do. *Doing* is what they do. They are to buy and sell stocks. If you're not buying or selling, you're not doing your job.

The finance lecture over, Jerry is back on the phone with another salesman. "What am I doing? I'm trying to get my goddamned computer to work. Every time I get halfway through something, the damn thing freezes up on me. . . . Amazon and Yahoo!? Jesus no, I wouldn't short them. . . . Advanced Fibre? I got my brains blown out on that the other day. So I bitched and moaned to Alex Brown. I said, 'Jesus Christ, who does your research there? You've got a company that does a preponderance of business with one company and no one calls them?' So, I was all pissed off at them. . . . A respirator? How old is he? . . . Yeah, well you have to be careful because infections on the outside go through the catheters that lead right into the heart. . . . You've got to ask when you have surgery—no matter what the surgery is—ask the doctor if they have any problems with infections. Last time I had knee surgery, I asked the doctor, 'You ever have any problems with infections with this?' Boy, was that a hot button!"

That's what Jerry is professionally trained to do—to push people's hot buttons, or at least find out what they are. He asks questions and he listens to the questions other investors ask. Sometimes the answers matter. Often, it is simply knowing what the other investors care about that matters. In this game, it is more important to know what other investors will react to than what the company thinks they should react to. On alert for the nuances, Jerry tries to determine—before every Wall Street analyst or investor knows it—what will and won't move a stock in the market. Like the surgeon's scalpel, it is just one of the tools Jerry uses to separate the stock from the company. It is a way to know what infections are out there, and to keep his funds protected.

Jerry is particularly aware of the insidiousness of a silent and slow-moving infection. His wife, Kelly, is an infectious disease doctor and keeps Jerry current with what new strains could potentially threaten the population. Her skill in studying, isolating, and determining infections is not lost on Jerry as a growth stock investor. He shakes his head in admiration when he rattles off her resume, and he frequently consults her on biotech and pharmaceutical investments and doctors' roles and policies in the world of managed care. Other times, Kelly offers her advice and conclusions unsolicited.

When Jerry and his five-year-old son picked up food from Boston Market to eat while they watched *Home Alone III* for the second and third times, his wife warned matter-of-factly, "Well, when you feel sick tomorrow, you'll know why." As far as glass-is-three-quarters-full Jerry was concerned, he and his son were having a fast meal at a good price. As far as his wife the doctor was concerned, fast food can often mean a fast ticket to a sick stomach.

As far as the stock market was concerned, ill health had been creeping up on Boston Market for a while. The very same week Jerry enjoyed his Boston Market dinner, the Nasdaq Stock Market was threatening to delist the company for having too low a stock price. Boston Market's stock debuted as Boston Chicken in 1993 to the most eager welcome any offering received that year. The shares jumped 143 percent, from $20 to $48.50, the very first day. Five years later, the wonder-IPO trades for a little over a dollar a share.

* * *

The stock market has been open for less than two hours, but things are already heating up this July morning.

"Go baby. Yeah, I love it," Marshall's voice rolls confidently into his speakerphone and spills out into the hallway. "Cyber . . . yeah, what is it?. . . Yeah, I'm owning it. I don't care what they do."

Within minutes, Marshall is in Jerry's office joking about this latest hot stock that the funds will own, no matter what the company does.

"The coolest name for a company ever," he announces himself inside the doorway. "I'm buying it, I don't care what it does. It's an online computer seller. It's called Cyberian Outpost. I love it. And the ticker symbol is gonna be COOL—C-O-O-L."

"It'll be hot for a while, then it *will* be cool," Jerry says, hardly glancing up from his screen.

"Yeah, then it'll be stone cold," Marshall says and moves on to stocks that are red-hot. "Look at CompUSA. Go baby." He moves both arms around in a circular motion in front of him, as though he's churning butter—a victory lap of the arms.

Jerry looks up to join Marshall's discussion and offers up a company he made an investment in, years ago, called Mr. Gasket. "It became Mr. Casket."

Soon, Marshall is back out in the hall asking after the whereabouts of his one o'clock meeting—and, more importantly, the lunch for his one o'clock meeting. It's the season of hot deals. There are companies to meet and free lunches to eat.

Jerry pulls out an IPO prospectus describing the company he'll be meeting next. He also takes out a full-size, lined notepad and a business card from his desk drawer. These supplies indicate that he's taking this meeting seriously, and also that it's a company or an industry he doesn't know much about. Sometimes, he will hardly read a prospectus at all—a sign that the deal won't exactly be getting a lot of attention from Jerry Frey and Delaware Investments. Other times, he simply takes notes and marks down a few questions and figures on the blank pages in the back of the prospectus, signaling that he knows the industry well and understands the dynamics, and his concern is at the level of detail.

But today's prospectus, Broadcast.com, requires a new pad of paper. Jerry opens the booklet and creases it neatly along the staples at the center of the document. These preliminary sales booklets are called "red herrings" or "the reds" because of the remarks printed in bright red ink alongside the spine of the cover. The term actually dates back to the woodlands and fields of fox hunting in England where dried, salted herrings were dragged across the fox's trail to divert the dogs' attention. Wall Street's red herrings may have less ill intent, but, in practice, they act as precisely the bait that gets investors hooked on a deal, despite the prominent warning in red ink: "Information contained herein is subject to completion or amendment."

Jerry begins to read the document, and the business card he uses as a ruler slides across and up and down the text, faintly rippling the thin tracing-paper-like pages of the booklet. The thin transparent paper is used for prospectuses before the deal is done. Thousands of copies are printed and distributed at this step of marketing and selling, so the thinner paper saves on both paper costs and shipping. The transparentness of the paper makes the deal or the company seem as if, at this stage, it's not yet real. It is just an idea that can be blown around by the air conditioner and is written in disappearing ink. When the deal is completed, a "final" prospectus is printed on heavier stock. The deal is live, the company is real, and it is trading in the stock market.

Jerry writes down questions to ask and underlines points or facts he wants to remember. "Internet 24 hours a day, seven days a week, 345 radio stations and networks, 17 television stations and cable networks, over 350 college and professional sports teams." He makes notes of numbers, how the business is run, how much stock is being sold, and who's selling the stock. In every deal, he wants to know who's selling, who's getting the money, and why. For Jerry, it is an important point. If the executives think it's such a great company, why are they selling so much stock? In other instances, his concern is: Why were the chairman's wife and nephew allowed to buy a million shares for a penny apiece? Often, the answers to these questions help Jerry decide whether a new company will be an investment or a trade for him. He likes to think he's putting his money with companies that are putting that investment back to work in new products, acquisitions of other companies, or the expansion of their existing businesses. But, if it looks like a sure-win, quick-boost-of-cash-to-your-mutual-fund kind of deal, he's not exactly against that either.

"There's not an officer of the company older than 39!" Jerry says aloud while reading through the prospectus. Broadcast.com is just one of many firms debuting in the late 1990s that are run by executives who were in college during the last stock market crash and recall little of life before the computer. When they hear about the "Nifty Fifty" stocks that were the must-own companies decades ago, they think, yes, that is "nifty"—as in "cute." The stock market, emerging technologies, and Americans' appetite for the next hot investment have created hundreds of millionaires and more than a few billionaires in their twenties and thirties.

It's a fact that offends many investors and even casual observers of the stock market. College-debt-laden twenty-four-year-olds are instantly worth $50 million, $500 million, or even a billion dollars if a company's IPO really takes off. Such instant just-add-IPO wealth prompts many spectators to cry "foul"—or at least "easy" or "lucky."

Jerry harbors no such displeasure or jealousy toward the new class of young and moneyed nerds high on junk food and stock options. In many ways, he feels his own success in the stock market and the mutual fund industry stems partially from a similar stroke of luck or happenstance. A case of right time, right place. He knows he could just as well be building factories for companies as investing in them. With a little more reflection, he would claim that a life—be it 24 years or 52—of working hard, doing the right things, and being the right person is what puts you in that "right" place at that "right" time.

"Heck, these guys are all bright. . . . They deserve it just as much as anybody else does. . . . I couldn't have thought of that. . . . It's actually really neat what they've come up with. . . . Yeah, and they're gonna make a lot more money for somebody else." These are Jerry's retorts to the summer's breathtaking IPO debuts and the sure-to-follow articles chronicling and calculating the latest whiz-kid Web zillionaire.

Jerry has no problem with the string of extra zeros and dollar signs the Internet has added to investors' vocabulary, but it's the lone exclamation point that bothers him—specifically, the Yahoo! exclamation point. "It's part of the company's official goddamn name. Why do they do it? To be different," he lectures during a lull in the market. "I tell you what it is. It's not different, it's just stupid."

While the exclamation point hasn't exactly caught on as a necessary part of corporate logos in the '90s, the period has. Jerry underlines the details about the company's changing its name, just two months ago, from AudioNet to Broadcast.com. "You gotta have a 'dot-com' on these 'cause that's what gives you the big multiple on your stock price."

Indeed, the dot-com name was becoming the name of the game in the stock market. All over the industrial map, companies were changing their names or their business plans to be seen—or at least invested in—as Internet companies. Back in the stock market's fledgling days, any company that could claim ties to the railroad industry garnered extra attention and eager investors. Now, at the end of the twentieth century, the same boomtown frenzy is on the World Wide Web frontier. Even real estate mogul Donald Trump has plans for an Internet access biz. And Zapata, which was originally an oil company founded by former president George Bush, unveiled its Internet strategy and named it Zap. And, when K-Tel International announced it would sell its record collections over the Internet, the company's stock price jumped 125 percent that same day. And now, here on Jerry's desk sits Broadcast.com, nee AudioNet.

While Jerry sits in the Broadcast.com meeting and listens to the pitch for on-demand audio and video, and for Web sites attracting 400,000 visitors a day, a swing band plays in the plaza forty stories below. The July sun is high, the Broadcast.com deal is heating up, and the band plays "In the Mood."

Three days later, when the shares of Broadcast.com are scheduled to debut in the market, Jerry's traders call to give him the news that the shares are indeed white-hot. The Wall Street firm handling the IPO set the price at $18 a share the night before, and word on the street is that the first shares will trade for $38 apiece when the bidding begins.

The opening of trading in IPO shares is usually delayed in order to give the trading desk of the investment bank that did the deal time to sort out everyone's orders and what they're willing to pay for those orders. It's like the excitement and buildup to the first sale of tickets to the summer's hottest concert. The company and its investment bank have traveled all over Wall Street, and through conference rooms and hotel ballrooms, meeting money managers like Jerry. The company's tune has been played through the media, on investing sites across the World Wide Web, and across the lips of every hot-stock junkie looking for the next IPO fix. The public has heard and likes the tune: IPOs are the easy way to make a fast buck.

So the company announces plans to sell 2.5 million tickets to the concert at $18 apiece. Jerry and other professional money managers are the season ticket holders who get to sign up for most of those tickets in advance, and will pay the price printed on the stub. Once all of the tickets have been spoken for, the investment bank buys the whole lot from the company for the $18 ticket price. This is the only money the company will see from the offering—no matter how fabulous a concert is put on at the stock market's opening bell the next morning or in the coming months.

On the day the IPO actually begins trading, it is the rest of Wall Street, the investing public, and, increasingly, individual investors who sleep out and stand in line at the booth for the chance to get tickets as soon as they become available. They know that not everyone who bought their tickets for $18 apiece really wants to see the show or to hold an investment in the new company. But the avid fans and stock junkies want it—and they'll pay up for it. They place orders with their brokers, sending them online to their Waterhouse Securities and Charles Schwab accounts. All of these get called in, by brokers or other traders, to the investment bank, which then has to decide how much those $18 tickets will be allowed to be scalped for. Then the trading desk overseeing the deal looks out the ticket window, sees how many times the line wraps around the stadium, how many fans are salivating with their wallets open. The investment bank in charge of the IPO declares the market price, the window opens, and shares are available for trading.

So, just like at a sellout concert, Jerry and other big investors will buy up their shares for Broadcast.com for the $18 price printed on the stub. The line of those fans who didn't get tickets, but want them, is long. When the buying and selling of the tickets begins, they will likely go for more than double what the season-ticket-holding professional investors paid for them. This is, of course, good news to Jerry and the rest standing on the other side of the stanchions holding their $18 tickets. But, Jerry got another bit of news about the deal. He was told that no, he didn't get the 10 percent order—250,000 shares—of Broadcast.com that he wanted, nor anywhere near that. He was given 6,000 shares. Sure, 6,000 shares of a 100 percent gainer on the first trade is nice, but it's a little like asking for a $250,000 mortgage for a house, and having the bank give you $6,000. It helps, but it doesn't get you far.

Jerry looks at the list of other investors who bought shares of Broadcast.com at the $18 price and how many they got. It was slim dishing all around—it's a hot ticket and there were lots of hands out. And, Jerry knows that there are indeed lots of investors who are not only not planning to *sell* their shares in the opening trades, but in fact want to *buy* even more shares and make an investment in the company. "I bet it'll close up at $52. Just looking at the allocations, it looks pretty skimpy. So everybody and their brother'll be fighting to get more in the aftermarket. They'll drive the price way up."

Two hours later, trading in Broadcast.com still hasn't opened, and Jerry is sitting in a small conference room, meeting with a hospital management company. The executives drone on about the balanced budget amendment, speaking in a swirl of government and medical acronyms and programs. BBA . . . Medicare . . . transfer rules . . . PPS.

In the middle of the meeting, Geri brings in a message folded in half and slips it to Jerry while the executives continue to talk about acquisitions not happening as fast as they expected. It is a call from the trading desk. He reads it and raises both eyebrows. He folds the paper back in half, creases it tightly, then folds it again, letting the news settle in with each movement. The indication for the opening price of Broadcast.com's shares has jumped from $38 to $60. It is now expected to be a 200 percent gain. On the very first trade. Jerry tries to turn his attention back to the conference table. The explanations of why growth is being pushed back another three to six months are little match for the pale pink memo resting in front of Jerry: 200 percent growth in about six seconds.

As soon as the meeting is over, Jerry heads to his office and calls Stu. "Broadcast.com. It didn't open, did it? . . . I said 50. Why don't you cut that back to 25. And do it right on the opening. I don't want to go too high with this one." Jerry will be one of the buyers waiting in line. He is willing to pay $60 a share to get his hands on another 25,000 tickets. He hopes to be able to sell these to the next round of interested buyers for even more. But these are higher prices than he expected, and the game is moving faster every day. Do it quick and don't be greedy.

* * *

Most of Jerry's and his group's days are filled with meetings, phone calls, research reports, sorting out information, looking at numbers, staring at computer screens, and deciphering what it all means. Most simply, does it mean a buy or a sell? Or maybe it means another call to another analyst, another salesman, or a competing company. Even if you get to the right answer first, will it matter if no one else cares that it's the right answer? You can do all your homework, produce the right number, and make the enlightened decision, and it may not be enough. The outside forces, the anonymous market, the intangible "they" and "there" may be the final factors that move a stock in one direction or another.

"Putting out fires all day long. That's all I'm doing," Marshall says to Jerry as the two pass on the circular staircase connecting the thirty-ninth and fortieth floors of Delaware's offices. "Outback Steakhouse is down. There was a report that came out saying that at one of the new restaurants some of the workers had hepatitis A, which is in and of itself not a big deal. They didn't get it from working in the restaurant or anything. But then this analyst goes out over his system and puts a report out saying that everything is okay, even though they got hepatitis B, not knowing the difference between A and B. So, I had to call him and tell him, now he's got to go out and retract it all."

An understanding of infectious diseases is not exactly a prerequisite for success in the stock market, but any edge can help. Any bit of obscure knowledge—a new way to look at things, or apply a fact, or ask a new question—can make the difference. And in this game, the subtle differences can count for a whole lot in the end.

The growth group, just like thousands of other professional investors in the market, spends its days searching for that edge. They are on the lookout for it everywhere: in research reports, on conference calls, during company meetings, and in announcements of hepatitis breakouts. Just as often as the group members trot their new piece of information or data through Jerry's office, auditioning for the tip-of-the-week spot, he brings ideas to them. Did you think of this? Did you see that? Did you try looking at it another way? It's an exchange of information, but it is also Jerry's way of mentoring and coaching his team. He lays out the plays and options before them, and then waits for them to choose whether or not to follow.

"You looking for me earlier?" Steve steps into Jerry's office, catching him off the phone for once.

"Yeah. I can't remember why I was looking for you." Jerry looks up from his computer and pauses. He is thinking, flipping through his mind's Rolodex of facts and data he has encountered, processed, and filed in the last few days. "Oh yeah, there was an article in *The New York Times* the other day on prisons. You see it?"

"Hmm. I think I had some analysts call me on that. Pretty negative, wasn't it?"

"It's *prison*. You didn't think prison was gonna be positive, did you?"

Smiling, Steve brushes the popcorn salt from his hands into the trash bin as he works up his response to Jerry's challenge. "Yeah, but they can be positive about the privatization of prisons—lower costs, lower recidivism."

"That's a big word. Where'd you get that?"

"From them," Steve says and tells Jerry about the prison tour he had on Monday of Cornell Corrections, a company the funds have an investment in.

At the end of the discussion, it is unclear whether Steve will take the direction Jerry has pointed—whether the article will be read, or that edge and those subtle differences will be sought and found. Steve ends the discussion. "It's a classic tailwind-headwind. It's a hell of a lot easier to do well when you have a tailwind."

It's just one of the many all-purpose phrases that business schools seem to pass out with their syllabus on the first day of classes. "Top Ten Sound-Intelligent Noncommittal Comments to Make about the Stock Market, a Company, or Business Circumstance." Tailwind-headwind. At the end of the day. Net-net. Thinking out of the box. Don't fight the tape. They are the slogans that twenty-four-year-old finance majors adopt as part of their vocabulary within weeks of arriving on campus. It takes even less time for the marketing majors of the class to silkscreen the phrases on the back of T-shirts and set up stands selling them for $15 apiece.

The Dow has closed up just under 100 points, and the Nasdaq is up six points. Jerry's head bounces back and forth between the daily performance sheet he received before the market opened and his screen showing today's prices after the market's close. He updates the printout in his head and can almost see the improved numbers appearing on tomorrow's printed sheets. It's nearly impossible to make the myriad calculations necessary to determine a fund's exact performance for the day, but Jerry does his best. He assesses the performance of the overall market and looks at his stocks in relation to that. It's more common sense than science, but Jerry announces the numbers to his team well before the computers post any final performance data. With confidence, he cites the numbers to at least one decimal place.

Math has always been one of Jerry's strongest subjects, and he even thought he might end up a high school math teacher. Those dreams disappeared when he started working on Wall Street, but he still has the slide rule he won as best student in Miss Lutes's eighth-grade math class. Jerry's oldest son was amazed to see the gadget being used on the big screen in *Apollo 13*. "Hey dad, there's that thing you have," he declared. Jerry smiles fondly when he remembers the prize. "It wasn't a cheap one," he says. "It was a really nice slide rule."

And now, decades later, Jerry sits with a Hewlett-Packard 19B business calculator open and waits for his up-to-the-minute computer to give him up-to-the-minute results. Until then, he has exactly three numbers—six digits—written on the top of a small, white memo pad.

"If you took Cendant and a couple of others out, we'd be having a pretty good year," Jerry says as he looks up from his calculations. It is as close as Jerry gets to a feeling of contentment over his number-one ranking performance so far this summer. "If 'ifs' and 'buts' were candy and nuts, we'd all have a Merry Christmas." He lets the performance sheet fall to the desk and picks up the phone to make a call.

Soon, the woman from Delaware's computer help desk is in Jerry's office. She and the other troubleshooters from the various information services that populate Jerry's desktop are surprisingly frequent visitors to his office—an office that oversees nearly a billion dollars worth of technology investments. Jerry's altercations with his computer are like a rehearsal for an IBM advertisement. It starts with a jiggling of the cords or flicking on and off of the power to the machines. The scene always ends with a phone call to the help desk or to Geri's desk—whoever might come sooner.

"You go to school for this? Where'd you learn all this stuff?" Jerry says, standing behind his chair where Linda is now seated, toggling away at the keyboard and the mouse.

"Yeah. I went to school for this. I'm a computer nerd."

"That is the only kind of nerd it's okay to be. Any other kind of nerd is, well, nerdy."

Marshall steps inside the door to make his first after-market appearance. "DelCap and Aggressive Growth had a kickass day."

"Well, I have some bad news for you. I sold some of your stocks today," Jerry says. "I sold more of mine than I did yours. Just housecleaning. No one else seems to want to do it, so I'm housecleaning." Jerry has been telling the group for weeks that they should have bigger positions in fewer stocks—know our companies better, participate more when they go up. "So I sold some Chuck E. Cheese."

"What? Chuck E. Cheese?" Marshall asks, confused.

"Yeah. P-Z-Z-A."

"Papa John's."

"Whatever it is. It was running, so I had 'em scale it up." To Jerry, the trader, this meant: This is something we have a small position in,

I have no emotional ties to the company. (How can I, if I don't know what it is?) The stock is going up, so the trading desk can sell our shares into an up-market—"scale it up." It's more fine-tuning of the core holdings. Build up where things are working, shave off where they're slipping.

"Well, whatever the case, we had a great day," Marshall gets back to the numbers on the screen—at least his, if not Jerry's, at the moment. Linda is still sitting at Jerry's desk clicking away.

"Yeah, it was working fine," Jerry says and turns his attention to his computer. "See, it was all left hand corrected and now it's all like this."

The alignment of numbers and letters on a screen is just one of the issues that trouble billion-dollar money managers after the stock market closes.

"Where's that guy that's always in here? The Bridge guy? He said I could call him any time I had a problem and he'd come fix it," Jerry asks. He figures if Linda can't fix it, maybe Bridge, the service that supplies Jerry and the other Delaware managers and analysts with their stock quotes, can help. He paces back and forth behind his desk while Linda calls "the Bridge guy."

"Just think, if Bill Gates had been interested in football or Little League when he was younger, we wouldn't be sitting here with this problem right now," Jerry says.

Linda gets up from his chair, her work complete. "Linda, you're a genius," Jerry says as he inspects the screen and finds it looking exactly as he wants. When she is out the door, he issues perhaps some of the highest praise doled out in American companies at the end of the 1990s, "She's the greatest person at this company. She fixes everyone's computers, and she's really nice about it."

Marshall is back, snapping his fingers as he steps through the doorframe. When Jerry raises his head, Marshall gives the thumbs-up sign with one hand. "One-eleven. Aggressive Growth, one-eleven."

"Yeah, that's pretty good." Jerry says, as a siren goes off underneath his window. Delaware's office tower is across the street from the Philadelphia Fire Station of Engine 43, Ladder 9, and is just blocks from two of the largest hospitals in the city. The screaming sounds of a fire engine or ambulance often punctuate his days.

"The Russell's up point-4," Marshall says. He offers this up for comparative purposes—the Aggressive Growth fund was up 111, or 1.11 percent, while the Russell 2000 Index—one of the fund's benchmarks—was up 40, or .4 percent.

"Let's see what that piece of crap—the S&P—did today," Jerry says, typing in the ticker for the S&P 500 index. It's nice to have trounced the Russell, but they were already beating that index when the day began. He wants to know whether they've gained any ground on the competition they were lagging.

Jeff walks in while Jerry is typing. "Veritas. HUGE. Microsoft, two cents better, Xilinx, a penny short. . . . Wanna hear Paul Sutton's numbers? Four-point-five."

"Four-point-five what?" asks Jerry, having missed a beat in Jeff's staccato, telegraph speak.

"Four-point-five mil. Nine million for two years," Jeff says, relaying the latest rumor on the pay package for a Wall Street technology analyst who has jumped firms.

This news stops Jerry. He drops his pen on his desk and leans back in his chair, giving the announcement more room to settle in with him. "Jeez. That's more than baseball players. That's more than Jaret Wright. Jeez, this is a crazy business. They get paid more than baseball players."

When Jerry was finishing college in the 1960s, he was asked to fill out a questionnaire on his expectations for his future:

Q: *What is the highest annual income you expect to earn?*

Jerry thought to himself. He considered two pieces of evidence. He thought about his father, who died when Jerry was twelve. He had graduated from an embalming school in Philadelphia and practiced as a mortician before taking a sales job with a local car dealership. He'd made about $4,000 a year. Jerry also thought of his own professional path. He was a good student, so figured he'd go back home and teach at the local high school and coach the Tunkhannock Tigers. What could be better? Sitting in that college lecture hall, he was pretty sure teachers made good money, and of course, he'd always thought enough of himself to place himself at the top of any field he entered. He picked up his pencil and wrote in a neat script that leans to the left:

A: *$17,500.*

For Jerry, as for many of the investment world's top managers and traders, it isn't the money. They have a passion for the ideas, the companies, and the constant challenge of the competition and the market. More than anything else, it is about getting it right.

At the end of the week, Jerry is sorting through papers and clearing off his desk when Geri sends a message in over the phone system. He takes his wallet out of his pocket and pulls out a dollar bill. It's time to play Delaware's Dollar Days. It's the firm's version of Liar's Poker, but instead of the goal being to show the biggest *cojones* of the office by betting a million dollars on a single poker hand, Dollar Days is about the luck of the draw, the game of chance, the ever-renewing optimism of Americans in the 1990s, and the desire to win. All in all, it is about a pot totaling around $70 or $80.

Those employees who want to play write their first name and telephone extension on a dollar bill, drop it into a bird's-egg-blue Tiffany bag that travels the halls each Friday, and wait. The lucky winner will get the call, the bag, the money, and the responsibility for rounding up the dollars the following week.

Jerry doesn't consider himself a gambler. But he does think he's lucky. If there's a game or a contest out there in which someone will be the winner, Jerry wants his chance to compete. He plays the lottery if it catches his eye, he bets on college football games, he strategizes over the office pools for the Final Four basketball tournament, and he plays Delaware Dollar Days every Friday.

He remembers the first time he played the game—in the first week or two he had joined the firm. He threw his dollar into the bag with all the others. At the end of the day, Jerry's was the lucky number. Even now, when he thinks about it, and the grand total of $80-plus that he won, he gets quiet. "I thought to myself, 'Holy shit. I can't believe I won.'"

CHAPTER 3

SHORTER THAN THE
LIFE SPAN OF A
STICK OF GUM

Half an hour before the stock market opens, numbers, prices, and strategies are starting to swirl through Jerry's head. His plans are stymied by an 8½-by-11-inch sign taped to his computer screen. Delaware's computer systems have been updated and Jerry hasn't.

"Everything okay?" A blond-haired guy from the computer help desk leans in the doorway.

"I haven't tried it yet," Jerry says as he stands behind the desk facing his keyboard, his screen, and the sign letting him know that his world has just gotten a little faster, a little more responsive, and a little more complex. He tears off the sign and throws it into the trash bin. A flip of the on–off switch starts the hard-drive grinding. Jerry types in a few keys and waits for a familiar response.

"Well, I'd better go find that guy right away," Jerry says and is out of the chair and down the hall before frustration sets in.

He returns with Linda, computer fixer extraordinaire.

"So we're up and running, right?" he asks her as they enter his office, as if her mere presence can fix the computer remotely.

"Sit down and I'll tell you how to get started," she says. Buckle up; changes are afoot, and you've got to get up to speed. She walks him step-by-step through functions he's practiced countless times, repeating each keystroke like they are the basics of the box step. "Okay, so just do *Start*, drag up to the user applications, go over to

Bridge Station, and let go." She directs, the computer grinds away, and Jerry just keeps chatting.

"So, how was your weekend, Linda? . . . Do you wake up dreaming about computer stuff?"

"I do. I do."

"You oughta drink more."

Then Lea comes in with the printouts of yesterday's performance, signaling that the race is ready to begin again.

"What do you think, Lea, we gonna make it through the day?" Jerry asks.

"Oh, I hope so," Lea says as she moves about his office distributing the mail, faxes, and trading sheets to their respective piles. "With this heat and all these calls."

Jerry and Linda both stare at his screen as though it is a 64-bit video game—watching the numbers and waiting for new programs to appear.

Jeff walks in. "Uh-oh. Surgery. This is never good. New PC? What'd you get him?"

"He's got a 6180," Linda says nonchalantly, as if the model number is as universal as saying it's a Dell or Compaq or IBM. And perhaps, to Jeff, it is.

"A 286?" Jeff asks sarcastically, knowing that the old 286-chip machines are the Studebakers of personal computers.

They all laugh. Ah, techno humor at nine in the morning. But in Jerry and Jeff's business, it's really not so funny, especially this summer. Technology is changing at a breathtaking pace, and more people are getting, using, and taking advantage of more of it. The competition is multiplying, and the rules are changing.

No longer are Jerry and his team battling only other mutual fund managers at firms like Fidelity, Putnam, and Janus. Now they are increasingly squaring off against individual investors for shares, speed, and information in the market. The promise—or threat—had always been that technology would level the playing field between professionals and individuals. This summer, the bulldozers were mowing that field down with force. Faster computers, multiple phone lines, and trading firms geared toward amateurs were enabling individuals to move in and out of stocks with nearly as much ease as the pros.

Making it even more complicated for Jerry and other managers, individuals seemed to be trading their mutual funds just as often as they were trading stocks. A couple of good days and the money comes in. A weakening market or a stalled fund and the cash pulls out like an undertow.

As Jeff likes to picture it, the market works like a complex game of chess—one with multiple layers, multiple worlds, and multiple players. The games are going on simultaneously on all of these boards in all of these worlds, and, to make matters worse, Jeff says, the players are all going out of turn. Companies make bids to take over other companies, new products come out to replace last month's debut, a hot mutual fund manager jumps firms, an investor posts a rumor on the Web, an executive sells a block of stock, an analyst issues a buy recommendation. They are all possible moves in the match that goes on every day in the market. It is a constant challenge to try to see and anticipate all of the moves on each layer as—or before—they happen.

According to Jeff, there's only one player who can do that. The chairman of Microsoft. Or simply, Bill.

* * *

Ten minutes later, Jeff is back in Jerry's office waiting for him to finish a telephone call. Jerry is in no hurry to end the call, nor does he appear eager to hear whatever news, tidbit, or opinion Jeff is bearing.

"N-W-H-S?" he asks his salesman and types in the ticker. "I may be asking too much trying to get this computer to work."

Jeff writes a note on the pad of paper he is holding and sets it on Jerry's desk. Jerry nods but doesn't look up. *Point taken, but it's not something I want to discuss.* Jeff picks up the pad and heads for the telephone in his own office next door, to dial the trading desk.

Minutes later, Jeff is heading back into Jerry's office when Jerry passes him on his way out. Jeff is clearly worked up by his news, but Jerry doesn't pause and nearly walks right into him.

"Analog miss their quarter again?" Jerry asks, with the air of saying "I told you so" rather than asking a real question.

"Yes," Jeff says as he breathes audibly through his nose. "Revenues are down 10 percent. . . ." He continues to cite the company's quarterly statistics and shortcomings, but Jerry is already halfway down the hall. The "yes" was all that mattered to him this morning. The company missed the quarter, the stock is down, we own the stock. The details are meaningless.

Four minutes before the market opens, Jerry is back at his desk, calling up to the traders. "Vinny? Stu? On that Broadcast.com— B-C-S-T—what've we got? . . . We've got 31,000 total? On the opening, why don't you sell that and then we'll come back and figure this one out."

This particular play in the game is happening a little too fast for Jerry. He wants the chance to stand on the sideline and review the moves. It's another game with multiple levels and multiple players. The shares of Broadcast.com's IPO have already doubled, and Jerry isn't sure whether he should stay in and go for more. What is everyone else going to do? Take their winnings and go home, and let the stock drop? Or keep buying more and chasing it higher? It's just as easy to get run over on the downside as it is challenging to keep up on the upside. He's looking for a little grounding, a little direction on where to stand.

"I better check in with my right-hand man," he says as he dials up his buddy Stew, whom he saw over the weekend. "What the hell you doing, taking human growth hormones or something? . . . You're looking good. . . . Yeah, my son Sam told me the other day, 'Hey, dad, you oughta take some of that Rogaine. You're looking thin on top. . . . You've got a real dirthole up there at school. What are you gonna do with the old school? . . . Oh yeah, that's gonna look nice. All the way down the back by Doc Bishop's house? . . . Huh, that's gonna look nice." Jeff walks in while Jerry is discussing building suppliers. Knowing this could take a while, he leaves. Jerry's phone beeps, and a message appears from Geri, letting him know that the trading desk is on the line. "Oh, I got my trader on," Jerry says instinctively—but then stays on, so that it doesn't appear that a call from the trading desk carries any more weight in his office than a call to his hometown. "How're the Indians doing? . . . Okay, I gotta hop. Good seeing you."

It is Stu from the trading desk. "Just called to tell you that Amazon you bought last week at $112, it's up six today. It's already up over $120." It is not a call asking about a clarification on a trade, nor is Stu calling to offer any new information. It is a call to say, "You're the man."

"Yeah, they've got a big meeting coming up. And either before or after they say something at that meeting, I want to get out. I just need to decide which one," Jerry says.

After a conference call and a few more trading calls, Jerry walks the seven blocks from his office to the Philadelphia train station for a slice of pizza and a root beer for lunch, and thinks about his next moves. The Dow is down 27 and the Nasdaq is up 10.

*   *   *

A little after one o'clock, the growth group gathers for its weekly meeting.

"Performance-wise, we're still hanging in there," Jerry opens the discussion.

"I think we moved up a couple of spots in the week," John says, looking at the peer rankings.

"You have to be cognizant of the positive cash flows in there." Jerry reminds his group to stay focused. We can't sit back and be content—shareholders are sending in more and more checks to us, and we've got to make sure we're doing the right thing with that money.

"What was the low in total asset size?" Jeff asks. Performance is the industry's first measure of success. The second is the ability of a fund, or manager, or group to attract new investors. How many people signed up to join you for the next round? How many mice have come out to follow the sound of your pipe?

"For all of growth, two billion was the low. It peaked in '96 at about $2.3 billion. . . . The numbers look okay. Aggressive Growth, when Delaware got it, was $6 million, then it went down to $3 million, and now it's up to $97 million," says Jerry. They've come a long way as a group, but they haven't set any records yet. They may be number one for the last twelve months in their peer group of 100, but winning the mutual fund game takes convincing a lot more than 100 peers. They've got to attract some attention in order to attract the dollars. And as of last month, Morningstar was willing to rate the fund only a fairly unattractive two stars. They would have to do better.

Jerry goes back to performance. "When you look at the numbers and you look at how much we're up for the year, if you annualize it, I'd have a hard time expecting that to happen," he says, with a hint of a laugh. Indeed, it would be difficult. The fund is up 25 percent in late July—a little more than halfway through the year. By annualizing that number, or simply multiplying by two to cover the second half of the year, a 50 percent gain in one year does seem, well, more than mildly aggressive. Most financial planners advise their clients to be pleased with a 10 percent return in a year. The S&P's 20 percent performance for the past three years has been extraordinary. It has been called unprecedented and abnormal. A 50 percent gain in one year would certainly be remarkable, and Jerry isn't necessarily looking at it as a realistic goal.

"So what do you do?" John asks.

"I think you look at the performance, and you look at your names, and you decide which names you'd buy more of if the market corrected 15 percent. We just want to make sure we're holding the names we really want to own."

"So, then if we make it through the summer and performance looks good, do you load up on cash heading into the fall?" John asks. The group is trying to construct some sort of road map, strategy, or schedule to navigate the unpredictability and volatility of the market.

"Yeah, you make it through the summer and then you hit October. . . . I was talking to a guy at Morgan Stanley about putting together some hedges against performance . . . some way to protect us when we get to October." Jerry looks around the room for reaction.

Hedges. Protection. Limiting risk on the downside. It's all covering your ass. Putting together hedges or trying to protect some of your performance in the stock market is a lot like buying insurance: you may not need it and it isn't free. Investors can buy hedges to protect their gains in case the market, a stock, or a particular industry or continent plummets. It can be something as simple as buying bonds while stock prices are high, in hopes that if stocks drop, bonds won't drop as much. If a fund is heavily invested in companies doing business in Japan, it might be active in the foreign currency market, to protect itself if Japan falls apart. Keeping more money in cash, as opposed to investing it in a volatile market, is probably the simplest way nervous investors protect themselves. But, as in climbing, being cautious can cost you. The extra tools, safety nets, and harnesses can weigh you down. They can make it harder to keep up in the climb to the top. Still, if the terrain becomes treacherous, those hedges, that protection, and those safety nets can make the difference between surviving and not.

So, as they do every other day in the market, Jerry and his group face a decision. They weigh their options, they calculate the risks, and they try to look forward to the future: the market's traditional August lull, the surprises of September and ominous October.

"And October's where big kahuna things are just waiting for you," Jeff adds.

"Well, it's hard to see a scenario where things just continue to go straight up from here," Jerry says. "In individual names, you've just got to watch out for the fires."

John asks about Cornell Corrections, the prison management company the fund owns shares in, and a fire he's been trying to put out for a few days. "We just can't get anything done. We can't even sell it down a buck. There are no buyers, only sellers."

"Well, it's better to shoot yourself than have someone else shoot you." Jerry repeats one of his frequent lessons: once things look bad, sell and don't look back. Don't be afraid to sell at a loss, and don't be tempted to wait around for things to settle. Trying to outlast the fire usually means you'll end up selling at fire-sale prices later. When a stock is trapped in controversy, it's a buy or a sell. It's not a hold, a wait-and-see. You don't say, "Let me be patient and watch how things play out." It is a time for action. Sell quickly at nearly any price to be rid of the burden, or have the conviction to pounce on more shares when other investors lose their patience and confidence.

"There's nothing there," John says.

"There's always something there. It just depends on what your price is. If you go down three dollars, is there something there?"

"People have been calling to see if we were interested in buying more," Steve says, attempting to back up John's position that there are no buyers out there. For Jerry, it provides another piece of the puzzle: What are the other sellers willing to do to get their shares sold? "How big's this other guy's piece?" Jerry asks, talking about million-dollar stock holdings as if they were slabs of beef.

"125,000."

"So he's smaller. You should control the price," Jerry says. If you wanted to buy his piece, you should be able to get it cheaper. No, you don't want to be left selling at fire-sale prices, but buying at fire-sale prices is an entirely different game.

"It just has that quiet-before-the-storm feeling," says John, refusing the bait Jerry has offered.

Jerry lets him off the hook. "You may own the best company in a poorly performing industry, and it's still gonna be tough to make money."

"Yep, tailwind-headwind," Steve says.

"Have you talked to the broker or the salesguy covering the company?" Jerry asks, still intrigued by the opportunity. "If you've got a lot of guts, buy his block down three. I like that scenario."

"But that's poker, right?" John asks.

Jerry smiles to himself, content with the prospect of taking a stand in the market and winning. John's question and the challenge to double down are left hanging in the air.

Some days, Jerry sees the stock market as an institution de-signed to raise money for growing and successful companies while rewarding shareholders for investing in the right companies. Other days, like many this summer, the market is a game. Because it's a highly lucrative game, Jerry says, it has attracted some of the brightest players. And that's what Jerry the competitor sees when he stares at the blinking numbers on his screen and must decide, "Should I buy or should I sell?" Facing his computer, he's sitting across the card table from the smartest players in the game. Should he fold or should he call their bluff?

After the meeting, Jerry calls Stu on the trading desk to check on Amazon. "Stu? Yeah, when it gets up twenty, we're gonna sell it. . . . They got this meeting this week, and I don't know if I want to sell or be really greedy and see how high it'll go." Again, should he take his winnings and go home? Or should he roll again and try to win big? Just minutes ago, he was encouraging John to be bold, be greedy. Now, what will Jerry do when he issues himself the challenge?

Nine minutes later, he is back on the phone. "Stu? Why don't you sell 25,000 Amazon."

At its core, the stock market represents capitalism in its purest form. On the surface, it is sheer gamesmanship. It is nuance and posturing. It is speed and positioning. It is bluffing and standing firm. And it is a game that can best be taken advantage of by the quick and agile. Like a Darwinian ruse, the soaring stock market of the late 1990s is doing its best to weed out the old-style investors who cared about such things as value, price, and history.

At 52, Jerry is doing his best to stay quick and agile. Unlike most investors who tend to be old school or new school, Jerry tries to straddle the middle ground. Building big positions in long-standing, solid companies that he understands well is the key to his strategy. But he isn't against working the newer, faster, less proven companies into the mix. As the head of technology investments for the group, he tries to keep up on the latest companies, products, and trends in the market, even though his own voicemail gives him trouble.

* * *

Just after the market closes, Jerry is in his office showing a salesman from Alex Brown how to throw a knuckleball.

"You've got to have fingernails. Dig your nails into the seam." Even if none of this advice will add to the salesman's ability to throw the pitch, Jerry likes saying it. He likes to feel that he is offering something different, from a different perspective. And who wouldn't prefer practicing pitching to working on a Monday afternoon in July?

"Keep your thumb on top and then you just pop it. . . ." He pulls his arm up alongside him, showing the motion of the pitch's release. "You turn your feet against the rubber, cause that's where all the power comes from." They both look down and watch his feet turn in his black socks and polished black loafers. "Then you just let go and pop it. It'll unload straight, and then it'll be everywhere along the way." Jerry flops his forearm from side to side like a fish struggling on a wet dock. The two are clearly enjoying the exchange. It is as fantastic as a major league pitcher's giving his catcher tips on buying mutual funds between batters.

That's what everyone is looking for—a guide, a little help, a secret pitch that unloads straight and then surprises everyone. Although it's no secret, one of the fastest growing guides to Wall Street and investing, during the past decade, has been the William O'Neil & Company empire. The company is a cross between an investment seminar sponsor and a publishing house. Most importantly to professional investors like Jerry, William O'Neil provides data—and lots of it.

Every month, three 11-by-16-inch William O'Neil books are delivered to Jerry's office. They pack nearly 2,800 pages of information, charts, numbers, and data. Jerry keeps the books stacked on his lowest bookshelf so that the overhang can rest on the floor. If he lets more than two or three months' deliveries stack up, he fears that the books will slide off and the millions of numbers and lines and graph points packaged so neatly inside will come spilling out onto the floor in a pile of indecipherable black ink.

Every week, no fewer than nine more William O'Neil books arrive in Jerry's office. Their data, again, fills well over 1,000 pages and another stack on the bookshelf. The books analyze stocks of specific markets, stocks of specific sizes, and stocks held specifically in Jerry's mutual funds.

Every day, Jerry receives from William O'Neil a facsimile that screens, analyzes, and highlights any changes in any of the stocks in Jerry's three funds.

Every minute of every day, Jerry has access to WONDA, William O'Neil Direct Access. WONDA has become the big-daddy database for most professional investors. It includes every data point published in William O'Neil's myriad books. The database is probably the simplest one-stop shop for an investor to look up such vital statistics as past performance of a stock, which Wall Street analysts write research on the company, and who else owns the stock and how much of it they hold.

All of this information, access, and ability comes at a price. It is no small subscription fee for the books, nor a simple access charge for the database. These are premium services that cost premium dollars. For the year, Jerry's group spends nearly a quarter of a million dollars on William O'Neil offerings. It is one of the group's highest expenses, second only to travel bills to visit companies and attend conferences.

For individual investors who don't have a quarter of a million dollars to spend on stock market data, William O'Neil publishes *Investor's Business Daily*. It can be picked up on any newsstand for $1. This, too, is delivered to Jerry's office every day.

When he opens one of the oversized maroon William O'Neil data books, Jerry first turns to the section that highlights companies whose stock prices are hitting new highs—stocks that are on the way up. "Usually, it's the stocks you don't own and are going up that are the most aggravating." He turns the pages slowly. His eyes bounce over the wavy lines climbing higher and higher as they move from left to right across the graph. "I go through these books and I see all these companies I owned and sold four years ago that are making new highs today, and then I look at what I still own personally, and they're probably at the same prices they were four years ago." He tears a page out of the book. "Quorum. New relative strength line." Just one more data point Jerry looks at. Does the stock climb or fall fast, relative to other stocks? What's its relative strength? "The stock's done well and we've made money in it—probably just not as fast as we've made money in some other areas, which is really sort of the business we're in. It's not 'Did you make me any money?' anymore. No, it's 'How fast did you make me money and how much money did you make me in as short a time as possible?'"

He continues paging through the book like it is an old high school yearbook stirring up memories of the prom or the model-car club. "Getty Images. Here's one I knew and watched and didn't get in on . . . so the stock's gone from ten to twenty-eight without me."

Jerry pauses to loosen his tie and unbutton the top button of his light blue oxford shirt. The daily scores are starting to post on his computer screen. "Hmm. We didn't do as well as I thought we did. . . . We were up, Dow was down, S&P was down, Russell was down close to a percent, and the Nasdaq was up slightly. In the grand scheme of things, it's the best of all worlds—everyone else is down and you're up." It was a strong day, and the Aggressive Growth Fund is up 0.6 percent. It has gained ground on all of the major indexes. But Jerry doesn't let his eyes rest on the green glow from the computer screen for long. Before he gets too pleased with himself, a page from the O'Neil book catches his eye. "Now here's one I did totally wrong— Guitar Centers, up 113 percent. We owned a little bit off the deal and then we sold it."

It is just two days later, but the mood and the market have shifted considerably. The Dow has closed down two days in a row and is off nearly 150 points. It is down already this morning, and Jerry is concerned.

July 21, 1998		
	Year-to-Date Performance	Rank
Aggressive Growth	25.3%	17
Trend	15.3%	25
Delcap	16.6%	50
Dow	16.2%	
S&P 500	21.0%	
Nasdaq	26.0%	

Just after the market opens, he is on the telephone with one of his salesmen. "I think we've probably entered the correction phase for a little while. . . . Jesus Christ, look at Amazon, up four. The market's getting hammered and this thing. . . ." He tosses into the air the pen he's been holding, and lets it land on the desk while he leans back from the screen in surrender to the market. "Yeah, I'm interested in Telebank, but I'm not an owner. . . . Oh I don't know—a week, a month, whatever. I'm not gonna flip it back to you the next day. . . . Yeah, if I get a decent allocation, I'd buy some in the aftermarket. If I get 5,000 shares, I won't, then it's not worth it. . . . Okay, I'll talk to you."

Jerry has just logged in his vote to the all-important "book" on Wall Street. When a company's IPO is being put together to begin trading, the Wall Street firm in charge of the deal calls around to take orders and get indications—to "build a book." First, the bankers want to know how many tickets you want to the concert and how much you are willing to pay for them, so that the investment bank can decide the official price to print on the ticket stub. But, they also want to know: Will you be standing in line for more, or will you be selling into the line—"flipping" your shares?

Salespeople and traders ask, "Will you be active in the aftermarket?" Will you be a buyer we can count on beyond the first trade? Unless he's a big fan of the deal and wants a guarantee of more shares, Jerry usually answers with a terse, "Yes. Yes, I will be active in the aftermarket." No need to show them his full hand, especially when it reads, "Yes, I will be actively selling the shit out of your deal in the aftermarket."

If everyone's a seller, the initial trading doesn't exactly look like the hot concert the investment bank wants to be known for promoting. They want investors to "support" their deals—especially those that are not so white-hot, and those that may have a very short line at the ticket window. But Wall Street is a two-way street. You support our less popular deals—hold onto your shares and possibly even buy more—and we'll set aside a nice-size block of tickets for you and make sure you get the nod for our next hot deal.

Just after ten o'clock, his first meeting arrives, and Jerry puts a stick of Big Red chewing gum into his mouth. The visitor is a salesman from a small research and trading firm in San Francisco. He's looking for his firm to get in on a little of the millions of commission dollars that Jerry and his team dole out to Wall Street firms each year. When they get useful research from an analyst or a timely tip from a salesperson, Jerry and his team send some trading their way. The firm then collects their fees through the trades done—commissions—rather than being forced to rely on investors' willingness to pay for reports written about the struggles in the software industry or the comeback of the oil and gas sector. It's the world of "soft dollars" on Wall Street. You send us the research and phone calls for free, and we'll let you know how much it's worth to us and send our trading orders your way.

The trading desks of Wall Street investment banks are where the cash registers just keep ringing. A desk collects a commission on every trade it makes, and the desk keeps the difference between what it sold the shares to Jerry for and what it bought the shares for from someone else. Jerry's group can turn soft dollars into millions of hard dollars at a firm's trading desk. And as a trading desk's relationships add up, so do those dollars.

In exchange for sending their trades and dollars to the trading desk, Jerry and his group earn credits with that firm. The credits can never be turned into hard currency, but are more like frequent flier miles that can be used to pay for things through that trading desk. Most often on Wall Street, commission dollars are used to pay for the countless research reports and calls that investment banks send out to clients. Or, a money manager can spend his or her commission dollars by calling up a trading desk and saying, "Great analyst panel you guys put on last week. Oh yeah, and we just got our bill from William O'Neil, why don't you send them over a check for a quarter of a million dollars?"

Some firms have let "soft dollars" get so soft and squishy that they are used to cover travel expenses of fund managers, and even phone bills and computer terminals. Jerry and his team follow strict rules on soft dollars—if that's possible. He has always had a strong sense of black and white, and now soft and hard. He leaves little room for the gray and squishy.

And now this salesman is sitting in Jerry's office, trying to convince him to start racking up some frequent flier points with his firm. The salesman sits across from Jerry. He is restless on the edge of his chair, and his too-big glen plaid suit hangs loosely on him. "Well, I just wanted to let you know what's been going on at the company. . . . We've changed a lot. . . . We've added a lot of new hires—an Internet guy from Volpe, a wireless guy from Soundview . . . so we're now up to six or seven tech analysts." Send some of your trades our way, get our cash registers ringing, and we'll mail you some research reports on all of our best investment ideas.

"Yeah, there's a fair amount of overlap in what we own and what you cover," Jerry says as he flips through the folder the salesman has brought. It contains several pieces of research the firm's analysts have written. As he thumbs the neatly printed pages, with their target stock prices, historical graphs, and colorful corporate logo, Jerry wonders to himself how many small firms look at a fund's holdings, start research on those companies, and then come calling, to offer their research and trading capabilities. It's the sort of skepticism most people reserve for personal injury lawyers loitering outside hospital emergency rooms or faith healers setting up near trailer parks.

It's just another component of the job. Filtering information, screening for an edge, reading a pitch. He's got to ask the right questions, look for the nuances, and determine the truth behind the story, the screen, the pitch.

Jerry closes the folder and lays it down in front of him. He has made his decision, and he will challenge the salesman to give him a reason to change his mind. "But, for us to buy it, it's got to be idea-driven. And we only pay for what works. We don't pay for someone to call me up and tell me what's in *The Wall Street Journal,* or that a company reported numbers last night. I can read the numbers myself. I pay for soft information."

"Well, that's kind of the way we work," says the salesman, perhaps thinking he is passing to the inside track.

They continue to discuss the structure of the trading firm—who the partners are, and what sort of deals the analysts are involved in. It is not enough to change Jerry's mind. When the salesman asks if Tom, the only analyst who seemed to pique Jerry's interest, can call him, Jerry replies, "Sure. I rely on voicemail quite a bit. That's an efficient way for me to get information." It's also an efficient way for Jerry to completely ignore an analyst or salesperson. Calls to Jerry's telephone number are immediately routed to voicemail, which Jerry's secretary retrieves and transcribes throughout the day. Being given Jerry's direct-dial number, instead of that of his secretary and gatekeeper Geri, puts you decidedly on the outside track.

Jerry shakes hands with the salesman as the two rise from the conference table. Before the salesman is even down the hall to the elevator bank, Jerry has tossed the folder and his piece of Big Red into the trash bin. The salesman and his firm were able to hold Jerry's attention for seven minutes, shorter than the life span of a stick of chewing gum.

Next in Jerry's office is Wayne Stork, the outgoing chairman of Delaware Investments. He barely steps in the doorway. "You want to call me later?" He simply looks at Jerry, not expecting a reply, knowing that there is only one way to answer that question, and walks out. Although Jerry oversees a team of professionals and manages more than $2 billion, he still has to report to someone. For the rest of the year, he will report to Wayne.

Today's meeting is to discuss compensation packages for Jerry and his team. In his mind, Jerry catalogs the faces of the people who work in the offices and desks around him. "All these people are loyal to me—all the way down to Geri and Lea, the secretaries—and I've got to make sure I look out for all of them. And yet I report to the chairman. I think a lot of times, at companies like this one, they're looking out for the greatest profitability in the short term. So I'm getting stretched in both directions." He wants to look out for the people below him, yet those above him want him to do that with as little as possible.

Now it is Jerry's turn to play the role of the salesman. He must sell himself and his team, and what they have done and can do for Delaware. Jerry isn't comfortable selling intangibles like the group's skills or expertise and experience, so he sticks to what he knows: the numbers.

Simplistically, money management firms take in money to invest and collect a fee for doing so. The more money they attract, the more fees. Strong performance, a proven manager, and a few stars from Morningstar can all combine to pull cash in like a magnet. In mid-1998, Jerry and his team manage about $2.3 billion. Collecting an average fee of .75 percent, they earn about $17 million for the firm. When expenses for things like travel, phones, computers, office space, and even those 600 reams of paper are taken out, there's still a hefty chunk left over from which to pay the group. The pay package has already been set for this year. It's a $3 million carrot, and, depending on how the funds do, the group can have some of that carrot or all of it. Sure it's a big number, but it's not unreasonable for the industry, especially for a group that has performed so well. Already Jerry is focused on next year's package. He wants to make sure that the better his group does, the bigger its share becomes.

The growth business has been expanding, and Jerry has been attracting more attention, but the other side of Delaware's business—the value side—has been slipping. The firm was founded on value, and most of the executives, including Wayne and the president of the firm's investment business, were groomed on value. Growth was viewed as the risky, the high-flying, casino kind of investing arena. Value had history; it was built on something, and it was built to last. Now, value stocks, value-oriented mutual funds, and Delaware's value business were all eroding. As in most firms, the erosion was slow at first, but the number of accounts choosing not to renew their contracts or pulling their assets all together has picked up. They are moving their money from value to growth or to index funds or private investments. Like everywhere else, investors are looking for more, faster.

So now, while Jerry watches his stocks and his own mutual funds on the rise, he worries that the weakening of his firm's business may perhaps stall his group's success. As Jerry might say, "Being the best player on the last-place team can only get you so far." Or, as Steve and his MBA colleagues might say, "Classic tailwind-headwind." To be blunt, will Delaware pay the growth group what they deserve when the firm is losing money elsewhere?

Jerry and Wayne are as opposite in their perspectives, interests, and tastes as they could be. While Jerry struggled through Bloomsburg University in rural Pennsylvania and shuttled between jobs as a construction worker, high school study hall monitor, and milk truck driver, Wayne is an Ivy Leaguer from Brown University and has donned a business suit at Delaware Investments' offices since 1962, when he was 25. Jerry is interested in college football, rifles, and carpentry; Wayne studies glass sculptures, buys up pieces from the New York school of abstract impressionism, and has a second home in Florida. Wayne wears cuff links, and he keeps his jacket on indoors. He sits in an office with a pair of sculptured lions from sixteenth-century China. A Delaware colleague says of Wayne, "That man is the board of health. He has every 'i' dotted and every 't' crossed." Jerry's "ts" are, well, less crossed. He has never worn cuff links to work, and on cooler days in the office he will put on a cardigan sweater from The Gap. He sits in an office with two dead cactuses in terra cotta pots from his son Sam. Wayne is a value investor; Jerry has always played in the field of growth. In spite of—or perhaps because of—these differences, the two men have tremendous respect, admiration, and even affection for one another.

Wayne shakes his head when he remembers the first time he met Jerry in New York, when Delaware was considering hiring him. "He walked in wearing a car coat and a hat. And he was not exactly charismatic, and I thought to myself, 'Oh, my God. And we're gonna pay this guy how much money?'" Now, knowing Jerry much better, he smiles and says, "He's very scientific in the way he thinks about things and puts them together, and not that many people are."

Professionally, Jerry would like to be known as a manager who thinks about things like not too many others do. But, the stock market and bonus aside, Jerry takes some pleasure in being the guy who makes you shake your head and say, "Oh my God." He still laughs when he thinks about a joke he told Wayne earlier in the year.

There's a guy driving by a farm and he sees a bunch of sheep. He pulls over and stands at the fence admiring the sheep. The farmer comes over and asks if he can help him.

The guy says, "Oh, I'm just admiring your sheep out there. You've got some very fine animals."

"Yep," the farmer agrees. "Got a good flock."

"How about if I guess how many sheep are in the field and I get my pick of one?" the guy asks.

"Sure," replies the farmer.

The guy takes a minute to look the flock and the field over. "637."

"That is exactly right," the farmer says.

So, the guy walks out into the field, picks up a female and brings her over to his car.

At this point in the joke, Wayne, sensing that Jerry might have a different definition of decorum than he, stopped him and asked, "Where are you going with this?"

Jerry continued.

Before the guy drives away, the farmer says, "Okay. Let's try this the other way. If I can guess your profession, I can win my animal back."

"Sure."

The farmer looks at the guy and says, "You're a portfolio manager. Probably small cap growth stocks."

"Yeah. Exactly right," the guy says, a little stunned. "How'd you know?"

"Cause you just picked the only fucking dog in the whole flock."

Jerry likes to say that he and Wayne are continually engaged in a game of intellectual ping-pong. They debate the market, the funds, growth versus value stocks, and new ways to measure performance. Most often, they discuss who should be paid and how much. They both have strong views on the subject and are not inclined to give any ground.

It's just one more battle in Jerry's list of challenges for the year: Attract shareholders. Beat the market. Make money for shareholders. Beat the competition. Make money for myself and my employees.

*   *   *

After lunch, Jerry walks into his office tossing John's baseball in the air. The familiar feel of the ball in his hand is comforting. He continues tossing it rhythmically while he sits at his desk and types in a ticker. "Gensia. It's a four-dollar stock. The chart on this thing is like watching the grass grow." He continues watching the screen and tossing and catching the ball. He punches in ticker symbols for prices, pulls up charts of historical performance, and even looks at listings of which investors own certain stocks. He has seen the numbers and screens so many times that, with just a single data point,

Jerry is able to reconstruct a company's entire trading history, product cycle, and stock market story.

Jerry's particular command of such corporate and market minutiae is partly due to his twenty years in the business, but the skill owes much more to his days trading baseball cards, not stocks. When the two were young, Jerry and his friend Stew made a game of having the most statistics at immediate recall. It was a Name-that-Tune version of baseball cards. They would take turns covering up random cards, and then slowly peel a finger off the corner, revealing just the border, or a hint of the photograph's background. Whoever could name the player and rattle off the endless statistics on the card's flipside was the winner.

Soon, Steve is in Jerry's office pulling a chair up to his desk. "I want to talk to you about a stock. You'll have some sort of two-sentence comment. You've been in the business long enough. You can crystallize it like that."

Jerry eyes the prospectus Steve holds in his hand. Before Steve has even asked a question or mentioned the company's name, Jerry opens the tutorial himself. Surely the prospectus came across his desk weeks ago, and he data-banked the pertinent information and issues without thinking. And now, he has glimpsed at least the cover or the corner of the prospectus, and he can name that tune. "Overnight Transportation? They were supposed to be the premier trucking company until Union Pacific bought them out. How much did Union Pacific pay for them?"

"I do not know."

"What's the industry growth?" Jerry asks.

"Top-line growth for the industry is 2 percent."

"That's exciting," Jerry says sarcastically. The growth group is used to looking at companies that are growing 30 percent and is not surprised to see companies growing at 50 percent or even 70 percent a year.

"Yeah, it's less than the GDP," Steve agrees. When the gross domestic product (GDP) grows 2 percent to 3 percent a year, it is considered a good thing. When the U.S. economy grows a few single-digit percentage points a year, it's impressive. When a company looking for attention in the stock market is an industry growing at 2 percent to 3 percent a year, it's less than impressive.

"But their bottom line is growing, like, 16 percent to 18 percent," Steve says. The top line—sales growth—is not that exciting, but the bottom line—the buck-stops-here profit line that shareholders care about—is up as much as 18 percent.

"How's it growing? Pricing?" Jerry asks.

"No. Efficiencies," Steve says. It is one of the corporate mantras of the '90s. We aren't making more money just because we can cut our prices more than our competitors. We're making more money because we're more *efficient.*

"I would call up Jon at Alex Brown and have him put you in touch with their trucking analyst. They have a good analyst. There's an index—I think it's called the Cass Index—that tracks trucking and is considered to be one of the early indicators of slowing economic trends. . . . Call up the analyst and have him get some info for you," Jerry offers, not saying yes or no to the deal, but trying to point Steve in a direction to find the answer for himself.

"I talked to DLJ for an hour yesterday," Steve says, showing the boss that he's done his homework—he's already spoken with an analyst from Donaldson, Lufkin, and Jennette (DLJ), another major Wall Street investment bank. "He seemed really knowledgeable. He said this is not a growth company and it's not a growth industry." Steve continues to detail the troubles in the industry and the weaknesses of this particular deal. "But somebody on Wall Street seems to think there are factors that could make this thing an earnings rocket for three years."

"Maybe," Jerry says. "Listen to what he says, 'This is not a growth company.' We are a growth fund. Keep that in mind."

They run growth funds that buy growth stocks in growth industries in a growing economy. They have no time to wait for a stock to catch up, to work through its problems, or to get back on the growth track. It's a game of getting ahead and staying ahead. The rules say: Do ruthlessly whatever you must to keep moving up as you move toward the end of the year. Nothing is personal. It's just the market.

When Steve leaves, Jerry turns back to his computer screen and the performance sheets on his desk. While the market and his computer whir away—hopefully, putting his fund another few pennies and a percentage point above his competitors for the day—he figures he might as well look back on the past. Jerry's character doesn't lead him to gloat publicly, or even aloud, but he does lean back in his chair and grin widely to himself as he looks over the numbers. It's the kind of moment that would call for the snapping of suspenders if he wore them. He flips leisurely through the six pages of the report, savoring the numbers, looking for things he hasn't noticed before, waiting for any answers he hasn't already thought of. There is almost no need for Jerry to go through the sheets to discover anything about his own performance—he knows exactly how he's doing. He's a little like a pitcher looking at his own box scores. Long before the presses roll, he has lived those statistics and gone over the numbers and all of their nuances a dozen times in his head.

No, Jerry (or any athlete or portfolio manager, for that matter) doesn't check the performance sheets or the charts in the paper to find out how he's doing. He studies the tables for the same reason he memorized box scores as a boy: to check out the competition. He questions himself and his abilities according to where he stands at various times of the year. How far ahead am I? How many games back from the lead am I? Is it possible to catch up? Whom do I need to look out for behind me? What would I have to do right, and what would the other guy have to do wrong, for me to catch up? Of course, thinking through these myriad scenarios does nothing to change his performance or his peer ranking. It simply helps pass the time until the new box scores are printed, or, in this case, until the numbers run across his computer screen.

This particular week, just past the halfway mark on the road to December 31, the numbers for the Aggressive Growth Fund look almost boring: rank for past eighteen months, number one; rank for past twelve months, number one; rank for year-to-date, number one. Below Jerry and his team rank ninety-nine of the most competitive funds with the same investment goal. There are no calculations to make, even in his head. At midseason, they are zero "games back," only games ahead. The only strategy issue is that of staying ahead—looking at and knowing where the competition stands, and not letting them make any ground. As Jerry's eyes pore over the names and numbers on the page, he often sees faces. The funds and performance numbers and rankings he looks at recall people with whom he has had lunch, flown on planes, traded analysis over the telephone, and they are even people he has worked with.

Halfway down the third page of the printout sits the Fremont U.S. Micro-Cap Fund. He decides to give Bob, the manager of the Fremont Fund, a call. Jerry has known Bob longer than anyone else he's known in the investment world, and he often and loudly credits Bob with teaching him everything he knows about the business. Bob was his mentor. He was his first boss on Wall Street. He was his roommate. And he was probably Jerry's truest friend when he arrived in New York from his small town in Pennsylvania—just one town over from where Bob grew up.

Back in the 1970s, the two had gotten to know each other over beers, laughs, and weekend sports games. Bob would leave his New York City investment job to spend the weekends back in Pennsylvania, near the hometown Jerry had been able to stay away from for only days-long stints.

It was probably after months of evenings that began and ended at the local bars, and enough teasing and good natured criticizing of one another to fill a high school yearbook, that conversation started to dribble out about what Bob did during the day and what Jerry thought about at night. Theirs wasn't a town or a crowd that discussed one another's careers—especially if the job didn't include a union and physical labor. Jobs on Wall Street and in high finance fell slightly outside this category.

By this time, Jerry was driving 26 miles three nights a week to Wilkes-Barre, where he was studying for his MBA. The extra credentials may not have been necessary to get ahead in his own town, but he was starting to think beyond those boundaries and its population of 2,200. Jerry took a collection of economics and statistics courses, but it was a finance and investment class that captured his interest—and, slowly, his wallet. As part of the class, the instructor organized a contest in which each of the students invested a mock portfolio during the semester. As months went by, Jerry began to talk to Bob more about stocks and investment strategies and perhaps less about the most recent weekend's bar adventures.

As the year was coming to an end, so was the job that Jerry worked on with a construction and engineering crew. They were just finishing the last phase of work on a 100,000-square-foot warehouse for the Procter & Gamble plant just west of town. The crew would be moving on to another job, and they had invited Jerry—who'd proved skilled not only with a tool or two, but with numbers, bookkeeping, and people—to come along with them. After the New Year, they'd be moving to Sartell, Minnesota, ninety minutes north of the Twin Cities. Average temperature in January, 6 degrees Fahrenheit. Jerry was not a cold-weather person. Besides, even with his limited career exposure, which included summer league softball for cash, test proctoring and substitute teaching at the local high school, and construction site management, Jerry was starting to think—or at least hope—that something else was out there for him. He grew up in the 1950s in a Jimmy Stewart sort of town where you believed opportunity was just around the corner. Or the next barstool.

At the end of the Wagon Wheel's polished oak bar, Jerry and Bob relaxed on high stools that could have had memorial nameplates on them after the cumulative hours the two of them and their friends had sat there.

They were having what had become one of the pair's routine discussions that wound from local chatter, their respective moments of glory in high school football, to investments, and finally to their lives. Neither remembers whether it was their second or third round of long-neck, seventy-five-cent Budweisers, but they both recall the conversation clearly.

"Well, they want me to come to Sartell, Minnesota, and work with them on a job there."

"Why don't you come to New York and work with me."

"Okay."

It is likely that, at this point, the next round of beers arrived and the dialogue had moved on, perhaps recalling the Thanksgiving game of 1963 or Tunkhannock versus Factoryville in the 1950s.

"Bob? It's Jerry." He smiles warmly and pauses, waiting for Bob to recognize the voice—and then to recognize its sincerity. It has been months since the two have spoken. After Jerry left New York two years ago, Bob had moved on to start his own firm. They had both been busy in their new roles and had little time for the friend-ship. Jerry wouldn't ever pass for the touchy-feely type, but he was at the point in his life where he could afford the time to work on his personal relationships. So many on Wall Street and in the invest-ment world have sizable egos and a lack of time for anything other than the markets. They seem to have the attitude, "Like me or don't like me. I have enough money and wield enough power (in my small sphere) that I don't care." But Jerry did care. If he respected some-one, he wanted at least respect in return. For the first time, Jerry was now very much in charge of his professional life, which was going well, and he could afford to give a little ground personally—for an old friend.

The two joke casually about what they know of each other's lives over the past two years—Jerry's move to Philadelphia, and a party Bob threw for his daughter's wedding. Slowly, the conversation turns to business, which, for these two who know each other so well, is personal. He's counting on the conversation's staying general and in the well-worn territory of investment cycles and an unforgiving stock market. But Bob turns specific and almost immediately men-tions the Internet stocks.

He laments the difficulties of being a mainstream investor when others out there are just chasing Internet stories. He discusses the ex-cesses in the market and he wonders about valuation. They are com-plaints he will offer more than once over the summer.

If the two had traded stock banter more frequently over the past few months, Jerry would've responded. He would've told Bob that in-deed it was Jerry Frey and his mutual funds who were buying up and trading those Internet stories—Inktomi, Broadcast.com, Amazon.com,

CNET. And he would have laughed out loud when he told him that his funds were making millions of dollars doing so. Instead, Jerry leans back in his chair and, with pursed lips, groans a series of noncommittal "um-hmms."

With his monologue, Bob has ceased to be Jerry's mentor. Even though the two hadn't worked together in years, and Jerry hadn't needed Bob's approval for even longer, Jerry had still worked in a faint shadow—even if he was the only one to see it. It's always reassuring—especially in an industry like the stock market—to think there's someone a few steps ahead, someone to ask questions of, someone to exchange ideas with, someone to look up to.

Jerry hangs up the phone after a few more casual laughs and wishes of goodwill. He pauses and looks out his office window before spinning his chair to face the computer screen once again. The Nasdaq market is down only four points, and less than two hours remain in the trading day on this Wednesday in late July. The sun hangs high just west of Jerry's building, casting not a single shadow on his thirty-ninth-floor office.

Five months are left in the year. Jerry's Aggressive Growth Fund is number one in the country. He is in the lead on the climb to the top. And now he is guiding his own team. There are no tracks for him to follow, and no one to take cues from in the months ahead. He is forced to rely on his own experience, his own analysis of the situation, and his own gut. Now it's time to see whether Jerry Frey has *It*.

CHAPTER 4

WHERE'S
THE PONY?

"Oh no, it's a sea of red today," Jerry says, looking at his screen. The market has been open for just four minutes and already most of the stocks blinking on Jerry's screen are trading down. Their tickers have flickered from white to red, signaling the trading direction as down.

It's late July, and the market is starting to wobble. The indexes are retreating, stocks are struggling, and the growth team's footing is slipping. At the end of the month, *The Wall Street Journal* reports that investors shorting stocks have set a new record. More people than ever are speculating that stocks will go down. Alan Greenspan, the chairman of the Federal Reserve Board and the country's economic guru who watches over what Americans spend and save, remarks that the single biggest piece of inflation in the country is the stock market. Everyone is betting that the bubble is getting ready to burst, and they want to be out of the way when it does.

"It doesn't look good. This is not good," Jerry says as he continues to stare at the screen. He hasn't touched his mouse or his keyboard to pull up any other view. The flashing red numbers on the screen are all he needs to see right now. "It's like brokers telling you you gotta see a movie, 'Oh, you're gonna love this one. You gotta see this movie. Just try it out.' They get everybody all packed into the theater and then they say, 'Oh, there's a fire in here.' "

Jerry doesn't sit down at his desk; he even stands back from it a bit, as if it's someone else's chair and he doesn't want to claim it. "On a down day, nobody calls. On an up day, everybody's calling. . . . I say to these guys, 'How come you love these stocks up here"—

Jerry puts his hand above his head, out in front of him, like he's measuring his height—"but you don't love 'em down here? Nobody wants to talk about it."

He walks back over to the newspapers on his conference table, hoping for at least a temporary distraction from the ominous numbers on his screen. "The Yankees are doing well." He moves from the sports page to the business page and back to the sheets ranking the competition's performance last week.

"The wind is getting knocked out of the theory that small caps are gonna come back. It just got knocked out for about the eighth time in a row. I think it's been a tough quarter for some people." Indeed, the indexes following smaller stocks haven't kept up with the major market benchmarks, and many of Jerry's peers struggled to keep up last week.

Jerry draws a small box on the front page of *The New York Times* and divides it into squares. He labels one side of the box as an axis for "small to large," and a connecting side of the box as the axis for "value to growth." It is an increasingly familiar chart to American investors, as they learn to categorize their investments and think about strategies like having some eggs in each square. Like mutual fund star ratings, the style boxes have spread and gained in importance largely because of Morningstar. Mutual fund investors have grown accustomed to seeing the nine-patch grid, with one square darkened to indicate a fund's investment style. For Jerry and other money managers, those boxes and their ever-tightening perimeters have become increasingly uncomfortable. Shareholders and their money are allowed to jump from box to box; fund managers are expected to stay firmly in their assigned or chosen squares. The funds have a duty to follow the style they promised to their investors—whether it's working or not. In addition, if managers were able to jump from box to box as the market favored one style over another, the fund industry's marketing departments and consultants around the country would have to constantly rewrite their books, their sales pitches, and their advertising—just to keep up. So managers remain in their boxes like mice in cages, even when the market has stopped doling out pellets to them and moved on to another square.

Jerry draws a circle in the corner he has labeled for small-cap growth investing, where his funds are categorized. "This is the worst place to be."

In the lower left-hand corner of the front page is an article on the twenty-state Powerball Lottery jackpot, which has risen to $250 million. This week, millions of Americans—even Jerry's babysitter—will ignore the investment boxes, the advice about saving for retirement, and the benefits of a long-term horizon. They will hand over their dollar in hopes of being dispensed a piece of the $250-million pellet. Sure, there are 401(k)s, diversified portfolios, and dollar cost averaging, but a number will be chosen and someone will get lucky.

*   *   *

After checking his screen again, just after ten o'clock, Jerry calls the trading desk. "Yeah, Vinny? I tell you, why don't you step back a little and see if you can get it a little lower. The stock's worked itself right back up here. . . . They reported good numbers. . . . So why don't you look for something to trade." Don't just go out there and buy it for me at any price; look for someone who wants to get out. Work it.

By the time Marshall comes in for the eleven o'clock meeting, the Dow is down 54 points and the Nasdaq is down 31 points.

"Is this the end of the world as we know it?" Jerry asks.

"I think it's the end of the world for the home retailers," Marshall says despondently.

"Yeah, I saw Home Depot announced something."

"Yeah, and Linens 'n Things, and Bed, Bath & Beyond have been acting badly." Generous praise is heaped on stocks on the way up, but they are scorned like disobedient children on the way down.

"It's tough to see where it's heading—if it's going to be a head-fake, or if it's going to come back. Then the question is *where* it's going to come back? What industries and what companies?" Jerry asks of the market overall.

"We're getting slammed today," Marshall says.

"Yeah, but the question is how much everyone else is getting slammed right along with us." Jerry leans forward in his chair to look at his screen. "Whew. They're sure gonna take those Internet stocks down today."

Jeff arrives for the meeting and takes a seat at the table. "The market's going down. The good news is: The problems are happening outside our names. The bad news is: It's taking down all of our names with it."

"Anyone making any money today?" Jerry asks. The response is silence and he gives out a "Hmmf" as he sets down a stack of research reports and stock chart printouts in the center of the table. "Performance-wise, I'm amazed. We did okay relative to the competition last week. I'd say today's gonna be a different story. It looks like they're taking everybody down."

"That was Merrill's call today—find places to hide: supermarkets, health care . . . ," Jeff says, relaying just one of the many calls from a Merrill Lynch market strategist.

Jerry interrupts, "That's a dumb idea. So you're only gonna lose 10 percent or 5 percent on the downside, but then things turn around and you've got no leverage to move up with, 'cause you're in the wrong place. I had a meeting with a strategist last week, and he was saying that Greenspan is focused on bringing the market down—and he's succeeding."

"Yeah, 400 bucks." Jeff says, his left leg continuing the steady bouncing it began when he sat down. The Dow had dropped 400 points—or "bucks" in Jeff's vernacular—last week. The Nasdaq was down just as sharply: nearly 5 percent in one week.

"Take a look at what you own. On the margin, lean heavier on the sell side rather than the buy side. I wouldn't be buying aggressively. You'll have a rally but it'll come back down. . . . Overall, the market is extremely narrow, and it is getting narrower. . . . There are some people that are really struggling this year. There are a lot of people in negative numbers—especially in small caps. . . . We've got to be looking at our names and thinking, 'Can I make a better trade?' . . . I told Vinny, 'What do we have on the desk? Be more aggressive on the sell side, and drag your feet a bit on the buy side.'"

"What about all these little IPOs?" Jeff asks.

"Clean 'em up," Jerry says.

"We've got a lot of those."

"There are a few we've got to hold onto because I promised up and down I wouldn't sell for a day, and I did a few on Friday," Jerry says. He wanted to get his funds cleaned up and clear any extraneous holdings off the deck to prepare for a possible storm ahead, but he'd given his word. Yes, I'll help you make your deal work. I will buy and I will hold—for one day.

The collective group swagger is gone, and Jerry senses it. He has spent far too many halftimes sitting in locker rooms and being lectured on poor performance. He can't ignore the importance of being bucked up before hitting the field again.

"Shit, performance was pretty damn good. Trend, holy-moley." They all agree and lighten a bit.

"Yeah, if only we could end the year here," Marshall says.

"Sell out and go to 100 percent cash," Jeff offers.

"Yeah, it's sick that the year's only half over," Marshall agrees.

Yes, Jerry knows about encouragement, but he also wants to stave off overconfidence. "Yeah, I remember back in '87. I thought I'd end the year up 100 percent. But then it absolutely crashed. I was up 2 percent for the year—maybe."

* * *

Before he heads out for lunch, Jerry makes one more call to the trading desk. "Stu? Vinny? How you doing? . . . They're getting cheaper, aren't they? I've got a few things for Aggressive Growth. Buy me 2,500 American Online, 5,000 Worldcom, 2,500 Snyder, and 10,000 Microsoft."

He's given the team the direction to sell, clean out the portfolio, shore up your positions, own only what you know and trust. Now, just twenty minutes later, Jerry is sending up orders to buy just under $2 million worth of stock. And positioning is exactly what Jerry is doing. Getting into position to participate and compete on the upside.

"For us, it's a question of do we shift our portfolios around and get really defensive, or do we trim back the number of names in the portfolios and be in the best companies that are prepared to rebound very well when the market returns? I think the trick is not to try to play gross defense, but to position yourself so that when the market does well, you do *extremely* well. One trick is to be a little more aggressive on the sell side—even when the numbers are down. If you have a $12 stock, you probably say, 'Oh, I don't want to sell it, it's down.' But you should say, 'Oh, I can sell this $12 stock and put my money into something better. When the market turns, that better stock may go up 20 to 30 percent, while your $12 stock may go up only 5 percent."

So now, with the market down, he is repositioning in some of those very best companies, preparing to rebound when the market returns. Worldcom and Microsoft are two of the most powerful stocks in the entire market, and America Online is said to be the most stable and the premier Internet name. Surely, they would be among those to turn fastest and farthest when the market comes back. (Every other money manager, amateur stock junkie, and passing viewer of CNBC refers to America Online's stock as simply "AOL," but Jerry insists on calling it "American Online." He may even flub the America into *American* on purpose. Getting entranced by lingo and buzzwords is one concession Jerry refuses to make.)

*   *   *

Just as Jerry and his team must prepare and position and strategize for battles in the market, so must the rest of the firm and the industry. Each has its arenas, its goals, and its opponents. Every year, as the dollars have climbed, the prize has gotten bigger, the opponents more numerous, and the competition more intense.

Nowhere has this been more evident than in the world of marketing for mutual funds. The game has changed from placing a few bland ads in a core group of personal finance magazines. Now, mutual fund managers appear on billboards, on television, and even on the back of Amtrak ticket envelopes. Mutual fund campaigns now feature celebrities and offer airline tickets as prizes to investors opening new accounts.

In 1998, there are more than 77 million mutual fund shareholders in America, and they have over $5.5 trillion invested in funds.

The challenge to every mutual fund marketing department in the country is to try to attract and woo those dollars to its firm's mutual funds. But as both shareholders and mutual funds have multiplied in the past decade, it has become harder for fund companies and managers to stand out. Mutual funds have become just one more commodity consumer product, like toilet tissue, breakfast cereal, or toothpaste. The industry has even adopted the lingo of consumer products. "We want strong brand recognition . . . it's all in the marketing . . . we're fighting for shelf space out there . . . nobody owns the customer anymore."

As another fund manager at Delaware explains it, "Fidelity is Crest, Putnam is Colgate. . . ." While he speaks, he reaches for the tubes on imaginary grocery shelves at eye level—the obvious choices. "And we're like UltraBrite. We still work, we're just an old brand." He reaches down a few shelves to the less obvious brands. Those shelves are crowded with several names fighting for attention, rather than one or two: UltraBrite, Aquafresh, Close-Up, and Mentadent. Or, in this case, fund companies like Delaware, Heartland, Strong, and Lord Abbett.

Jerry, like all fund managers, absolutely needs marketing professionals who will go out and promote the funds to institutions or to the public, so that money managers have something to manage. As the Aggressive Growth Fund continued to log extraordinary numbers throughout the summer, marketing set up more and more appointments for Jerry to meet with clients and institutions considering pledging money for his team to manage. The meetings are essential to attracting new money, but the more meetings Jerry has to attend, the less time he is in the office focusing on the market and the funds' performance.

The cycle can quickly turn into a treadmill that is prone to derailment. Fund has good performance. Fund gets good rating from Morningstar. Fund attracts new shareholders and more money. Fund company collects more fees and can pay managers better. Fund manager spends more time marketing and less time managing. Fund performance slips. Morningstar stars are taken away. Shareholders take their money away. And it all starts over again: Fund manager is left trying to beat the market and attract some attention.

Yet, despite the dependence on marketing, Jerry—like most fund managers—has absolutely no respect for the department. "They are late to catch on to changes in the market. . . . They don't understand the investment process. . . . They don't value my time. They want to talk only about hot stock ideas. They care about selling your funds only when you are on top. . . . They care more about getting their Powerpoint slides right for presentations than they do about getting an investment strategy right for shareholders."

Now, with just three trading days left in July, and the market down more than 400 points from its all-time high at mid-month, Jerry sits in a conference room with a half dozen people from Delaware's sales and marketing departments. They are preparing a sales push for the growth group's funds and wanted the chance to talk with Jerry in person. They are seated around an oblong conference table and have left the head open, presumably for Jerry. He takes a chair off to the side, certainly at the end of the table, but decidedly to the side. The two people leading the meeting continue to field detailed questions on the promotional material—details that befuddle Jerry.

"So the new brochure will address the basic issues—'Why Delaware?' 'Why Small Cap?' 'Why Growth versus Value?'" the woman says as she stands flipping through a pamphlet, Vanna White-style, for the rest to see.

"We want to position ourselves as pure small cap growth." Her partner points out the handy slot for the salesperson's business card, where the performance charts will be printed, where the brochure will fold, the clever way the pages will stagger. "And we saved on cost because we avoided gluing."

Jerry sits silently watching the performance, likely wishing he had brought something to read.

"Will that flap be anchored?" someone asks.

"Will it be die-cut?" someone else says.

Finally, it is Jerry's turn to speak. He opens up broadly. "What we do is small cap growth."

"To you, what's small cap?" comes the first challenge.

"We have a median market cap of $600 million. You want to buy small stocks that become big stocks. And we don't sell them when they reach the top of some arbitrary range." He goes over the facts and details of such classic growth stocks as Dell Computer, Staples, and Cisco. They were all, at one time, small companies that have now grown into very large companies. That in itself is not enough of a reason for Jerry to sell. Sales and marketing and money management consultants can tell him he has to stay in his box, but he gets to say exactly where the lines are drawn around that box. Jerry has to follow his funds' rules on when he can buy companies, but he gets to determine when to sell.

Jerry discusses the investment team and he talks about risk. He explains how the stocks are chosen and what kind of services and computer screens the group uses to help them do their jobs. "It's like planting a garden. We're constantly pulling the weeds and planting more flowers."

Few are taking notes on such details, although to Jerry these details are the difference between his fund and someone else's, between trying to responsibly make money for your shareholders and not. His voice fades in and out, and at certain points he talks more to the performance sheets in his hand than to his audience. Marketing has tried to send him to speech school, or have a professional presentation consultant come in and work with him. They want him to tell more stories, they want him to have more charisma, they want him to sell. To Jerry, these suggestions are an insult. He would agree he's not exactly up for election as the next head of Toastmasters, but he finds it insulting that his performance and his track record aren't enough to stand on their own. The numbers have to be spun; they need multimedia presentations, and staggered pages with die-cut card holders; they need to be marketed. When Jerry thinks of the countless times he's been told he should work with someone on his presentation skills, he says aloud, "Fuck you."

He continues to talk about the challenge of earnings estimates, turnover, time horizon, and stock price ratios such as return on equity and return on investment. He talks about the complexities of investing in the health care sector and the basics of the retail industry. "With consumer stocks, you want to know: What are the economics of a box? Can that platform be replicated? Like Pollo

Tropical. It's a restaurant chain in Miami. It's very successful there, but will it sell in Wisconsin?"

"That's what we do." He says as he looks around the room, trying to determine whether they have heard or have simply listened. "It's not rocket science. We just do it every day." It's like an ad for the Marines. We look after billions of dollars, and we buy and sell stocks with it from 9:30 in the morning to 4:00 in the afternoon. It's exactly what thousands of other Americans would like to be doing—every day.

Jerry is thanked for his time, and the marketing guy sees him off with the words, "When we go out in the field, we'll want some general portfolio themes. We always need a couple of stories to back up the sales pitch." Maybe they were listening, but they have not heard.

As Jerry waits at the elevator bank, CNBC is on the television set hanging in the corner of the floor's lobby. The news of the morning is that the market is off slightly, and housing starts are down. Someone else from the marketing department joins Jerry in the elevator bank just as the car arrives. "Hey, what's the market doing?" he asks, the catch-all conversation opener in this building, this industry, and much of the country this summer.

"It was up this morning. It was down yesterday but up this morning, and it's struggling right now. Housing starts . . . ," Jerry says, parroting the television report.

"And Asia and Clinton . . . ," says the marketing guy as the two get on the elevator.

Jerry continues talking about consumer confidence, but the marketing guy interrupts before Jerry gets too settled into such dry government statistics as the consumer price index and housing starts. Like most market watchers, he figures, why waste time talking about what's down when it's so much fun to talk about what's up.

"Yeah, well, performance has been excellent," he says.

"Nasdaq was down a couple of percent yesterday," Jerry quickly counters. "The trouble is, you work for months to get up a few percent and then it's wiped out in a few hours. But we're hanging in there."

"Yeah, it can be gone so fast," the marketing guy says as the elevator reaches the ground floor. "Well, we're out there banging the drums on Aggressive Growth, so we may call you and try to do something. We're working with Norwest, so we may like to get you out in front of some people."

Jerry nods and gives a noncommittal response with a measured enthusiasm he seems to reserve specifically for marketing professionals who propose meetings he must travel to or changes to presentations he doesn't want to give.

He shakes his head as he walks out of the building. The market is down 5 percent in the past week and this guy's out there banging the drum? Don't they realize that waving the victory flag in the heat of the battle is just an invitation to get shot down?

* * *

Just after noon, Jerry is back in his office talking on the phone to Jeff, who is at a technology conference on the West Coast. The market has dropped 300 points in the past week.

"They took it down, then they took it back up, then down again, and now they're trying to settle. We got pummeled yesterday. . . . Yeah, everyone got pummeled yesterday, so I think what'll happen is, people will sell everything and see what settles. . . . I think it's gonna be tough to make headway for a while." He continues looking at his screen, trying to determine who's selling and buying what and why. "I tell you, they're sure putting a lot of fluff into these PC stocks—Dell, Compaq, Gateway. . . . Okay, I gotta get ready for this GeoCities meeting."

The rhythm of the market and its machinery continues. Numbers flicker from white to red to green and back again on Jerry's screen. Jeff will meet with more executives of the companies that bounce all over Jerry's screen, and Jerry will meet with officers of new companies looking for their chance to dance across that same screen.

Jerry holds the telephone receiver to his chest, the only mute button he uses, and calls out to his secretary, "Geri, can you pick up Jeff? I'd do it myself, but I don't want to screw it up somehow."

As he begins paging through the prospectus for his afternoon meeting, one of his regular salesmen stops in to tell him about another IPO he's bringing by to meet with John.

"They do NT-based systems for small banks—under $3 billion—and credit unions . . . conservative revenue recognition . . . they've got a backlog right now of $10 million . . . just wanted to tell you about it and that John is going," the salesman says.

"Haven't you guys given up on the IPO market yet?" Jerry asks him, the group's favorite salesman and the one they good-naturedly rib to his face most often.

The salesman laughs the client laugh and John arrives toting his prospectus for the banking software company. "No, apparently not," John says. "Not when they can sell 2.8 million shares at $10 a share." When the market begins to stall, IPOs are always the first deals to get put off. Already, a few banks were putting some offerings on hold and considering rescheduling others.

As John and the salesman walk out of Jerry's office into the hall leading to the conference room, John says, "You didn't pitch this thing entirely honestly."

"What do you mean?" the salesman asks.

"You didn't tell me this was a piece-of-shit little company that doesn't make any money and nobody's gonna care about."

"No, that would've been dishonest to say that." And the two laugh as they go to meet a few entrepreneurs looking for $28 million to *really* get their business going.

The investment world seems to thrive on skepticism and enthusiasm. Managers need a storehouse of each and they alternate drawing on each, depending on the market and their mood. This season, John is the skeptic and Jerry the enthusiast.

Marshall comes in while Jerry is reading the GeoCities prospectus.

"I got one of those touchy-feely deals that's probably right up your alley," Jerry says with a smile.

"Yeah, I sat through one of those yesterday. I'm gonna do it because the salesman says it's absolutely red hot, but I'm gonna sell it in the first ten minutes. They were a bunch of flakes. They couldn't even answer my questions. At least those Amazon guys could say,

'Well, we're not gonna tell you because of this or that.' These guys couldn't even do that."

Jerry reads aloud from the prospectus, "Founded in 1994 as Beverly Hills Internet."

"Beverly Hills? What the hell are they selling?"

" 'GeoCities offers the world's largest and one of the fastest growing communities of Web sites on the Internet,' " Jerry reads.

"Well, it's an old company—1994," Marshall says.

" 'The company pioneered the first large-scale, Web-based community for Internet users to express themselves, share ideas, interests and expertise, and publish content accessible to other users with common interests,' " Jerry keeps reading.

"That sounds like something out of California."

Jerry continues to scan the document, reading aloud things that strike him. As Marshall steps out the door, Jerry calls out, "Homesteader. Do you want to be a homesteader? Whatever your prurient interest, you could create a little community. So you can have little Internet communes all over the place."

"Let me tell you, the emperor's new clothes sounded more plausible than that," Marshall concludes.

Jerry is entertaining himself with the prospectus—even the pages of additional information that many investors never turn to. It's like reading footnotes of a textbook for pleasure. He is a man who enjoys his job. "CEO . . . since April 1998." He raises his eyebrows. "He's been there a long time . . . COO since May 1998 . . . from Universal Studios Hollywood . . . another guy from Disney . . . they probably know what they're doing . . . maybe they don't . . . it's a lot of media moguls . . . there are more stock options in this deal than you can imagine. . . ."

He closes the prospectus on the desk and walks over to the window to pause on his way out to lunch. "God! I hate to buy these things. But it's gonna go up, so what do you do? You just remember why you went into the whorehouse in the first place."

Outside his office door, on the file cabinets in front of Geri's desk, he sees the trays of leftover bagels from a breakfast meeting. "Oh, lunch. Should I have jelly or cream cheese? Which one is worse for me?"

He looks over the offerings and bobs his head back and forth as if he's reciting eenie-meenie-miney-mo to himself. Like a red-hot Internet IPO, both the sugar and the fat will give him the quick boost he's looking for. He knows that he might be better off opting for something of more complex substance that will sustain him longer. But these are here for the taking, they may not be here tomorrow, and he wants the boost now. His head stops bobbing and he reaches for the jelly.

*   *   *

Two hours later, when Jerry returns from the meeting with the GeoCities executives, he is clearly energized. "GeoCities. Why didn't I think of that?" he asks himself. "No, I don't get it. I'm not the right person for this. I'm not into chit-chat."

Jerry's funds have made millions of dollars from their investments in the Internet. Almost every company the group invests in is focused on having some presence on the Web as part of its business strategy. Jerry has ordered books over the Internet and has retrieved research materials online. His stepfather has his own Web site, and billboards in Jerry's hometown invite visitors to "Put Tunkhannock on Your Desktop. www.Tunkhannock.com." Yet Jerry, like so many, is still a bit skeptical, a bit uncertain, and maybe a little uncomfortable with the whole World Wide Web and all of its promises, promotion, and imperfections.

He remembers a conversation, years ago, with an analyst who was hired away from an investment bank by a venture capital firm focused on putting money into private Internet startups. "They offered him wild amounts of money to come, and I said, 'This is all bullshit.' He got very serious with me and said, 'Oh no. It's going to be huge. And there are some guys that are going to be phenomenally successful with it.'"

And Jerry had just met a table full of them. Nine days later, GeoCities shares would price at $17 a share and trade up to $37 on their first day. He bought 20,000 shares for the Aggressive Growth Fund and sold them two days later for $44.67 a share, a profit of over half a million dollars.

Just five months later, GeoCities would be bought by Yahoo! for $5 billion in stock, or about $124 a share. That's a 629 percent profit. In five months. Okay, it was five-and-a-half months.

*   *   *

Just after the market closes, the Bridge technician stops in to help Jerry with the system that provides him with his indispensable stock quotes and charts. Jerry pushes his chair back from the desk, and the Bridge guy takes a minute to look over the screen, like he is getting his bearings under the hood of a car.

"So what'd you do?" The Bridge guy clicks the mouse a few times before giving his diagnosis. "Oh, boy. You been minimizing news stories instead of closing them?"

"Is that what I've been doing? God knows, I'm sorry for that."

The Bridge guy leans in closer over Jerry's keyboard and methodically clicks the mouse. "So, you got tickets for the big event tonight?" he asks. "The big lottery?"

The multistate Powerball Lottery jackpot has climbed to $295 million, the biggest American lottery in history, and the numbers will be picked just hours after the stock market closes. And holders of 210 million tickets will wait to find out if they have the lucky one.

"No, but my secretary Geri has ten of 'em. She says if she wins, she'll stop by tomorrow and open an account."

"Yeah, I been keeping a list of my clients I'd put money with. You're on my list," the Bridge guy says. The two men continue to click away at buttons on their machines. Jerry punches in numbers on his calculator, and the Bridge guy closes items on Jerry's computer.

"Yeah, I don't have tickets for tonight. I had 'em for Saturday, but now the lines are too long," says the Bridge guy, keeping the conversation going.

"Too bad. There's a ticket there with your name on it," Jerry says with a smile. He works all day, every day, in a market where there is money out there for the taking. You've just got to know how to put your name on it.

"What would you do with all that money?" the Bridge guy asks rhetorically. "Ah, I've thought about it. Even if I gave my brothers and sisters $3 million apiece and told 'em to use $500,000 for a new house and some cars, they could still just live off the interest. I've thought about it. I know what I'd do with it."

In his head, he has divided the jackpot, he has calculated the interest, and he has likely taken taxes into consideration. Like so many Americans, he dreams of and talks about hitting the jackpot, yet he has no ticket in his pocket. Instead, like Jerry, he is at work on a sunny and clear Wednesday afternoon, chatting with a client and enjoying his job.

A dollar will buy you a lottery ticket, and an IPO may give you the chance to win big. But real investing—building a fund for performance that will last—doesn't rely on luck or chance. It requires going to work every day, doing the right analysis, punching in those numbers, and pushing the chair back to get your bearings on the world around you.

His shareholders may play the lottery every week, and Jerry himself may buy a ticket or two when they catch his eye. But the money he manages in his funds is for investing. His shareholders want it in the market, working for them. They want Jerry and his team to be the ticket to a secure retirement, not instant riches. But Jerry, who has the confidence and desire to deliver more than is expected, wonders sometimes to himself, "Wouldn't it be nice to be able to do both."

A few minutes before five, Marshall stops by Jerry's office for the second time since the market has closed. Jerry's computer has once again thwarted him from getting his information and forming his own assessment.

"I broke my computer again. How did I do that? How the hell did I wipe out my whole Bridge?" Jerry says as Marshall walks in. The Bridge technician left Jerry's office just forty-five minutes ago.

"That took talent." Marshall walks around Jerry's desk to get his own look under the hood. "'Your briefcase?' What the hell is that crap? Okay, okay. Get out and go to 'My Computer.' What have they given you?" Jerry keeps clicking and sliding the mouse, and Marshall keeps inspecting.

"There you go, there it is. How the hell did it get over there?" Crisis averted, Marshall steps back to give Jerry some space. He looks out the window. The afternoon sun rests on rusting train rails at Philadelphia's train station. "It looks like it's shaping up to be a pretty decent day. Relatively."

"Yeah, Trend is down only point-three," Jerry says.

"Some of these other guys are down over a percent," Marshall says. So, for today, the growth group may have made up some ground—Trend was only down .3 percent, DelCap was off .6 percent, and the Aggressive Growth fund was knocked back .8 percent. But, as Marshall and Jerry know, as bad as being down feels, it doesn't feel nearly as bad when others are down more than you are. "Mike Garrison's down sixty-four beeps," Marshall says and gestures with his hand out the window, presumably in an effort to point north to where Mike Garrison works, but his hands are pointing west. It doesn't really matter where or who the competition is. What matters is that they're out there, and we're doing better.

"Huh," Jerry pauses, perhaps creating a mental picture of the stocks on his competitor's screen, as opposed to his own. "And they're pretty low beta—they're not that aggressive." Beta is just the market's term for volatility. High-beta stocks rise and fall more than the market, low-beta stocks, less.

"Yeah, they're not that aggressive and they're such lousy stock-pickers," Marshall says on his way out the door. They both laugh.

The market continues to slide, ending down more days than it closes up. Jerry is looking for answers, looking for clues, looking for guidance. "You got any good ideas?" he asks one of his salesmen who is calling from a stock conference in Napa Valley. "The market? What do you think? Is this it? I

July 28, 1998	Year-to-Date Performance	Rank
Aggressive Growth	17.3%	19
Trend	9.4%	17
Delcap	10.3%	49
Dow	13.0%	
S&P 500	17.4%	
Nasdaq	20.8%	

tell you, it can't seem to catch hold. It's hard to tell if this will be one of those things that will roll downhill or if it's just a correction and will turn in the other direction. . . . So what are you hearing at the conference? Anything good? Bad? . . . Yeah, I bought a little of that at 23. I'm gonna sell it tomorrow at 25. . . . Yeah, I just don't know if it can hold up. . . . Oh, some piece-of-shit company. . . . Boy, I just don't trust this market. If it starts going down, there's just no bottom to these things. . . . The Internet stocks in general—Amazon, Yahoo!— they're just waiting to catch hold, establish a base here."

While Jerry tries to prepare for the market's continuing to go down, others try to make excuses as to why these few down days are the exception. Jerry shakes his head while he stares at his computer screen and repeats the familiar arguments. "These guys always say, 'Well, it went down on no volume.'" For many, the line is welcome reassurance. It's a way to write off the down days in the market as meaningless: It wasn't broad; not everybody thinks things are going down—it's just a few investors who have lost their confidence.

Jerry disagrees. "That's how bear markets start. If there's a big problem out there and the market is going down, I'm not worried about that. At the end of 1990, the market was going down, down, down. When the war started, the question was, 'What are you gonna sell?' I said, 'No, that is in the market.' We knew about the war. You've always got to be more concerned about what you *don't* know in the market."

It could be political. It could be an affair between the President and an intern. It could be a financial crisis on the other side of the world. It could be millennium fears. It could be a destructive natural disaster. This year, as with any year in the market, those unknown issues are out there. And Jerry's got to find them before they find him.

"Some days I'll have a gut feeling. . . . Other times, I just don't have a real high confidence, and I don't have a feel for where things are going."

* * *

It's the last day of July, and shares of the Cyberian Outpost— C-O-O-L—IPO are scheduled to begin trading today. Marshall takes a salesman's call that resembles that of a bookie more than it does a top Wall Street broker.

"Just wanted to let you know you got 30,000 of Cyberian Outpost and it came at $18—up from an expected $13–$15 filing," the salesman says. The stock hadn't even opened for trading yet, and it was already worth 30 percent more than investors had expected.

That's what hot deals do. Bankers give a range when they're out on the road selling investors on the idea of buying shares; then, as demand heats up and the actual deal approaches, that original price—the filing range—is upped even before the stock begins trading.

"Just don't forget to put your sell order in," the salesman's instructions come over the speakerphone, while Marshall types tickers into his computer. "There is absolutely no institutional sponsorship of this thing whatsoever." No one actually wants to *own* tickets to this concert; everyone will be scalping them right back to the line as soon as it opens.

"What's the price again? Where do you think it'll open?" Marshall asks.

"The chatter on the Internet is that people like it a lot and it should be a hot deal. But, like I said, just don't forget to sell. This thing'll be under the offer in a week."

All the signs and calls were adding up to one of those times when Jerry didn't have high confidence. He had no feel for where things were going. His gut wasn't telling him anything, or if it was, it wasn't good.

And now, Marshall was waiting for Jerry to arrive for the day, so he could deliver one more piece of bad news.

"The market is going down big time today. Big time." Marshall says this as if it is an unequivocal fact.

"Oh, because of that . . . ," Jerry stammers, trying to get his bearings in his office and the market. He tries not to appear ignorant. What can Marshall be so certain of at nine o'clock in the morning?

"Cowboy Bob," Marshall says and throws both hands up in the air in defeat. "Cowboy Bob died."

It is half an hour before the market opens. The Dow is 4 percent off its record highs of two weeks ago; Cyberian Outpost is red hot—as far as the first trade is concerned; and Cowboy Bob of Howdy Doody fame is dead.

About an hour after the market opens, Jerry sits alone in his office. It is a Friday, the last day in July. People are trying to leave early for the weekend. And there is little activity other than selling on Wall Street. The Dow is down 56 points and the Nasdaq is down 13.

Jerry looks around at his computer screen, his telephone, and the performance and competition reports on his desk. He is in no hurry to go about them in any particular order. He doesn't expect many interruptions.

"It's gonna be a quiet day today. And it's only gonna get quieter. I have a bad feeling about this market."

Knowing that the market is something he can't control, he takes the cap off a pen and turns his attentions to the printouts of his own funds—perhaps something he *can* control.

*   *   *

With the Dow on its way to closing down 143 for the day and the Nasdaq off 47, Jerry looks over his screen. "The market is awful and my stocks are shit . . . crappy."

"So I came at a good time?" says Jon, Jerry's salesman from Alex Brown, as he walks in holding a stack of prospectuses—new companies that will promise to change Jerry's fortunes.

The two talk about specific stocks, recent troubles in the market, mergers, and investors' shortening horizons and increasing expectations.

"So what's the conclusion? That there are no investors today? I think that's never been truer," the salesman says. "It's all, 'What's the last data point out there?'"

"Yeah, it's 'What was the last quarter, the last month, the last week, the last day, the last data point? Is it better? If it's not better, sell it.'"

Soon, Marshall comes in to join the discussion. He plants his hands firmly on his hips, and his tie rests just above his monogrammed silver belt buckle. "I am not in shape for a bear market. I've got to sell all my stocks today. I'm gonna sell everything," he says in mock panic.

It is an opening for one of Jerry's lessons and a joke that gets passed around by those on Wall Street, and in corporate America, who are looking for the silver lining.

"It's like the little boy that goes into the room of shit. The older brother comes in and he's a pessimist, so he says, 'Oh, this place is full of shit.' The younger brother, he's an optimist, and he's going through the room, rifling through all the crap. His mother comes in and says, 'Ugh. What are you doing?' The boy says, 'With all this shit in here, there's got to be a pony somewhere.'"

They all laugh. Jon leaves some prospectuses behind, and the three go back to work. With the 11,000-plus publicly traded companies—and these few that this salesman hopes to bring by for visits in the next several weeks—there have got to be at least a few decent stocks out there.

And Jerry, the optimist brother, turns back to his screen, his performance sheets, his position holdings, and his calculator. He's determined to find the pony.

CHAPTER 5

HURRICANE SEASON

When Jerry was injured in high school and unable to play football, he took on other roles for the team. He would go and watch games and scrimmages of rival teams and report back. He would scout out their strengths and their vulnerabilities. He would watch and learn their plays and see which players were the fastest and whom to look out for. Back with his own team, Jerry would sometimes tell the quarterback what plays to call, and the coaches would let him. His coaches said that, even at seventeen, Jerry possessed a greater vision and understanding of what was going on around him than others had. He had a sense about the game, and he could see things others couldn't, *before* they would happen. His quiet confidence and easy way with people made Jerry one of the leaders—particularly in the background—of any team he joined.

And now, in the last few months of the year, Jerry is faced with the same challenge in the stock market. He needs to see things others can't, *before* they happen. He sits in front of his computer, facing the screen. He is trying to assess the market's strengths and vulnerabilities. Just like on the field, he wants to determine what will move the fastest and what might surprise him.

* * *

In the past two weeks, the market has bounced around—up a day, down two, then up another. On Monday, the Dow fell 97 points, and Tuesday it was down 299 points. It was the biggest one-day drop investors had seen all year, and it was the third largest point drop in stock market history. August has only started, the market is already down 396 points for the month, and September and October are still to come.

Jerry says he wouldn't be surprised to see the market go down big on the opening. He also says he wouldn't be surprised to see the market jump up big on the opening. There are explanations for each scenario he can envision, and historical precedents for every direction in which the market and investors can react.

While he was in the shower this morning, Jerry was thinking about the stock market. It was 6:30 A.M., and hot water and ticker symbols and flashing prices were keeping him company. "Would this time be like 1987?" he asked himself. "When the market started slipping, would buyers come in to try to prop it up and convince everyone everything was okay? Or, would investors flee, fearing the worst?"

The first few minutes of the stock market's being open give him his answer. The Dow is up 21. A moderate climb that signals stability to Jerry rather than irrationality. Investors are willing to stay calm this time. For now. They are willing to buy stocks and support the market, but not artificially so.

Jeff calls in from San Francisco, just a little before seven o'clock in the morning, his time.

Jerry reads him the group's performance numbers for last week. "Year-to-date, Aggressive is up 13.2 percent, DelCap is up 8.1 percent, and Trend is up 7.9 percent. So we're in line with most of the crowd there. For the quarter, that's a different story. Aggressive Growth is the one sort of getting pasted. You know, there's just so much beta in it. On an absolute basis we're not doing well, but on a relative basis we're in the ball park. . . ."

Then it is Jerry's turn for questions and an update from the West Coast. What are other investors saying? Are they buying? Are they selling?

When he hangs up, Jerry heads for the trading desk. On his way, he stops in to see Steve. What's he been hearing, what kind of calls is he getting? Anything useful? It's the same exercise upstairs with the traders. What's your feel for the market right now? Where are these things headed? As the market continues to climb during the day, Jerry thinks more and more about a bigger decline that could be brewing just below this surface of investor confidence. His mind toys with numbers as high as a 40 percent downfall in the market in the near term.

In the October 1987 crash, the market plunged 22.6 percent in one day, and on Black Tuesday in 1929, the crash that heralded the Great Depression, the Dow fell 12.8 percent. A 40 percent drop in the market, like that which Jerry imagines, would truly be catastrophic.

Such a fall would knock out all of Jerry's performance for the year and then some. The past seven months of climbing to the top would be for naught. The group would have five months to work their way out of a deep hole or end the year with negative performance numbers next to their names.

All of Wall Street seems to be going through a cause-and-effect analysis of a stock market crash. Everyone seems to be getting ready to prepare for the worst. The business papers are reporting an increased use of puts—investors' bets that certain stocks, or the overall market, will go down. "Puts" and "calls" are just two kinds of options in the stock market—two hedging strategies, or ways to look for a little protection on the downside and a little juice on the upside. Buying calls is a little bit like putting down a deposit to reserve a spot on a cruise at a set price. When the price goes up, you can buy your spot for the price at which you made your reservation. If the price drops, or you decide not to take that cruise, the deposit is forfeited. Puts and calls don't come with rain checks. You pay for them and you either act on the opportunity or not. Options expire, and you don't get your money back.

Options have traditionally been the playground of professional traders who have the experience, savvy, and equipment to move quickly and without emotion. But as more investors gain better access to information and become more knowledgeable, the use of options becomes more widespread. Now, everyone is looking for a little protection, or that extra edge. Being invested in the market—owning stock in a company, buying shares of a mutual fund—is no longer enough. People want more, better, faster in the 1990s. Can I buy options on it? Can I juice it?

* * *

At lunchtime, the Dow is up 74 points. Jerry takes some calls, returns others, and goes through his personal bills. He writes a postcard to his five-year-old son, Jonah, who is fascinated with getting mail.

By the time the market reaches its last hour of trading for the day, it is down. With just thirty minutes to go, the Dow is down 104 points.

"This is a pain in the ass," Jerry says.

His attention has jumped around his screen as his cursor and mouse land on each new stock ticker. He is reading news items, looking at who's selling what and for how much, and talking with analysts and salespeople over the telephone. It is the daily search for insight and clues, if not answers.

"I was good until I talked to you guys. How can you do this and then let the stupid thing drop like a stone? . . . We sold a little the other day, and then Montgomery came out with some comments on it and took the thing out and absolutely shot it. . . . Yeah, the numbers are great, but the stock is just flat down. The numbers are good, everybody's pushing it. They're saying it's the best name in the bunch. . . . If the market was acting better, I think I'd do it. . . . Do I have a higher confidence that Microsoft will make their numbers than these guys? Absolutely. I think the risk is all in the earnings estimates. . . ."

These are lines, criticisms, and conversations that Jerry will repeat throughout the year, but especially during earnings season. "I have absolutely no confidence in analysts' estimates. I haven't for ten years," Jerry says. "They have no idea what the numbers are. The stock goes down and the next thing you know, the analyst cuts his estimates. The stocks are leading the estimates."

The business has evolved; the rules are different and the dynamics have shifted. Perhaps most dramatically, the numbers have changed. Twenty years ago, there were about 450 Wall Street analysts publishing estimates for all to see. Now, there are more than 5,700 analysts making calls, writing reports, trying to get noticed. With the field so crowded, it's harder and harder for those calls and reports to make an impact, to get noticed. Now, analysts and Wall Street react to a stock's move just as often as a stock reacts to an analyst's call. There are investor chat rooms, newsletters, television shows, insider buying and selling, and avaricious day traders that all move stocks. The Wall Street research analysts, who used to be the source for information on stocks, are now left to play catch-up—catch up and protect yourself. It's far easier to revise estimates in line with where the stock actually *is* trading than it is to take a stand on where the stock *should* trade, and wait for investors to agree or disagree. It's a game where *looking* right at the end of the quarter and the end of the year has become even more important than *being* right.

*   *   *

Just before four o'clock, Steve comes in to talk about a few stocks and a new IPO.

"I talked to the salesman about it, and he says the management is good. They're bright guys," Steve says, as he confidently holds the prospectus and his notes in one hand.

"Is it an IPO?" Jerry asks.

"Yes."

"Sure, go ahead and see them."

"I already saw them. But the salesman hasn't gotten back to me on how the book is coming together," Steve explains. The all-important IPO order book. What does the line outside the ticket window look like? How many people are waiting? Do they look eager, and did they bring their wallets? The salesman is still calling around to find out—will you hold, are you gonna sell immediately, would you be interested in buying more?

"I think that's the more important issue here," Jerry says, knowing that, for many IPOs, the key is not what the company does or who the management is and how good they are. So often it is, instead: Does Wall Street want it and will they support it? "Call the salesman back and tell him you want 250,000 shares at $10."

Steve stares in disbelief. Is Jerry bluffing? This major salesman at an important investment bank is trying to sell a deal at $16 a share, and Jerry wants Steve to call him and essentially say, "I think your deal is shit, but I'll buy it at $10."

Jerry lets the silence hover in the space separating Steve from Jerry and his side of the desk—the side that is in charge, the side that makes the final decisions. "It's just interesting how they're gonna get these deals done in this kind of market. I talked to some guy today pushing a little stock. I said, 'Why would I own that in this kind of market when I can buy Microsoft?'"

"And I've looked at three of the major competitors in the last week or so, and they're all trading at twelve times and this one wants to trade at thirty times," Steve says. Steve is always prepared to take and defend either side of a company or issue in each of his discussions with Jerry. He has the history, the numbers, and the issues on instant recall. Mostly, he ends up agreeing with Jerry and his twenty years of market experience, but Steve is always armed with his own reasons for coming out on that side. He is an aggressive learner in an aggressive business. Today, the reason just happens to be valuation—this new company thinks investors should pay a whole lot more for their shares than buyers are willing to pay for those of any other competing company. Other days, Steve decides that it's not the right industry, or the business model is flawed, or the cycle has turned and the opportunity has been missed. In still other instances, Steve's analysis determines that the company and its executives are just too cocky for him to want to own it.

When Jerry and Steve finish discussing the capriciousness of companies, their executives, and the investment bankers and salesmen looking to do deals, the stock market is closed. The Dow ends the day in positive territory, up 59 points.

Up 74, down 104, up 59. As Jerry said, "It's a pain in the ass." On countless days this year, the market has swung wildly between positive and negative territories. Analysts are saying it's the most volatile market in 65 years. And volatility can make it so much harder for Jerry's team to get in and out of stocks, and so much easier for them to get run over by the market.

By the middle of August, the market has stabilized. Investors are writing off the down days earlier in the month as "the usual summer lull" and "the pause that refreshes." Individual investors have heeded their own advice to "buy on the dips." Since the day of the 299-point drop, two weeks

August 17, 1998	Year-to-Date Performance	Rank
Aggressive Growth	13.5%	14
Trend	4.6%	16
Delcap	4.1%	52
Dow	8.4%	
S&P 500	12.7%	
Nasdaq	15.8%	

prior, confident shareholders have sent the Aggressive Growth Fund over $6 million in new cash to invest. A stock market crash has been averted, and Jerry and his team are looking for ways to spend that cash. Jerry is back to screening for new ideas, and screening old ideas for new problems. Sometimes he screens stocks to find any that have insider buying. A good sign: They are confident and they know more than I do. Other times he'll look for changes in management, or stocks hitting new highs.

After lunch, he runs all three funds through one of the screens he created to look for stocks that have hit resistance on their climb higher. Today, only the pizza restaurateur Papa John's shows up as a candidate for a sell.

"I'll have to catch up with Marshall on that one later," Jerry says when he reviews the results. He fits himself with this casual tone and interest when he looks into problems, especially those in which he must challenge other people. Don't accuse, don't put them off, don't make them defensive. In a business where egos and hubris rival the millions and billions of dollars tossed around in the market, feelings are hurt surprisingly easily. It's a business where you are putting your intellect, your insight, and at least your self-confidence on the line every day by what you buy, sell, and hold. And tomorrow, your performance will be published for all to see and criticize in the local and national papers.

Jerry treads such waters with the gentleness and reserve of a mentor, rather than the brashness of the Wall Street trader and mutual fund boss that he is. When he asks Marshall about Papa John's, he doesn't specifically seek him out and corner him. Instead, he waits for Marshall to come to him with questions about an upcoming presentation. Casually, Jerry brings up the stock like it is an old car engine the two have been tinkering over for weeks.

"So, what's going on with our friends at Papa John's these days?"

Leaning against the bookshelf in Jerry's office, Marshall turns both palms up and gives an open shrug. "I don't know why it's down. Actually, Pizza Hut is suing them over advertising. Which I think is good news—free advertising."

"When we were driving in Tunkhannock, my nine-year-old asks, 'Why don't we move to Tunkhannock and live here all year?' I asked him, 'What would mommy and daddy do if we moved?' He said, 'Well, mommy could be a doctor.' And just about this time, we were driving past the fast-food restaurants. He looked out the window and said, 'See that Pizza Hut? You could work there. Then I could come in and get free pizza for lunch.'"

Jerry and Marshall both laugh. Jerry has raised the issue. He has let Marshall know that he is concerned—and watching.

"Huh, so Pizza Hut is suing Papa John's?" Jerry asks.

"Yeah, I figure it's free advertising. Then there's also talk that cheese prices are going up. This happens every year with the back-to-school lunch programs. Cheese prices go up so the restaurant industry can raise prices. I wish I had more dry powder, it's a great buying opportunity," Marshall says. It's one of the advantages of knowing your core holdings well. The group can use price drops in the stock market to build up positions in companies they know, like, and want to keep as part of a portfolio's foundation. Marshall has owned shares of Papa John's since before he joined the growth team at Delaware. He knows the management, he understands the cycles, and he can read the market's reaction to the stock.

Jerry is satisfied with Marshall's analysis. The group might know something computer screens don't. There is no data field for rising cheese prices. "We've got room in Aggressive Growth and Trend," Jerry offers to Marshall.

*   *   *

At the end of the day, Marshall is back giving his regular recap of the performance of the group and the market.

The Dow and the S&P are both up 1.6 percent for the day, and the Nasdaq, which the group's funds compete against more closely, is up just over 2 percent—significant gains by almost any measure. The growth group logged in gains of 2 percent in Trend, 1.9 percent in DelCap, and a weaker 1.7 percent in Aggressive Growth—the fund that should have participated most fully in the day's run-up.

"I guess that's what you get for having cash," Jerry says. You've got to pay to play. You've got to have your money in the market to make money in the market. But, the team had gotten cautious during the recent weeks of volatility and had let the Aggressive Growth fund go to about 18 percent cash. Certainly, on the market's down days, having that much money protected was a help, but when stocks are running, cash just can't keep up. Like that extra $20 bill in the back of the wallet or a purse's unused zipper pocket, most funds like to keep about 5 percent in cash to be ready for emergencies. Like the emergency buying opportunity where you want to buy something but don't have the time or desire to sell something else to raise the cash. Or emergencies like mutual fund redemptions—shareholders who are selling their shares and want their cash back. Fund companies want to be able to return the money quickly, without being forced to sell something just to raise fast cash.

But letting a cash position drift to 18 percent signaled something more. The market was making Jerry nervous. He was preparing for either a big spiral downward in the market, or a heavy round of investors selling out. Either one would not be good for his fund.

Along with sending more than $6 million into the Aggressive Growth Fund in the past two weeks, shareholders had taken out just over $1 million. For over a year now, the fund has had more coming in than going out, but Jerry can't know when the scales might tip the other way.

"Well, I put about a percent of that cash to work today," Marshall says. "I bought Barnes & Noble."

Jerry looks up from his screen. "Christ! Buy Amazon if you're gonna buy books."

"Hey, I'm just trying to make a quick 15 percent here. I'm not even looking for 30 percent, just 15 percent. I heard something from someone who heard something. . . . Someone was hearing they were thinking of accelerating their earnings announcement. They're gonna make the numbers, and apparently they're gonna say something about their Internet book business," Marshall explains.

Marshall and Jerry—like all professional investors and even casual stock pickers—"hear things." And now, Marshall was hearing things about Barnes & Noble. It's up to him to be the filter—to decide whether what he's hearing will have an impact on the stock price. He has to decide: Is what he's hearing true? Does it even matter whether it's true, as long as enough people are hearing it and believe it might be true?

Marshall decided that this latest information will affect the stock, and so he spent just under $1 million buying 27,000 shares of Barnes & Noble. He will sell it in two days for a profit just shy of $100,000. A nice pop for a few days' investment and the right phone call. But, it's the kind of trade Jerry is trying to steer himself and the group away from. He wants the team to invest with conviction. To be willing to buy bigger when something is down, and hold on longer when it's climbing higher.

"In Aggressive Growth, what you're looking for are stocks that can make you a significant amount of money. You're not looking for 10 percent. You're looking for 40 percent, 50 percent, and doubles and triples and ten baggers," Jerry often lectures.

Marshall is just trying to keep the group going into the next inning. After selling out of the Barnes & Noble shares, Marshall will say, "It's fine when you can trade like that, but you can't build a business on it. But if you can add a little around the edges—like Barnes & Noble—I probably added 15 beeps. If I can do that ten times a year, that's 1.5 percent, and if we can all do that, it's 6 or 7 percent."

And he's right. The game is won by steadily making your way around the bases just as often as it is by hitting home runs.

* * *

"This is a good day to be pouring concrete," Jerry tells Marshall. The pre-market discussion between the two, as August comes to a close, has centered around the building of a new addition on Marshall's house. "It's hot and humid out there today. If it's too *dry* out, just the top layer will dry, and it'll flake off later."

While other kids at Jerry's high school had spent their summers fishing, or working on their cars, Jerry had tried to persuade his mother to let him buy his own cement mixer. He figured he'd start his own business rebuilding sidewalks and other small projects. At seventeen, he wanted to be the guy to call for odd cement jobs around town. Would she please let him have a cement mixer? Just a small one? His mother said no.

"The Romans invented concrete," Marshall offers back to Jerry. "How can they build the Pantheon and we can't have an overpass?"

"You know the secret to good cement? A little Portland Cement," Jerry says, and explains just the right ratios and mixing orders for the perfect compound like he is explaining the delicate steps of getting a soufflé to rise properly.

For Jerry, it's a skill that has translated well into the world of mutual funds. Jerry's bosses at Delaware frequently cite his understanding of portfolio management theory as one of his strongest assets. They like to contrast Jerry with mere stockpickers—those who do exactly that: pick a few stocks, put 'em in the fund, wait for them to go up or down. They like to say that Jerry knows how to "really build a fund." He lays a foundation of sizable positions in some core stocks to help him keep up with the market. Then he adds other names to the fund—knowing just how much room there is for technology; when health care should be pared back; or when to let cash build up. He considers the risk he takes on with certain stocks that the indexes don't. He demands that the additional risk should come with the promise of greater return. Portfolio management theory is a way of checking the blueprint, knowing which walls can be moved, where an extra beam is needed for support.

"I wish I knew more about cement," Marshall says. And he means it. These are two men with varied and eclectic interests. "Churchill was a bricklayer. He found it very therapeutic."

Jeff has been standing in the doorway during the final exchange. "I'll remember to wear my hardhat next time," he says before he moves on to subjects that are far more concrete to him—earnings estimates for semiconductor companies and upcoming technology conferences.

* * *

Just after lunch, the group gathers for the weekly meeting.

"Considering last week could've been a total disaster, it wasn't. But people seem to be playing in the same sandbox as us. We did give up a little ground; you can take a look." Jerry lays the peer group performance sheets from the past two weeks down on the table. It is his gesture to let the group know that they've slipped a few notches in the ranking. They're losing their edge, and they've got to get it back.

"If we're really believers in 'em, we've got to get in line," he continues. "We've got some cash. I'm not saying we need to rush out there and wallow around with the rest of the hogs, but just be aware. If there are big blocks up for sale, be ready to buy. . . . When I look at the daily performance, it's 'Are we keeping up? Are we keeping up? Are we keeping up?' And we're not. We've done extremely well on the downside, but we gave up some last week. If you look at the performance, we are definitely not out of it. Overall, we are doing well."

"I think there's no way to have a portfolio that has all the juice on the upside and can stay ahead on the downside," John says, defending the group.

"It's next to impossible, I agree," Jerry nods. "But I'm willing to try."

The conversation turns to year-end bonuses and "protecting what we've already earned. . . . Maybe move more of the funds to cash? . . . Lock in some of the gains so far. . . . How to protect the performance until December?"

"The only other thing we've got to live through is the reporting period. That's the last thing for the year," Jerry says. Perhaps it is a challenge he is issuing to the team to show some confidence—don't look for protection and simply be concerned with what you already have. We've got another four months out there—sure, we can lose money in that time, but we can also make money. "If we get through that period, we'll probably perform like the market performs. . . . We can start asking around, noodling around, getting some information. Are you ahead of plan or behind plan? Call some analysts. Ask them if they've talked to the guys at the company lately. If they say 'No,' then tell 'em to get a new job."

Then, on to the schedule of upcoming conferences, meetings after Labor Day, the yield curve, and the world of bonds.

"Well, we're in positive territory for the year," Jerry says.

"Not after today," Marshall retorts quickly.

"Not after today," Jeff repeats.

"When the market gets like this, people have a tendency to not do anything. They say, 'Jeez, I'm just gonna stay out.' . . . We've started to see redemptions," Jerry says.

"Cowards," Marshall accuses loudly, leaning back in his chair.

"I think the other day I heard you make that call," Jerry says as he turns to give Marshall a smile. And indeed, just two weeks ago, Marshall had announced to Jerry that he had moved part of his retirement money from stocks to bonds.

"You're damn right. Damn right," Marshall says.

Marshall was starting to get cautious. Sure, he comes to work every day and buys and sells retail and restaurant stocks because that's what shareholders pay him to do. But with his own money, it might be time to take a little out of the stock market. It's time to change his allocations, to diversify a little more, to spread his eggs into a few more baskets.

* * *

Mid-morning on the last Wednesday of August, the market is down 113 points.

Looking at his screen, Jerry sees two green stocks and two white stocks: two up for the morning and two flat. Every other stock and index on his screen is red.

Marshall often says that he likes to be able to "see" his screen. His monitor sits opposite his office window, making the red tickers and prices difficult to read when the sun is shining. The red blurs with the black background, making the green and white letters and numbers stand out all the more. On a morning like today, Marshall would claim that he "can't even see his screen." He would need to squint, to look harder, and to really search to find something that was trading up.

When Jerry looks at his monitor, it seems the entire screen is nearly black, as more and more stocks trade down and turn deep red in the act. They vanish one by one as he watches them. Just as he spots a stock that is trading up and smiling back at him in bright green font, he loses hold of it. It's like the reassurance of finally seeing a familiar face in a crowd, and having that person move suddenly. The movement is followed by frantic scanning and searching with the whole head and neck extended, accompanied by a quickening of the heart rate. Give me something to grasp, some grounding. Don't let things start spiraling around me, don't let my world go too dark.

Jerry has had such a feeling before—in 1954, when he was walking home from school as an eight-year-old boy. It was only mid-afternoon on a fall day, but already dark skies were settling in. Everything seemed quiet and peaceful, but the sky continued to grow blacker. Hurricane Hazel was on her way. And she had no regard for the fact that Jerry and his hometown in rural Pennsylvania were supposed to be far from the path of any tropical storm. The hurricane made her way up the East Coast killing 95 people and causing $281 million worth of damage. She was so vicious that the name Hazel was retired from circulation—at the time, only the second name to be removed from the rotating list of hurricane designations.

Now, 44 years later, Hurricane Bonnie, the first Atlantic hurricane of the season, is making her way up the East Coast. She hit land in North Carolina, bringing with her winds of up to 90 miles per hour. The wind and water are headed north toward Delaware, Rhode Island, and Massachusetts. Residents all along the East Coast are preparing for the storm.

While a cloud of gloom and gray settles over Philadelphia, Jerry turns his attention to the performance sheets for his funds. He looks over the holdings in each: How much do I own, how much are they down, how much will that one hurt me? Instinctually, Jerry makes the calculations that tell him exactly what the last day of the year looks like, at least from the vantage point of a morning in late August. His eyes rest on the funds' performance for the year so far: DelCap up 1.93 percent, Trend up .74 percent, and Aggressive Growth up 11.78 percent.

"By the end of the day, two of the three will be under water," he says matter-of-factly.

"That's not bad. Yeah, that's pretty good," he says, trying to convince himself. Trying to be satisfied with simply surviving. And he almost was—until he looked further down the page. "Yeah, and the S&P is up only 14 percent for the year. Goddamned friggin' index."

Reports had shown that the market's swoons of early August hit mutual funds hard—especially those focused on smaller stocks, as most of Jerry's funds were. *The Wall Street Journal* had run charts showing that more than 80 percent of small-cap funds were negative for the year, and 45 percent of mid-cap funds were in the red. All three of Jerry's funds were still up for the year. But it wasn't enough. Investors buy funds according to a style box, and they expect managers to invest according to the lines drawn around that box. But when it comes to performance, they want it all. Investors want funds to beat everyone outside their box as well. It's not enough to beat the direct competition, which Jerry was doing handily. Shareholder expectations also pitted him against the overall market. And the market was winning.

*   *   *

At eleven o'clock, the technician for the Bridge system is showing Jerry some new features.

"Now I can turn red to green, but that doesn't mean the prices will go up," Jerry says, looking from his screen to the technician, looking for some answers or guidance from somewhere. "You guys ever gonna try to go public?"

"Next year. . . . We're busy buying everything up right now, so that when we do it we'll look a little more attractive. It's not gonna be the parent company Welsh, Carson going forward, it'll just be a spinout of all the Bridge stuff." His voice grows increasingly enthusiastic, as the consultant trained in computer programs waxes about the world of the stock market, IPOs, and spinouts. "Yeah, I'm waiting for my options. So when I have stock options and we go public, then I'll come see you with my money."

"You know what happens to your options when the stock goes down?" Jerry asks.

"Yeah, you can lose money too. I know."

"Yeah, if the stock goes down, your options aren't worth anything."

"Yeah, but it's going up. It's going up." The Bridge technician says this with a laugh, doing his best to will it to be true. He is just one of millions of Americans for whom the definition of "options" has drastically changed. It used to be, "Well, I'll consider my options. . . . It's nice to have a few options. . . . I have the option to go back to school." Now, options means stock options. Options are the new alchemy. Like turning lead into gold, stock options can turn pennies into dollars. Options can let an employee buy a million shares for a nickel apiece, shares that may well rise to $15 or $20 apiece. Or higher. Stock options mean equity, IPOs, and early retirement.

By the time the Bridge technician leaves with his dreams of options and quick IPO riches, the market is down 90 points. Jerry is thinking more about his shareholders, individual investors, and people like the Bridge technician, whose eyes and wallets are being hypnotized by the markets.

"People's expectations have gotten way too high. *Way* too high. Too many people think 20 percent returns are standard operating procedure, which is ridiculous. But I think there are enough people out there who are willing to condone that belief. There are brokers that say, 'Oh yeah, I can get you 20 percent.' . . . That's where the rub is for me. These guys are saying they're 'financial advisors' or 'investment advisors.' I don't care what you call them, they're brokers." He says this with the disdain people save for used car salesmen.

Jerry's hometown paper, *The New Age Examiner,* used to come out once a week when he was growing up. It was filled with the news of the day, the high school football highlights, and the bowling column. The ads were for tractors, three-bedroom homes for $8,715 or $58.73 a month, and the pancake supper and dance—75-cent donation. The paper reported Procter & Gamble was moving to the area, bringing with it thousands of new jobs. The plant would open up worlds and opportunities that most in the town had never seen.

Now the paper comes out twice a week. There are color pictures, and the paper runs to two sections. It still follows the high school football team and news of the local quilt show. But now the ads are for Merrill Lynch, Morgan Stanley Dean Witter, and American Express Financial Advisors. The ads call out to the citizens of Tunkhannock: "You don't have to earn big bucks to retire in style . . . Free consultation . . . Above Gables Bakery . . . Estate Planning Workshop . . .Even with an ordinary income you can make extraordinary plans for retirement . . . Attention Procter & Gamble Employees: Retirement Planning Hotline." Many of the locals who took those new jobs with Procter & Gamble some thirty years ago are entering their mid-fifties and have accounts full of P&G shares. Wall Street has come to let them know that the stock market can open up worlds and opportunities most in the town have never seen.

"I know some really smart brokers out there, but a lot of these brokers don't even know what they're selling. They know they just need to sell. They don't have any regard for who they're selling it to."

His screen continues to stare back at him, tickers blinking red, green, and white with every trade that takes place. He has a phone message on his desk from a recently widowed woman with two young children who was calling for a little financial guidance.

"But what's a contractor in rural Pennsylvania gonna do? They're not gonna call up a partnership or a hedge fund, and they're not gonna get word of mouth, from any friends they know, about a good money manager. They're gonna look in the paper, and they're gonna buy a mutual fund. Or they're gonna go with a broker who calls and says, 'Yeah, let me put this package together for you. . . .'" He shakes his head and lets his attention drift back to the screen and the share-holders who have sent their checks for him to invest for them.

When the stock market closes, the Dow is down 79 points, and, indeed, two of Jerry's funds now have negative performance records for the year.

"People are gonna come back from vacations and see this market and they're just going to want to get out," he says as he leans back in his chair. The market is closed for the day, and philosophizing and predicting is all he can do, until it all starts over again at 9:30 tomorrow.

Jerry had planned to make the last weekend of August a long one with his family at their cottage in the mountains of Pennsylvania. While he willingly changes work commitments to make more time for his family, Jerry rarely lets meetings or work concerns change his plans.

As the last week of August wears on and stocks continue to decline, Jerry, in a rare move, lets the market dictate his social schedule. On Thursday, the market drops 357 points and on Friday it falls another 114. Jerry decides he should cut his weekend plans short and come to work on Monday.

Watching his screen, looking at his performance sheets, and seeing the rapidly declining numbers, Jerry is forced to admit that the market is in control.

"It doesn't look good," Jerry says, shaking his head and looking at his screen. "In '87, they took it down like this and then they tried to hold it up."

*   *   *

On Monday morning, the last day of August, Jerry proceeds with the same routine as on any other workday: a muffin, a cup of freshly squeezed orange juice, a few sips of coffee, and one aspirin.

A little more than half an hour after the stock market opens, it is down 50 points.

Jerry sells some Amazon and buys some Ascend Communications. And he watches his screen. He sells some CNET and buys some Chancellor Media. And he watches his screen.

Another thirty minutes and the Dow is down nearly 100 points.

Jerry takes a pause from watching the screen to have lunch with the newspapers at his conference table. Lunch is a near replay of his breakfast from the Au Bon Pain in the building's lobby, only this meal is a bagel with cream cheese, a root beer, and an orange. No one stops in to see him and he takes no calls.

The market drops another 75 points.

As the afternoon progresses, so does the market's decline. Down another 20, another 50, and another 30, and it is headed for what feels like a free fall during the last two hours of trading.

Jerry is ready to take a stand. He thinks the selling is overdone, the market will come back, and all those nervous sellers today will be eager buyers tomorrow. He calls the trading desk to put in a buy order for some Spiders. It's not a new stock he's been following or a company he's been trying to build a position in—it's a bet on the market. "Spiders" is the nickname for Standard & Poor's Depository Receipts (SPDRs). Investors can buy or sell Spiders just like they would any stock, only the SPDR Trust isn't just one stock. It is an investment that holds shares of all the companies in the S&P 500. It's put together like an index fund, in that it holds all the stocks in the S&P 500 and is supposed to mimic its performance. But, Spiders act like a stock—they can be bought and sold and traded throughout the day. It's one way a fund manager like Jerry can bet on the market. Selling a Spider is a bet that the S&P—and, by representation, the overall market—is going down. Buying a Spider is a bet that it will go up.

It's a bold move when the market is down several hundred points. But that's what Jerry has been telling himself real achievement demands, especially in the stock market. You've got to be willing to do something different, sooner, faster, and with more conviction—and more money—than the next guy and the next mutual fund.

When the growth group leaves for the day, the stock market has closed down 512 points. The Dow has lost nearly 6.5 percent in one day, the S&P is down nearly 7 percent, and the Nasdaq is off almost 9 percent for the day. It is the second largest one-day point drop in history.

And Jerry leaves the office with his $2 million bet that the market will rebound.

Like most nights, he thinks about the market, stocks, and strategies on his drive home. He arrives to a quiet house because his wife and three children stayed behind in the mountains. Leaving his Ford Expedition for his wife, Jerry drove back to Philadelphia in the pickup truck he keeps at the cabin. And now, the $2 billion money manager, having endured the biggest drop of the year in the stock market, stands outside his house, alone, with no key to get inside.

He pays a visit to the neighbor with whom an extra house key has been left for just such emergencies. He chats with the woman about the weekend, and of course about the market. He tries to downplay the day's drop, giving counterreaction to all of the market commentary and doomsday scenarios that have been broadcast over talk and news radio during everyone's commute home, and are, as Jerry stands in his neighbor's house, the subject of countless news reports and special analyses on television. It is his attempt to calm individual investors, to try and convince Americans—one by one—to take a long-term view of the market and of their investments. His neighbor is having none of it.

Jerry still laughs about the conversation. "So she says to me, 'This is great. Just great, because we've been wanting to get into the market. This is probably a great opportunity for us.'"

He has to smile that, on a day when he has lost nearly $125 million for his shareholders, others see opportunity. The market has taught him to appreciate the paradox. His sell is someone else's buy. His buy is someone else's sell.

With the market closed for the evening, the debate remains. Eager investors hoping to buy on the dips wait for the market to drop further. Jerry, with his $2 million Spider investment, waits for the market to climb back up. In just hours, the market will decide who is right.

CHAPTER 6

FEVERS OF
UNKNOWN ORIGIN

The next day, two Delaware colleagues discuss the market in the elevator taking them to the thirty-ninth floor, where Jerry and his team work.

"Some volatility, huh?" the first guy asks the other, with the precise tone and interest he might reserve for elevator talk about the weather.

His colleague shuffles his feet a bit. He sighs and laughs nervously through his nose. "A lot of people are saying it's over."

"Well. . . ." It is the first guy's turn to shuffle nervously. No one knows what the market will do, and now this guy is saying the market is over. Or is he saying the volatility is over? It is a conversation of miscues and ambiguities between two professionals in an industry that deals out performance and answers in black and white—or rather red and green—down and up.

"A lot of people are saying that the bull market is over, I mean." He clarifies just as the elevator reaches the thirty-ninth floor, where Jerry and his team are already in their offices, ready for a new day and a new market.

"Is it a lady or a tiger?" Marshall announces himself in Jerry's office.

"Stu said they marked the futures up this morning." Jerry has already

August 31, 1998	Year-to-Date Performance	Rank
Aggressive Growth	-5.5%	29
Trend	-14.5%	19
Delcap	-12.9%	53
Dow	-4.7%	
S&P 500	-0.4%	
Nasdaq	-4.5%	

checked in with the trading desk, and the anonymous market (the "they") was already out there buying up futures (bets that the market would go up).

"I betcha it's not gonna rally. They'll probably try to mark it up hard, early on."

"You're gonna have to be fast if you want to move anything," Jerry says. The two exchange predictions and trading strategies as though the market is a video game that can be over just as soon as the quarter is dropped into the slot.

"I'd rather have another severe day, rather than this constant erosion," Marshall says as he picks up the sports page from Jerry's table.

Jerry looks back at his screen. "There's still this enormous diversion in the market. The Russell 2000 is down 25 percent, and the S&P year-to-date is down .4 percent." Less than two months ago, the two indexes were up more than 6 percent and 22 percent, respectively. Investors have gotten nervous, and the last place they want their money in a down market is in small-cap stocks, those that the Russell Index tracks.

Jerry is standing at the trading desk while the television over his shoulder counts down to the market's opening. The CNBC clock shows 6 minutes and 44 seconds to trading, on the day after the largest drop of the year. Which way will the market go? Jerry scans his traders' monitors and looks over the sheet of orders he's brought with him.

"Vinny, why don't you take 6 Amazon to go." He looks down at the paper again, where he has listed companies and single-digit numbers. The 5s and 6s mean thousands of shares and multimillion-dollar positions. On a day with so much built-in uncertainty and volatility, all the trades are sales—"to go"—as though they are deli sandwiches to be eaten on the run. "Take 5 AOL to go and 5 CNET to go. . . . You should probably be ready if they mark these things up early." Have your hand on the joystick when the bell goes off. Be ready to sell as soon as they go up, because they may come back down just as quickly.

"They marked 'em down hard yesterday at the closing, but they'll bounce this morning," Stu says, offering his boss reassurance that his bet on the market was the right call. You'll see. In fact, in less than six minutes, you'll see.

Fifteen minutes later, Jerry is back at his desk, watching the first minutes of the day pass on his screen. "This is even what it *looked* like in '87. Numbers blinking all over the place. People just trying to get some bids out there. Trying to find something that's real to hold onto."

For the first 25 minutes of trading, the market climbs sharply, up nearly 100 points.

Soon, Jerry is on the phone with one of his regular salesmen. "They're not gonna hold up. . . . It's a question of where you want to buy. . . . Look. Like fucking Amazon—that could be 20 as well as 78. Who the hell knows. . . . The market is just flopping around like a dead carp with prickly heat—just flopping around in the sun."

A siren is heard as a fire engine drives by on the street, thirty-nine floors below Jerry's windows.

Jerry calls up to the trading desk to check on the status of his bet that the market would rally. "Stu? On those Spiders, how you doing? . . . What do you think? Just hold on to them and see what happens? . . . Why don't you sell ten."

Another siren screams as it passes below the windows. It announces to all that there are emergencies out there that need attending to.

Just before ten o'clock, the market turns and starts dropping.

It's back to the morning call with the salesman. "Then Merrill came out with a sell on Amazon. . . . They say they are the most expensive of any of the book retailers on the next twelve months' revenues. They say it's hard to make money no matter what you do. . . . And you know, they're exactly right. Thank you, Merrill Lynch. I didn't even know they had an analyst on it. . . . I don't know who it is, but that'll go out to every analyst under the sun, and that's not going to help matters. . . . Yeah, it's a fad; you don't want to own a lot of this stuff. . . . I think going forward the numbers are too high, not just in retail. I think *all* the numbers are too high. And I think that's going to continue into the future. Analyst estimates will be cut back. It's not going to be pleasant. . . ."

Research analysts have their own language when it comes to rating stocks. None uses exactly the same words, so there is a host of terms to describe the investment opportunity of a particular stock. Top-rated stocks get a "strong buy" or "accumulate aggressively." As they cool off, they become "attractive," "buy," and "accumulate." Stocks that are going nowhere soon euphemistically become "neutral," "market performer," or "hold." "Speculative," "long-term buy," and "venture" are thrown in to give analysts some more flexibility— and creativity.

Wall Street research serves the dual purpose of guiding investors on what stocks to invest in, and acting as a calling card to companies looking to hire an investment bank. Thousands of investors use analysts' reports to understand a company's past and to get a sense of its future. But analysts' research reports are also some of the best advertising for an investment bank's services. The laudatory reports say, "Look what we can do for you."

The exchange most commonly works like this: The investment bank collects millions of dollars in fees for taking a company public or helping it to buy another company or to pursue its "strategic alternatives." Thirty days later, a handsome research report is issued with charts and logos and predictions that highlight all of the company's selling points and its advantages over its competitors. In the interest of keeping the investment banking business banking, it is extremely rare for an analyst to issue a report with a "sell" recommendation. Not only is a "sell" or "reduce" not exactly a beacon for new business, it also says to customers that the analyst follows companies not worth investing in.

*   *   *

By 10:15, the Dow is down 82 points and the Nasdaq has dropped 5.

"Stu? Vinny? Some of those things I gave you, where are we? Amazon? . . . We're out? How about America Online? . . . We sold 10? CNET, we sold 5? Okay, how about take another 5 AOL and sell that, and take another 5 CNET and sell that."

Calls can be heard from the offices of the other members of the growth team. More orders for Stu and Vinny to take care of. "How about selling me 50,000 Royal Caribbean? Please." . . . "Let's move some more of that Sterling."

Minutes later, Stu calls down to Jerry. He wants to know if Jerry has any buy orders to go with those sell orders. "It looks like they're gonna turn here. Now they might be on the way up," Stu tells him.

Jerry looks over his screen and its constant blinking. "I think maybe the best thing to do here is to watch."

A little after eleven o'clock, Steve comes in to see Jerry.

"Hey, you're just the guy I'm looking for," Jerry greets him. "You've been missing all the fun."

"Yeah. Isn't this fun?" he says sarcastically. "Yeah, well now you older guys won't be able to give all your talk, 'I was there in '73, '74.' "

"Why?"

" 'Cause guys my age will be able to say, 'I was there in '98,' " Steve replies.

Jerry doesn't even take his eyes off his screen. "Ah, that was nothing. It didn't even make the top twenty in percentage losses."

"It's the seventh worst since World War Two," says Steve, always armed with the facts and data and opinions to back up any line of argument he chooses to pursue.

"Most of 'em are in the last ten years," Jerry says, letting Steve know he is not impressed that this is a survivor's story. "Looks like they're gonna bring it right back up. Up 104. It's all over the place. I think it's best if I just do nothing. It's lunchtime. It's never supposed to go up at lunchtime."

*　*　*

The market bounces wildly for the rest of the afternoon and closes up 288 points, or 3.8 percent. Just before five o'clock, Marshall walks in to announce the group's performance.

"It hasn't come up on the screen yet, but I can just tell you, Trend was up 4.5," he says with satisfaction. It is a number to be pleased with. In just one day, the Trend fund was up by an amount that can take months to achieve.

"What was the Russell up?" Jerry is quick to remind his team that it doesn't matter how well we did; it only matters how much better we did than our competitors and the market.

"Like 3.5."

Jerry nods. "Three. The Nasdaq?"

"Like 5."

"Five-point-one. I need some more indices on my screen," Jerry says, having run out of flashcards for today's quiz round.

"DelCap was up 2.6 and Aggressive Growth was up 3.35," Marshall says.

Steve comes in with the performance sheets for the month of August, and Jerry looks over the printouts, again paying particular attention to the peer group rankings. When he asks Steve about a fund that had been listed as a competitor all year long and was now followed by a row of blank boxes for its performance, Steve replies simply, "It went away."

"It went away?" Jerry asks, unsure that this is explanation enough.

"Yeah, the fund is gone. But I'm not gonna take it out of there because it's still our peer group. One percent of our peer group just couldn't hack it," Steve says with the swagger of a plus 288-point day in the stock market.

"So you'll just leave it in there until the end of the year and then take it out?" Jerry asks.

"Yeah."

"Hmm." Jerry raises his eyebrows and nods as he walks back around his desk to look at his screen. "I guess I'll buy off on that logic for now."

"But be ready with another one when you ask for it," Steve says, confident of Jerry's train of thought as he walks out of his office.

The mood and fortunes of the group have turned with the help of just one big up day. Jerry has tried to be the voice of caution and reason and even a little doom as they've each checked in with him, recovered and unscathed from yesterday's 512-point drop. But, looking at his screen, even Jerry is not immune to rolling with the market's swelling tide. Just before five o'clock, he leans back from his screen and throws both arms up into the air. He flares his fingers from fist to five and back to fist a few times. "Holy shit. Our biggest position in Aggressive Growth is up five."

Citrix Systems. The fund owns 50,000 shares of the networking software company. That five-dollar jump adds a quarter of a million dollars to the fund. A single stock adding .3 percent to an entire fund—a number it often takes all 59 stocks in the fund to achieve. It is a commendable job that deserves the grin on Jerry's face.

*   *   *

The next day, the market continues to climb steadily all morning. Jerry makes calls and trades and sorts through research reports before lunch.

During the noon hour, a reggae band is playing a summer lunchtime concert in the courtyard of Jerry's office building. The water fountain that usually sprays a choreographed show is turned off while Lenny and the Soulsenders drum and sing for the crowd. The first hour concludes with the band's version of the 1980s hit song, *Down Under,* by the Australian band Men at Work. The performance ends with the last lines of the chorus repeated while the cymbals and drums fade out. "You'd better run, you'd better take cover . . . you'd better run, you'd better take cover. . . ."

Upstairs on the thirty-ninth floor, the men at work are watching a stock market that is up 140 points in the Dow and a whopping 50 points in the Nasdaq. Many of the stocks the group bought yesterday are up big—Gateway up $4, Dell up $6. It was just the sort of turn they'd been talking about and preparing for: Be in the stocks that are going to climb first and fastest when the rally starts.

Looking at his screen, and seeing the green tickers and prices flicker higher, Jerry gets increasingly concerned. So much energy has been spent in trying to get out of the way of a down market for the past few weeks—build up some cash, be aggressive in selling, don't be in a hurry to buy. Now the challenge is getting back in the moving market fast enough—be in the right stocks, put your cash to work.

"Back in '83, we went to about 40 percent cash mid-year, and we did really well for the year because the market tanked. But we didn't put it to work fast enough in '84, so we got run over that year," he reminisces, while the stocks and indexes on his screen continue to move higher. He rolls his pen around in circles in between his top and bottom teeth while he watches. He sighs, leans forward, and punches in a ticker on the keyboard. Again, he leans back with the pen on his teeth. Another deep breath and another sliding of the mouse.

The stock market continues to climb higher until it hits an intra-day high of up 125, and then it slips the rest of the afternoon and closes down 45 for the day.

*   *   *

One week later, Jerry is sitting at his conference table reading *The New York Times* sports section as he eats his breakfast. The last three trading days have sent the market down 100, down 42, and up 380.

"You mean to tell me that Roger Maris is not in the Hall of Fame?" he asks the paper aloud. "He had a great arm. People forget that he could really play. People wouldn't run on him. Most people don't realize that. You get no credit for defense in this world."

From where Jerry sits—atop $2 billion on the thirty-ninth floor of a Philadelphia office tower—that is true. Over the past two weeks, his funds have lost less than the overall market has lost on down days. Yet, he has lost a few spots in the rankings, and his perfor-mance numbers are slipping little by little. It is all because on the market's up days—like yesterday's 5 percent climb in the Dow and 6 percent jump in the Nasdaq—Jerry's Aggressive Growth fund was up 4.5 percent. You get no credit for defense in this world.

"Everyone says they want to be in this for the long term. People who are buying or recommending say they look for long-term perfor-mance—services like Morningstar. But really, you blow a quarter as a manager and they'll rip you to shreds. You blow two quarters and you're probably looking for a new job."

Jerry's dour outlook continues when he is talking on the phone later to a salesman. "One thing I think they should do is shut down the IPO market for a year or so. That's the best thing that could hap-pen to the small caps." It is no matter to Jerry that this salesman works for Alex Brown, one of the most active investment banks in the IPO business. "That's one of the things that has killed our end of the market. Every time you turn around, another investment bank is bringing out some piece of shit. That's just flooded the names on our end. There are just too many names."

They talk about the business, the market in general, and specific stocks. "Amazon . . . a lot of people argue that for every book they sell they lose a dollar," Jerry continues. "The question is, how much does it cost to acquire a customer? And will that customer come back? Will they order again? So the most important stuff is the stuff they don't say. They won't tell you these things—I know because I've asked 'em about 18 times. . . . People tell me the real benefit to Amazon is their execution and delivery. People order it and they've got it in a couple of days. If it takes ten days to two weeks, forget it."

People want their books and they want their mutual fund performance *now*. If you can't give it to me, I'll take my money somewhere else.

By two o'clock, the Dow is down 140 points and the Nasdaq is off 18. Jerry's phone is quiet, and he is working on a monthly letter to investors about August's performance.

"What do you say when you're down 18 percent in the month? Is there *anything* you can take from that?" He gives a little snort and shakes his head. He looks at the paper in front of him as though it is an essay question on the pleasures of root canal.

It is another down day for the market and for Jerry's funds. Yesterday, his numbers had flirted with climbing back into positive territory for the year, but a 2 percent loss today confirmed it: He had worked for nearly eight and a half months, and he had lost money for his investors.

Mixed in with the stack of research, IPO prospectuses, and conference invitations Jerry received in the mail today was a royal-blue bumper sticker from an analyst at Prudential. In bold white lettering, the sticker asked, "Have you hugged your small-cap manager today?"

* * *

Just after five o'clock, Jerry takes a call from a broker who is considering recommending the Aggressive Growth Fund to his clients. For this call, Jerry must switch to sell mode—a not entirely comfortable position for him. He must be able to say with confidence, "Yes, our funds are down for the year, the market has lost more than

9 percent in the past two weeks, but yes, by all means buy in, and buy in with me."

Jerry speaks in a monotone as he recites his resume to the broker. "I've been in the business since 1980. Basically, my whole life I've been managing growth stocks. Prior to that, if that matters at all, I was in engineering and worked for Bechtel Corporation. I sort of like to brag about that part because I actually understand the way these things work, as opposed to just picking up the Wall Street research reports and saying, 'Yeah, that makes sense.'

". . . The market has cooperated. We've made some good picks. We didn't have any mistakes and we've done very well. . . . Now we're just waiting to see what's going to happen in the market. We've bought into some S&P Spiders, so we do have the ability to try to limit our risk on the downside. . . ."

When he talks about actual performance numbers, he lists the indexes he's lagging first, rather than boasting about those he's beating and then mumbling the others under his breath.

It's just one more example of the way Jerry thinks things "should be done." Focus on the challenges ahead, not on the accomplishments of the past. Focus on your weaknesses; your strengths should stand for themselves. Jerry enthusiastically points out the abilities of others, while his own confidence and character keep his own achievements quiet, if not entirely to himself. "Now *he* was a tremendous athlete," Jerry says emphatically when speaking of his friend Stew, who was drafted by the Pittsburgh Pirates after college. When he speaks of his own athletic prowess, Jerry's eyes quickly dart around his office. Quiet and serious, he says simply, "I was fast." Almost as an afterthought, he adds, "And I was exceedingly aggressive."

* * *

The following Monday, Steve stops in to talk to Jerry about a stock he and John have been following: CBT Group, a company that sells interactive training software.

"I just talked to John. We're not sellers here, but we don't want to get in the way when it's going down. We want to wait 'til things settle before we buy."

"You're a buyer?" Jerry asks with notable surprise in his voice.

"Yeah, maybe this afternoon," Steve says confidently. "John says he's been waiting to buy this thing in the 40s, and here it is. So I'll talk to H&Q and see what they say."

"Yeah, why don't you talk to H&Q before you buy," Jerry says, not telling Steve whether to buy or sell, merely suggesting that he get a little more guidance from a Wall Street analyst or salesman first. Find out what they know, find out what they're telling people, anticipate what the stock is going to do.

Once Steve has left Jerry's office, Jerry shakes his head. "CBT. Those two are looking at it on a fundamental basis. This stock does *not* trade on fundamentals. There's a lot of fast money in this stock—it is completely momentum-driven. And they want to buy more." He looks back at CBT's ticker on his screen. "And I need to convince them that they should have sold it all on the opening trade."

By the afternoon, the stock is down $10 to $45—well into the $40 range where John and Steve were looking to buy. They froze. They didn't want to buy, but they didn't want to sell. The group owned 200,000 shares and they wanted to hold. They continued their research and analysis and avoided making a hasty decision. To Jerry, when a stock is moving as much as CBT, and conference calls, analyst estimates, and questions regarding quarterly earnings litter the market, it is either a buy or a sell. It is not a hold.

Jerry listened to John and Steve confidently tell him that the company would make its quarter and that Wall Street analysts would support the stock. If they didn't have the conviction to make the trade, Jerry did. He called up the trading desk and put in an order to buy another 300,000 shares—a $12.6-million position. He told himself it was a trade. He'd sell it the next day whether it went down or up, but it was a stock that required action.

As John and Steve predicted, an afternoon conference call tried to assure investors that the company would meet the quarter. But, upon explanation, it came out that most of the dollars would be coming in at the end—the company would be pushing it to make the quarter. The expected support from analysts didn't come, and the stock dropped another seven points. With little hesitation and less emotion, Jerry called the trading desk and ordered Stu to sell 400,000 shares. In the time between when Jerry put in the buy order and when he decided to sell, those 400,000 shares lost $2.7 million in value. In less than one day.

"These guys keep saying it could be a really big company in the next few years." He is speaking quietly and seriously; he rarely talks about colleagues. "The next few years mean nothing to me. The way the money management business is today, you are sold on a quarter-to-quarter basis. You are judged by the day, the month, and the quarter, and that's the reality of it."

Sometimes a hold should be a sell. Or a buy should be a sell. At other times, a sell should be a hold. No one is always right in making those decisions—even Jerry, with his twenty years' experience and unemotional attachment to stocks and companies. But, he takes it as his job to teach his team to make those decisions. Whether you are right or wrong, you've got to learn to recognize when to take action. Then take it, and learn from your mistakes and by feeling your way around.

"I'm selling a little Network Appliance today," Jeff says just inside Jerry's doorway.

Jerry cranes his neck to find the ticker and price for Network Appliance on his screen. It is down $3 a share. "Is that you leaning all over your own stock today?"

"Phew, no. There were some sales out there at $54, and then the next trade," he slaps his hands together, "down three bucks. . . . So we're selling a little."

Jerry looks over his screen, and rocks in his chair slightly. "If you're gonna sell, I'd control the trades. I would scale up on this one." If you want to sell, go ahead, but I think it could go up—so at least sell when it's on the way up.

"Yeah, I'm just paring back a bit, maybe a quarter percent in each of the funds," Jeff says. "You think, we've owned the stock for four to five months and it's up 50 percent. Not bad."

"Why do people buy stocks? Because of the opportunity. . . . I'm just trying to separate technologically what's going on with the companies and what's going on with the stocks," Jerry says, mulling over his thoughts out loud to Jeff. "I just wouldn't be in a huge hurry to sell."

"Hey, we've had a 50 percent run," Jeff says and leans up against the door.

"We could have a 100 percent run. They could split the stock and it could go higher. You don't know that."

"I'm just taking a little bit off the table," Jeff says. I understand your argument, but I'm taking some of my chips home so I have at least something tomorrow.

Jeff, John, and Marshall have gathered in Jerry's office for the weekly meeting. Steve is traveling, and Lori, back from maternity leave for two weeks now, is already booked with analyst and company visits.

September 18, 1998	Year-to-Date Performance	Rank
Aggressive Growth	-0.4%	32
Trend	-9.0%	22
Delcap	-5.7%	51
Dow	-0.2%	
S&P 500	6.3%	
Nasdaq	6.0%	

With just over a week to go before October hits, the Dow is flat for the year, and all three of the group's funds are negative.

"Well, for a sort of week-in-review here, I don't have any great thoughts as to which way the market is going," Jerry starts off. "One scenario is that they address some of the international issues at this G-7 Summit coming up, and the market goes up; another is if they don't and earnings fall apart; and the third scenario is. . . ."

"Is this the three-handed economist?" Jeff interrupts. "When I was up at the Salomon conference, people were ready for doom."

"The market could rally, but the rally could be in things you don't expect to rally—business services, health care," Marshall adds. "But is this gonna be like '91? Hell no, that was the twilight of the gods for health care stocks."

"Things like the money centers will be the bellwether indicators," Jeff jumps in. "If they turn, that will indicate that South America's not over and that the world will stabilize. 'Cause your sectors have been the worst in this." Jeff adds the last bit as he turns to face John. It is not meant to be a personal criticism, and the whole team knows that John can't exactly be held responsible for the performance of all of the banks, insurers, and credit card companies out there. Besides, John had done his research, assessed the direction the stocks were heading and pared back the group's holdings. He'd made the right move when much of the industry hadn't. But, the funds are down, the group is slipping, and it's human nature to want to lay blame somewhere.

"My sector's only been a reflection of the weaknesses in your sector," John replies. "I'm a mirror of your stocks."

Jerry gets up and walks over to his bookshelf, looking for a piece of research that might draw the debate away from weakness and underperformance.

"We may not get a big rally here," Marshall says, filling the void. "This thing could chew its way sideways."

"Where do you think the concern is? Are the worries in technology, that they'll start missing the numbers?" Jerry asks. He's trolling for insight and answers—any of the puzzle pieces that will help the group decide what to buy and what to sell.

"I wouldn't stray too far from the indexes in technology," Marshall says. He is not willing to go out on a limb here. Let's keep right in line with everyone else's holdings in technology; that's not where we want to make a big bet one way or the other.

Jerry agrees. "Yeah, the risk is if you have a rally, you'll be so far behind the eight ball you'll never get out of the hole." It is the familiar mantra: You've got to be in the right stocks when the market starts to move.

"There are some concerns out there that companies will start missing the lowered numbers for the quarter," John offers.

"Yeah, it's not like you miss the number by a few pennies, you miss the *whole* number," Jerry says.

John mentions a few credit card companies whose stocks have doubled recently. The group is not in them, and he is wondering: Should we get in there? He doesn't trust the industry right now, but he doesn't want to miss out on any more doubles.

"You run a huge risk in those things if the market goes down," Jerry cautions. It's a cycle that's easy to get caught in and hard to dodge. When the market goes down, consumer confidence goes down. Consumers' spending and their subsequent credit card bills go down with it. When the credit card companies and the banks are left without new loans to collect interest on, their earnings and stock prices both drop. (And, of course, it all happens in less time than it took to read this paragraph.)

"You hear all this anecdotal evidence that banks are making more and more loans on less and less asset base," Marshall adds. As the quality of their loans goes down, the banks are less likely to get those payments back. Their profits go down, and eventually the stock price catches up and comes down right alongside.

"Yeah, the latest numbers on housing sales in Princeton was that people were buying houses on 5 percent down payments," Jeff says. As the market climbed higher heading into the summer, so did consumer confidence, and buyers went from paying 20 percent or 10 percent down for homes to being willing to take on mortgages for 95 percent of their homes. The economy is good, the stock market is up, and I've got a 401(k). What could go wrong?

"Yeah, and housing starts were slow," Jerry adds. The business is cooling off, and the consumers—and individual investors—may be the last to know.

"It's sloppy out there."

"And Toll Brothers said they're gonna miss the quarter," John offers his own housing market data. Toll Brothers, one of the nation's largest home builders, gets caught in the same cycle as the credit card companies. Down market equals less spending equals fewer new homes. "Some sort of convoluted reasoning—building mix—more Texas, less New Jersey."

"For now, I guess we've just got to keep our nose to the grindstone. Keep our heads down 'til we get through whatever this is we're going through," Jerry says. "I've started going through my names and trying to figure out which companies are gonna make it, which companies might make mistakes. We've got to be out there."

Jerry moves on to the business mix at Delaware Investments— more growth, less value. The board has been talking about starting some large-cap growth funds, in addition to the small-cap and mid-cap growth funds that Jerry and his team run. Management is happy with the team's performance, and costs are a little tight to be hiring a new large-cap team, so they're thinking of adding it to the responsibilities of Jerry's group.

"We can really build it and run it off screens, and use what we already know," Jerry explains. "So, I'm more inclined to drag it in here rather than let it wander off somewhere else."

"I'd try to grab as much territory as possible as fast as possible," John shows he has an aggressive streak as well. He encourages Jerry—with words that could have come from any business plan of the growth group's stocks. "I'd try to be in charge of as much assets as possible, make yourself as important as possible."

Jerry and his group need to take advantage of their own cycle while they can. Good performance equals more attention and more shareholder dollars. More shareholder dollars equal more fees for Delaware and a bigger piece of the pie for the growth group.

*　*　*

One week later, the performance sheets on the table in front of the group show that the team has climbed five spots. The Aggressive Growth Fund is now ranked twenty-seventh for the year-to-date. All three funds were up every day but one. They climbed into positive territory in the Aggressive Growth Fund and were inching their way up in the DelCap Fund.

"Well, another crappy week for us last week. Poor management," Marshall says sarcastically.

"Marshall says we got two more stars from Morningstar. Where'd you see that?" Jerry asks.

"I read the paper every day." Jerry simply smiles when Marshall says this.

The fund-ranking company has bestowed two more of the all-important Morningstar stars on the growth group—one more for the DelCap Fund and one more for the Trend Fund. Now DelCap has two stars and Trend has three. An improvement, but still not enough to get noticed. The Aggressive Growth Fund is holding steady with three stars. But who wants steady in the greatest bull market in history?

"Performance—you can look and see everything's moving along fine there. Cash levels are coming down—there are a couple of things going on there. One, we've put more to work; and two, when the market goes up, your equity percentage goes up and your cash percentage comes down," Jerry says.

"And three, redemptions," Marshall laughs—as if anyone would even consider taking money out from under the guidance of the growth group.

"Well, actually, funny you should say that," Jerry says. "Out of Trend, someone popped out a $19-million piece."

"Idiot," Marshall says.

More investors are trying to time the market and trade their mutual funds accordingly. They want to try and call when the market is going to come back down and when it's going to start to climb. They want to move in advance of the market's shift from growth to value or from tech to oil and gas. The challenge for Jerry is that the more his shareholders move their money around, the less mobility he has to move money in, out of, and around the market. And, the more he and his group have to worry about cash coming in and out of the funds, the less attention they have to focus on the market. Now, with $19 million being taken out of the fund, the group has to take $19 million out of the market to cover the withdrawal. That's $19 million worth of moving around, and $19 million less mobility for the group.

"Performance issues—you can all read the numbers," Jerry continues his post- and pregame analysis. "The end of the quarter is coming up. Call the companies, call the analysts, call your mother, call anyone you can think of. Make sure earnings are on track. Because after the quarter, that's all the data points we're gonna get—all things being equal—'til after the end of the year. And that's what compensation is going to be based on."

The last item gets their attention: compensation—this is what we've got to do to get paid.

John leans in closer to the table, and Jeff's knee starts bouncing a little faster.

"We've got cash, so be willing to step up and buy more. We've had a rally, so you can look at your names and see what works in a rally, so that when the market goes down you know what to buy. . . . In the Aggressive Growth fund, we've sort of focused on the story stocks. We've gotten into a lot of the Internet stocks. Jeff and I do most of that, and it's really more gamesmanship than investing. . . ."

"Sectors aside," Marshall says, "this is a stockpickers' market."

"And it's only gonna get more so," Jerry agrees.

"And as we start to see some blowups, it's gonna be fewer companies that are gonna move," Marshall continues.

"If you see good ideas, we could use 'em. Just try to be a little bit of a market timer—a sharpshooter on a short-term basis. Some of these things can go down 10 percent in a day, and we can take advantage of that. . . . Greenspan . . . IMF. . . . You need to be a little cautious because you're not at the bottom; we've had a bounce, but earnings are going to change things. . . . Am I totally euphoric about the market and do I think things are gonna go straight up? No. But do I think it's so bad we don't want to play? No."

Jeff offers up the invitation to meet with a technology analyst who is coming in to see him later in the week. "He's unbelievably connected in Asia-Pac. It's well worth your hour."

Jerry isn't buying it, even if this guy is so connected with the entire Asian-Pacific region he can call it Asia-Pac. "We've got to keep in mind that what we do is pick stocks, pick stocks, pick stocks. And we do that against the backdrop of what's going on in the rest of the world—so you need to be looking at and understanding what you own first," he says. He wants the team to stay focused. There's too much confusion in thinking from the outside in. Keep it simple. Think from the inside out.

The coach has called the plays, and each team member knows the positions to take. As they get up from the table to leave, Jerry adds, "Hey, did you guys see—on DelCap, we're in the money now?" As usual, he can't let them go without some word of encouragement—we're doing well, we just hit bonus round in another fund.

"Oh, that is sweet," Jeff says.

"Yeah, in the year to date and in the twelve months," Jerry adds.

From just outside the door, John jokes, "Let's go to 100 percent cash, close it out, and lock in a 1 percent gain for the year."

* * *

It is the last day of September, and Jerry has yet another meeting with another analyst to discuss more industries, trends, companies, executives, and numbers. As he stands up to greet the analyst at the door, he sees the trays of bagels, mini-Danishes, and croissants left over from someone else's breakfast meeting.

"You want any donuts, coffee . . . ?" Already, this meeting is off to a different start than most. He is the first to offer something. True, it's only free food that seconds ago he didn't know was his to offer, but he likes this analyst. She covers pharmaceutical and biotech companies, she has her PhD, she's quick and insightful, and she knows all of her numbers cold.

She goes methodically down her list of companies, citing pros and cons of each, as though she's helping Jerry put together a table seating of people he might like to dine with.

"It's so hard to find things to be long in right now; they've all run up," she says, after a string of cautionary remarks.

"You're too worried about valuation," Jerry chides her.

Valuation. It had become one of the most debated measures in the stock market. What's the company worth? Is the stock too expensive? Is it cheap? If it's cheap, does that mean it's a good buy or, well, just cheap? The most common way to measure valuation of a company is its P/E, or price-to-earnings ratio. It sounds pretty technical, but the measure really answers the question: How much do investors expect to get out of the company at a given price? Should you buy the $80 shoes that will last two years, or the $40 pair that will wear out after one year? Simple math says they both have the same P/E. But to a shopper or an investor, it's not that simple. There's a chance the cheap shoes could last two years, which would make them a real bargain. Or will the soles on that $40 pair fall off sooner than a year? Maybe the $80 shoes are worth the extra money now, if they are better for your feet. Then again, the $80 pair may be out of style before their utility is up. Do you look for value today or growth tomorrow?

As the name would suggest, value investors look for stocks that appear to be good values. Growth funds, on the other hand, are concerned more with a company's growth prospects in the future than with its current valuation. Value investors look for the $10 and $20 shoes that are good solid buys and have the potential to last longer. Growth investors are willing to spring for the $80 shoes and even the $200 pair, believing the claims that the more expensive kicks will outlast the others, help you jump higher, run faster, and lose weight. They're willing to pay more for the potential of those shoes.

Valuation is one measure that has a lot of investors spooked. Just like the conversation ping-ponging across Jerry's conference table today, for every claim of "It's too expensive" there's a new buyer theorizing that "Valuation doesn't matter anymore . . . that's not what the market cares about. . . ." Buyers have stopped looking at the price tags and are just listening to the promises and the pitches.

Jerry continues to listen, and the analyst proceeds with her list of what she *does* care about in the market. "Coulter . . . Pathogenesis . . . Millennium Pharmaceuticals . . . Agouron. . . ." Where other women would have a small kerchief showing in a suit coat's breast pocket; this analyst has a dollar bill, likely change from the taxi fare from the train station to Jerry's office. The money rises higher and higher in her vanilla suit's pocket as she gets more animated in talking about stocks. "There were the ABCs of biotech—Amgen, Biogen, and Chiron; now, it's Amgen, Biogen, and Centocor . . . vaccines . . . ptosis, hepatitis C . . . viral companies. . . ."

They talk about trends in the pharmaceutical industry—more manufacturing moving overseas—and about an IPO that was just postponed due to "market conditions." The meeting is casual and friendly; they trade thoughts and quips on multibillion-dollar companies and multimillion-dollar IPO payouts. Jerry has even trotted out his favorite phrase for describing symptoms with no diagnoses, sicknesses with no names: FUOs, fevers of unknown origins. By the end of the meeting, they have laughed over the biotech industry and discussed the challenges of investing in the current market. And, when the analyst stands to leave the office, the dollar bill inside her pocket has climbed so high that it is only inches from her face. It is undeniable. I am here to talk about biology, about diseases, about cures. I am here to talk about money.

*　*　*

As the market closes on the last day of September, Jerry is on the phone with an old colleague. "Horrible. . . . Yeah, these last few days I've been getting the crap whaled out of me. . . . This sucks. . . . I hope in my lifetime it does come back. . . ."

And indeed, the screen shows it. The market closes down 238 points for the day, and all of Jerry's funds are down. The Aggressive Growth Fund is near the zero percent range again. And there are only three months left in the year. Unfortunately—for all investors—October is one of them.

The two stock market crashes of the twentieth century happened in October: October 29, 1929, and October 19, 1987. The month is always approached with trepidation and historical baggage, and it often doesn't disappoint. In 1997, the market dropped more than 7 percent on October 27—a 554-point drop that was the largest single-day point drop in history. Tomorrow, the group will begin to discover whether the October jitters are merely superstition.

Steve steps into Jerry's office and takes a piece of gum from the bowl on Jerry's table. He sits down and puts his feet up on the table. He laces his fingers together, indicating that he'd like to pursue a philosophical or historical discussion about the market. The sunlight streaming in through Jerry's windows catches Steve's gold bull-and-bear cufflinks. They were a gift from a friend for his thirtieth birthday earlier in the month. "CBT. Short covering today?"

"No, I heard there's some talk out there that they're gonna put in a poison pill. Probably some short covering too. . . . You know, just a dead-cat bounce," Jerry says. It's a particularly colorful Wall Street phrase used to describe a cratered stock that falsely looks to have some sign of life. Even a dead cat bounces.

"Yeah, that's what I thought," Steve says. He continues to work the piece of gum around in his mouth. "Here we have all this talk about the market overreacting to things, and yet we have all these examples of the market *underreacting*. Like CBT, it was down in the 30s, now it's 10-ish. . . . Cendant, here we thought it was the biggest over-reaction when the stock went to 16. Where's the stock now? Ten?"

"Yeah," Jerry says.

"That's actually what I came to talk to you about. Cendant. Did you hear what they're calling it? AIG 2—Accounting Irregularities Galore." Jerry hardly gives it the guffaw the coiners of the phrase might have been hoping for.

"It could be interesting, but I don't want to have to explain it to my shareholders," Jerry says. It could be a great buy, but people are only aware of the problems right now. If I buy it, it shows up on my list of holdings, and shareholders will be alarmed and ask questions about it. Jerry lives and invests by simple rules. Make money for your shareholders, but make sure that your shareholders are comfortable about the way you're making that money.

* * *

Just before six o'clock, Jerry is packing up his bag to go home—a bit of research, some faxes, his checkbook.

"We hung right in there today. Picked up ground on those indexes we were lagging," Marshall says as he enters.

"In the world of relative gamesmanship, it could've been worse," Jerry says and pulls out a pamphlet from the side pocket of his canvas briefcase. "My wife doesn't have a diamond, and I want to get her one." He opens the cover of the Tiffany booklet *How to Buy a Diamond*. "It needs to match the gold ring in here, but do you think that one's ugly?" Marshall can come to Jerry for advice on the secret to the right concrete mix, and Jerry turns to Marshall on buying jewelry for his wife.

"Oh, a bezel setting? That's nice."

Jerry looks up at him accusingly. "You know this stuff?"

"Sure, and I know some guy in the diamond district can get it for you for half that price."

Jerry closes up the book and slips it back in the bag, where he has been carrying it, along with the manual to his new rifle, for the past several months. He doesn't yet have the confidence or the certainty to call in the buy order. He's been married for over ten years now, and he's always wanted to buy his wife a diamond. It would be an easy purchase for a $2-billion money manager in a bull market, but Jerry doesn't want it to be easy. It's not like a fast-buck IPO to get in and out of in a day or two. It's got to be the right one, the right time, and he's got to be in the right mood. He's pulled out the pamphlet several times in the past few weeks and inspected the photograph. He's starting to think that this year may just be the right time.

"We didn't do too badly," Jerry says, returning to the usual end-of-day exchange.

"That's what I came to show you," Marshall says, and holds out a handwritten sheet of competitive funds and their performance numbers for the day. "These are some of the other funds in our decile."

"Yeah, it looked like we did pretty well," Jerry nods. He is satisfied that, on a day when the market is down nearly 240 points, he and his team made up some ground against the competition.

Marshall, knowing that the day-to-day numbers are worth less than the paper he has written them on, balls up the sheet and throws it in one of Jerry's trash bins.

CHAPTER 7

THIS USED TO
BE FUN

As his maroon Ford Expedition weaves through the traffic on the way into Philadelphia, Jerry is thinking about the stock market. The market isn't due to open for nearly another two hours, but he is already going over numbers, strategies, and scenarios in his head. He had left work thinking about his funds, went to bed wondering about specific stocks, and woke up this morning pondering the stock market in general. Now, sitting in traffic, he pictures the market as a vehicle in motion: a train.

He envisions the whole market as a long train of railroad cars climbing up a steep hill. Investors of all varieties are spread out among the cars. Hedge funds—those funds that are allowed to short stocks and bet *against* the market—and maybe the faster, momentum money investors are in the front cars. Most mutual fund shareholders and individual investors are riding in the rear cars or even in the caboose. For most of the year—most of the past ten years—the train has just kept climbing up and up and up the hill as the stock market has risen higher. Individuals have continued to invest more money in the stock market, and they send bigger checks to mutual fund companies. It was almost as if Jerry and all the other professional money managers on board could hear the rhythmic chanting—"I think I can, I think I can, I think I can"—that is *willing* the train and the ride and the Dow to climb higher.

It wasn't until August, or maybe even September, that some of the train's cars started to reach the top of the hill. When funds invested in Russia fell apart, hedge funds started to report losses, and big banks and insurance companies were warning of difficulties ahead. But these front cars were so far from the back that investors in the rear seemed to persuade themselves, as they so desperately wanted to believe, "Oh, that's a different train. . . . We're not connected at all. . . . That's not the direction I'm going in. . . . I think I can, I think I can. . . ."

But as he moves along the highway today, Jerry admits to himself that his car in the train had reached the top of the hill. In fact, its stay at the top was so brief that he is already feeling the wind rushing by his face as the descent begins. He knows that the speed of the descent will only increase when all the adjoining cars carrying millions of individual investors and shareholders behind him crest the hill and add to the momentum on the way down.

He is so taken with the image that, later, he sketches it out on one of the notepads that has *Gerald S. Frey* printed across the top. It's not a bad drawing. It's a big hill, but the train is definitely strong enough to climb it. And there are two arrows pointing to the railroad car that is just teetering, ever so slightly, on the downside of the hill: the Delaware growth group's car.

"We absolutely got the shit kicked out of us yesterday," Jerry tells one of his regular salesmen over the phone. "Yeah, we were down 6 percent. And I run a relatively high-test portfolio."

Marshall comes in to start the day's dialogue just a few minutes before the market opens.

October 1, 1998		
	Year-to-Date Performance	Rank
Aggressive Growth	-3.8%	27
Trend	-13.3%	18
Delcap	-11.3%	45
Dow	-3.5%	
S&P 500	2.8%	
Nasdaq	2.7%	

"Where's your belt?" Jerry asks him, skipping over any formal morning greeting.

Fridays are casual at Delaware, and Marshall is wearing blue jeans and a navy-collared knit shirt. He explains that he has simply forgotten his belt. Many of Marshall's shirts are monogrammed in meticulous, crisp script. His suit coats have handkerchiefs peeking out at just the right distance above the left breast pocket. He has a suede brush at home, knows how to use it, and is considering buying a second one to keep at the office. Something is occupying Marshall's mind or he would not simply forget a belt.

"Piper Jaffray has a negative call on the market," he says.

They both laugh. The Dow was down 210 points yesterday, their funds fell more than 6 percent each in one day, Russia is defaulting on billions in loans, money managers are preparing for the possibility of a recession in the economy. And now this particular analyst sends out a piece of research saying he has concerns about the market.

"Yeah, this guy's the Oracle of Delphi," Marshall laughs. "And he also has a negative call on consumer."

As an investor following restaurant and retail stocks, Marshall takes this forecast on consumer stocks as an insult. It's like a bad review in the paper. It's tough to get people to line up at the box office once the publicity is out.

"It's a technical call?" Jerry asks.

"Yeah, it's technical."

Some calls are fundamental, some are technical. If a report says, "Papa John's Pizza is going to have a difficult quarter because cheese prices have gone up faster than the restaurants can raise their prices," that's a fundamental call. A report that says, "The stock can't go any higher, because it's reached an inflection point in its 52-week history and the yield curve on the 30-year Treasury is weakening"— well, that's a little more technical.

"I'm just wondering if we shouldn't take some off the table." The past few weeks have ushered in some of the swiftest declines Marshall has seen in his career on Wall Street. He's looking for a little consensus.

"You're hearing all the calls now—it's over for retail, it's over for semiconductors. Now Peoplesoft, it's over for software. Gold is the only place to go, but you could never explain that—'We're aggressive growth, and we're in the ultimate disaster sector—gold.'" Jerry smiles as he pictures himself standing in front of the Fund's board and telling them that he's opted out of the stock market and instead is stashing gold bars in a safety deposit box. "We've moved things around and we have a more aggressive portfolio than we did, but there's a flip side to that. And we saw that in spades yesterday."

"Well, when Linens 'n Things has 11 percent comps and the stock is down 10 percent, I say 'Screw you.' I'm not selling the stock just because it's down," Marshall says.

Another fundamental-versus-technical battle. Fundamentally, the company is doing well. It has just reported that its comparable sales, its comps, are up 11 percent over the last period. Technically, the stock is down 10 percent, so things must be getting worse; sell.

The two talk over apparel cycles and some of the other stocks Marshall owns. Marshall is confident in his sector, but yet, like most investors this first week in October, he's nervous on the whole. Jerry consents to cutting back some of the funds' positions in Abercrombie & Fitch and American Eagle.

"You and I both know that apparel stocks are a lot like disk drive stocks. There just comes a point. . . ."

"Well, I just want to feel my way along," Marshall says. "I feel like when you're little and you go to the county fairs. You go in the funhouse maze and all the walls are painted black and you can't see where you're going. And every once in a while there's a chink of light in the wall called truth, and you just feel your way along. And it was always easier if you were with someone. So I'm just gonna check in here throughout the day."

Jerry looks at his screen. The stock market has opened and the numbers are flickering from white to red to green and back to red. Little chinks of light that will guide them through the day. "We'll just hang on and see what happens."

The New York Times sits on Jerry's conference table, spread open to a multipage article on the demise of Long-Term Capital Management, a hedge fund thought by most in the investment business to be among the savviest of funds. Hedge funds are funds available to wealthy investors who presumably have a little more understanding of and tolerance for risk. Hedge funds can short stocks, use other strategies average mutual funds can't, and may even invest in private companies. For their higher risk and higher fees, hedge funds attempt to deliver higher returns. Certainly, Long-Term Capital's investors were mindful of the risks in the stock market. But, the firm boasted two Nobel prize-winning economists among its ranks and was led by John Meriwether, long considered one of the great trading minds of Wall Street. Long-Term Capital was supposed to be untouchable. And now, it was at risk of losing billions of dollars and had to be rescued by a team of Federal Reserve masterminds and 14 investment banks pledging a bailout package of $3.6 billion to the fund. Long-Term Capital must have been in the lead car of the train as it headed over the hill. The car had now settled at the bottom.

The sight of so many bright investors and so many billions settled in the wreckage at the bottom of the hill has the rest of the market terrified. Could the demise of one hedge fund be the lead domino in a series of market-toppling financial crises? Many strategists had been saying there was something out there that could bring the bull market to a screeching halt. The collapse of the Russian economy didn't do it, an extramarital affair of the U.S. President didn't do it; would it be this high-minded, high-finance vehicle in high-net-worth Greenwich, Connecticut?

*   *   *

Thirty minutes after the market opens, the Dow is down 13 points. Marlene, one of the assistants from upstairs, roams the hallway lining the growth group's offices. She is carrying the Tiffany bag and collecting bills for "Dollar Days." She steps into Jerry's office knowing he is one of the game's regulars—one of the few fund managers who plays. "It's a waste of a dollar . . . it's all luck . . . I never win . . . I don't like games of chance" the others say, and they keep their wallets to themselves. Before Marlene has even announced herself, Jerry takes a dollar from his wallet and drops it in the bag. He figures this may just be his week.

He continues checking his screen and returns calls from his salesmen.

"There are no places to go and hide right now. . . . Yeah, I talked to some hedge fund guy yesterday, and he said they spent the whole day just talking to clients, telling them what they're doing. People are saying they're gonna take their money out. . . . The market just turned around and it's heading the other way again."

The Dow is now down 70 points and the Nasdaq has dropped 26. A 57-point fall in the twenty minutes since Jerry dropped his dollar into the Tiffany bag.

He calls the trading desk. "Stu? Network Associates. I own 245,500. Sell it." Jerry is selling the Network Associates to make room for the 15,000-share Microsoft order he placed with the trading desk before the market opened. "That's what we do here. We try to trade up. We're constantly upgrading the positions and shifting into higher-quality names," he explains.

It's easy to picture Jerry shuffling the stocks around in his portfolio like so many playing cards spread across his bedroom floor. It's like a high-stakes game of gin with multiple decks: I've been holding this pair of sixes for a while without seeing a third. Should I give up a six for a pair of threes, in hopes of getting another three? Once the six is discarded, it seems that, inevitably, the next round produces a six.

* * *

After lunch, John takes an oversized red apple from a box of freebies some broker or salesman sent the group. He looks around the hall and addresses no one in particular. "You bought growth stocks at growth multiples, and now there's no growth." He walks back into his office shaking his head. "Brutal. It used to be fun."

The Dow is down 244 points for the week, and the growth group has lost everything their funds had made for the year and more.

Jerry has survived these swings before. He'd been in the business seven years when October 1987 hit—a 23 percent drop in the Dow in one trading session, and an even larger drop in his team's portfolio in a single day. But back then he had others to look to, he followed guidance from above and alongside him. Now he is the one being looked to. Most in the group weren't working on Wall Street in 1987. Lori and Steve were in college, and Marshall and John had left jobs on Wall Street for business school.

Other than Jerry, only Jeff was working in the investment world that fateful fall. Even though he was building spread sheets and wasn't involved in looking at companies or making decisions on stocks at the time, Jeff can talk about 1987 like he was on the front lines. Jeff approaches the stock market, earnings season, and company presentations like a Navy SEAL on a reconnaissance mission. There are clues hiding everywhere. It is not entirely implausible to expect to see Jeff wearing night-vision goggles while he listens to quarterly conference calls.

"I just came in to tell you something truly useful. Dolly Parton called Clinton a 'horny little toad.'"

Jerry looks up from his screen to acknowledge Jeff inside his door only briefly. "Fore Systems, up 1⅝. Network Appliance, up ¾."

"EMC has already issued the time and date of their conference call. It's interesting, because they will never give anything away before the quarter's over."

"The stock's been a great stock." Jerry leans back in his chair. "But, you know what? Deep in my heart I wonder about them."

Jeff weighs his next words carefully, wanting the last word without insulting the boss. "Hmm. I've been with them since '92."

"Try '90," Jerry says curtly and lets his chair snap forward as he leans in to look at his screen again.

"Well. Good news is they released their phone number for the conference call. The quarter's done."

Jerry says nothing and Jeff walks out. Once he is out the door, Jerry cocks his head to address the space where Jeff just stood, "Maybe."

As the market continues to drop, Jerry looks at his computer screen and moves his mouse in small circles around the red foam pad it rests on. The pad was a company giveaway a few years ago—maybe an IPO deal toy, maybe a holiday trifle. The pad shows a photo of a Humvee driving across a barren desert landscape and the logo and motto for SEER Technology, "We've been there before."

It seemed SEER had indeed been there before—and was maybe still there. The software company came public in the summer of 1995 at $18 a share. The stock slipped for the next three years, and now trades at around 75 cents a share.

*   *   *

Marshall announces himself in Jerry's office by biting into one of the apples from the green-tissue-paper-lined box in the hallway.

"Now Gene Autry's dead. What is it, a plague on cowboys? First Roy Rogers, then Cowboy Bob."

"Gene Autry's dead?" Jerry looks up with genuine interest.

"Yeah. It just came across the tape."

"The tape" has advanced from a running printout of stock prices that is later shredded for confetti and sprinkled upon the heads of heroes during parades to an omnipotent source of stock quotes, news, rumors, and announcements. Now, "the tape" is used to refer mainly to news items from the Dow Jones Newswire that continually appear on the screens of most fund managers throughout the trading day. New headlines appear every few seconds, detailing the current status of the market, world affairs and events, and the passing of beloved cowboy movie stars.

Although confounding at first, it is not uncommon for a money manager to cast aside a newspaper's front page and business page and turn immediately to the sports section in the morning. This is the news that took place after the close of the market, after "the tape" stopped ticking for the night. By vigilantly reading "the tape" throughout the day, a money manager would miss nothing by skipping the evening news, daily newspapers, and even *Time, Fortune,* or *Business Week.*

"You ever go to his movies?" Jerry asks, letting his thoughts drift back to the days of Gene Autry and his horse Champ.

Marshall shakes his head no.

"I used to. There was a theater in the middle of downtown, and every Saturday all the kids'd go to the movie. It cost 20 cents to see the movie and 10 cents for popcorn."

The two join in the familiar duet of nostalgia, known to everyone who remembers a different time, cheaper prices, and an easier life. Movies for under a dollar, and gas for 15, 16, or 17 cents a gallon.

"When I first started driving, you'd say, 'Here's a buck, fill 'er up.'"

Marshall lobs back, "I remember getting two cents back for empty Coke bottles. Unless you got the big ones, then you got. . . ."

"Five cents back," they say in unison.

It sounds almost like a foreign language in an office that speaks in terms of "mills" and "bills" and often leaves off the last three zeros when writing numbers in the thousands on notes and memos.

Jerry likes to keep one foot in the offices of big and fast-moving money, while the other is firmly planted in a world of Saturday matinees and soda bottle rebates. As he often does, Jerry has plans this weekend to take his family to their cottage in the mountains of Pennsylvania. They will hike the trails, throw stones in the lake, and maybe see a high school football game. The County Chamber events hotline for the area is promoting the Fire Company's Spaghetti Dinner, $5 for adults and $2.50 for children ages five to twelve. Then there's the annual fall fair—the Ferris wheel is said to be the biggest in several counties.

Jerry's allegiance to the land of spaghetti dinners and Ferris wheels helps him keep the world of "bills" and "mills" less anonymous. It helps him keep the shareholder side of the equation in balance with the Wall Street side, as much as one can from a corner office on the thirty-ninth floor in downtown Philadelphia. That allegiance is the part of Jerry that gives him the most strength. It's where his confidence comes from—from the football fields, the classroom, and the community. He has the unique opportunity to be a very successful investor and fund manager without needing to be a big fish on Wall Street. He is already a big fish in his hometown—and he goes back to visit the pond frequently, to get his fill.

Years ago, he took a coworker and close friend from New York back to his town of 2,200 for a Friday night high school football game. "It was like he was a famous astronaut," the friend says. "Everyone knew him, everyone wanted to talk to him, to touch him."

Not a politician, a movie star, or a famous athlete, but an astronaut. Someone who has reached for the heavens, touched the stars, and returned to tell of it.

*   *   *

It is only minutes after the market has opened, and Jeff is in visiting Jerry for the third time. "The one piece of news we did get today is that Motorola actually looked pretty good for the quarter."

"Who the hell cares. That's a total piece of junk."

"I'm just saying that this was a company people had given up for dead, and it's not *that* bad. And semiconductor numbers are up sequentially quarter to quarter. It may be the first time semis have been up Q-2 to Q-3 this decade. . . ."

"Well, I don't want to have anything to do with Motorola. I think it's a one-trick pony and I'm not gonna chase it today."

"I'm not here to buy Motorola or even recommend it," Jeff says, his pace quickening. "All I'm saying is, here's a company that was never expected to make a quarter again, and they actually beat the numbers."

Jerry refuses Jeff's enthusiasm and continues to read the pages Geri transcribed from his voicemail this morning.

At eleven o'clock, Jerry is in a conference room on the fortieth floor, greeting two executives of one of the fastest growing technology companies to wow the investing public in the past few years.

The executives of Qwest Communications, a high-end telecommunications company, are touring the country with their investment banker and a research analyst as simply a reminder of the good news their company has brought investors. Most companies go on roadshows and meet with big institutional investors like Jerry when they are going public and selling their shares for the first time. Or, perhaps when the stock has been battered, they will hit the conference table circuit to rally support around the shares. At other times, a company might be preparing to sell shares to the public a second or third time, and so its bigwigs are out updating and improving their story.

But, as far as Jerry—and the rest of the investment community who will be hosting Qwest's executives over the next several days— knows, this meeting has no such purpose. Qwest's cross-country tour this season is more of a victory lap. The company's stock has done so well in the past year that its shares have already "split." A stock split is exactly that—one share of stock on sale for $2 splits into two shares of stock on sale for $1. A split lets buyers who couldn't afford to buy shares at $2 buy shares at $1. Or, in Qwest's case, it can make a stock that has risen to $64 a share sound cheap at $32 a share.

Qwest's current round of meetings gives its executives the chance to meet with investors who participated in the IPO and say, "Thanks for the support . . . we've put those millions you gave us to good use . . . keep buying those shares." To those investors who didn't get in on the 190 percent gain so far, the meetings serve as a reminder, "See what you missed out on? It's not too late. There's room on the train—step up to your local trading desk and buy your tickets. Just $32 apiece. Sure, prices have gone up in the last few months, but no telling what they'll be going for next year. We're moving fast, get on board."

In meetings like this one, Jerry likes to—ever so gently—say, "Indeed, you may be moving fast, but not too fast for me."

"Oh, so you've got a new phone number?" Jerry asks in the shuffle of shaking hands, clicking briefcases, and trading business cards.

Both executives stop their movement toward the brown leather chairs and look at Jerry. They are executives of a company that will have 18,000 miles of fiber optic cable laid across the country by next year. They lead a company that does business in "ubiquitous non-zero dispersion fiber—the technology everybody wants to ride on." And this guy who sits behind a desk in Philadelphia wants to know if we've changed our phone number?

"Three-oh-three, nine-nine-two . . . ," the executive starts, almost in disbelief.

"Yeah. Yeah, you've got it written in here," Jerry says, pointing to the handwritten numbers on the business card, knowing that his moving finger is really silently drawing a small hash mark in the air—chalk one up for Jerry Frey.

It's a trick he tries in nearly every meeting. Most businesspeople slip business cards into a shirt pocket or a wallet or datebook immediately upon receiving them. It is as if to say, "I'm definitely keeping this. You can count on it, I've got your card." Jerry uses a reverse approach. He places the cards loosely on the table in front of him during a presentation and may even rotate them slowly during the meeting, more a signal of, "You are simply small pieces of card stock I can slide around my conference table like pawns. I may even forget and leave you behind after our meeting." He inspects every card upon receiving it, not so that he can repeat the name five times to himself, as so many career counselors or public relations agents might advise, but rather to look for an edge, an opening for Jerry to gain some ground, for the balance of knowledge and power to tilt in his direction.

In a meeting earlier in the year, Jerry recognized the address of a particular office tower in Cambridge, Massachusetts, where the visiting company was headquartered. "One Kendall Square. Who else is in that building?" he asked, inspecting the card. The officers from the company exchanged puzzled looks as they cited the collection of companies located in the tower. "Genzyme. That's right. I knew they were up there," Jerry said when the name was mentioned. It is his way of pointing out to those who have come calling and asking for money, "I watch the details. I remember things. I am not a pushover."

With the score settled for now, today's meeting continues with Jerry sitting perhaps a little taller in his supple leather swivel chair. One executive speaks while the other picks his teeth with a folded yellow index card.

"We're not interested in the $19.95 a month, all-you-can-eat dogfight kind of Internet business. . . . We're in the higher-end space . . . the new bandwidth enabled applications—these are the perfect applications for OC-48 IP. . . ."

Jerry is moderately interested in the perfect applications for OC-48 IP, but he is more concerned about numbers—cash flows, capital expenditures, analyst estimates. These executives have told him where the *company* wants to go; now Jerry is trying to figure out where the *stock* might want to go.

The business cards that sit on the table in front of Jerry have Qwest's logo and motto printed in silver ink: Ride the Light. Hanging on the conference room wall across from Jerry is a painting of General George Washington riding a white horse, his black cape flowing behind him. The painting, "America Must Go Forward," was done by N. C. Wyeth in 1932 to commemorate the two-hundredth anniversary of Washington's birth. Delaware's founder bought the painting in the 1970s from a Philadelphia gallery. It was hung in the company's lobby during the country's Bicentennial in

1976. The founder liked the painting, and was also said to fancy himself as having a bit of an eye for art as well as investments. He bought the painting for $18,000, and less than twenty years later it was appraised at $85,000. More than a 350 percent appreciation, or about 19 percent a year.

An admirable gain, until considering a painting that hangs in Delaware's legal library just six floors below. It's about half the size of the Wyeth and is a contemporary abstract painting—a collection of pastel colors on canvas. One of the women who oversees the supply and placement of office furniture and equipment at Delaware bought the painting for $110 in 1987. She was out shopping for lamps and accessories for the offices at a suburban mall and saw the painting in JCPenney. The painting hangs in a simple brass frame and was appraised just seven years later at $1,200. An appreciation of 990 percent, or about 140 percent a year.

* * *

Back in his office after lunch, Jerry discusses some of the intricacies of the stock market with Marshall. "August was terrible, September was good, and October is disastrous."

John steps in from the hallway to join the pair. He turns his Hewlett Packard calculator over and over in his hand while he waits for an entry point to the conversation.

"I'm not gonna change what I do. My companies are knocking the lights out in sales," Marshall says, giving John the opening.

"Anything you sell Linens 'n Things for would be a lesser company."

"I got to own something. When I bought it a year and a half ago, the stores made $160 to $165 a square foot, now it's $180 going to $200. Screw 'em."

"I'm with you."

"Besides, I got to think of my mutual fund shareholders. They're gonna see a loss for the year, why am I gonna turn around and give 'em a capital gain to boot?" With this, Marshall takes the proverbial high ground of mutual fund investing: If the market is bad enough for the year that we have negative performance, why sell stocks that are going to generate capital gains for shareholders?

In the stock market—as with any place where money is being made—there are taxes to be collected. Instead of taxing the funds or the companies that run the mutual funds, the government bills the fund shareholders, the actual recipients of those earnings. But taxes need to be paid only on those earnings that are "realized"—shares that have been sold by the mutual fund and profits taken. So, the longer a fund can hold onto its winners, the lighter the tax burden it gives its shareholders.

A tax burden is exactly what Marshall is trying to avoid by holding onto his shares of Linens 'n Things. He doesn't want to sell out just because the market is slipping, and then have to turn to his shareholders and say, "Not only did your shares lose money this year, but I did some short-term trading instead of holding, so you'll be needing to send a check to Uncle Sam because of my decisions. Better luck next year."

Jerry trumps Marshall's effort to think about the shareholders by reminding him that the market is no chicken-and-egg debate. The market acts, mutual fund shareholders react. "On the flip side, do I think the stock market's going down? Yes I do."

Marshall pauses and then nods. "We may have entered a period of long-term secular deflation. And then we won't know what to do." Ah yes, long-term secular deflation. Who *would* know what to do?

"My problem is in technology. The companies are good for a while, or they have a good product for a certain window of time, and that window's getting smaller. So even if I have the best companies now, in six months they may not be the best companies. So that's one way retail is a little bit easier on the downside." Jeff walks in to join the group while Jerry bemoans the challenges of being the main technology investor of the growth group. Sort of a professionally correct "my job's harder than your job" assertion. Jerry continues, "It's so volatile that when it goes down, these things slide off the end of the earth never to be heard from again."

"So you wonder, why the hell do you even dink with it?" Marshall asks rhetorically, his head bobbing in agreement. He leans up against Jerry's wall, settling in for a longer stay. The market is going down, and looking out Jerry's window means that he doesn't have to watch the red stocks on his screen.

" 'Cause when it works, it can work phenomenally well. You can find a Microsoft."

"Or a Cisco or a Gemstar. It can make your whole career," chimes in Jeff, second to Jerry in technology investment decisions, first in technology trivia.

"It's a lot like love," Marshall begins waxing philosophical. "When it works it's great, and when it doesn't it's awful. You love it or you hate it."

"Yeah, and if technology is like love," Jerry counters, "then retail is like sex. It's always good. Sometimes it's great, sometimes it's just good."

The conversation moves from sex to recession and the end of the bull market. The Dow is negative for the year and the group is down more than 10 percent for the year. Going back to their offices would feel like returning to the locker room after losing the pennant race, and having to pass by the cases of unopened champagne bottles that need to be returned. They'd rather stay in the dugout and relive the highs and lows of the season and their careers, play by play.

"Electronic Arts. That stock is such a piece of shit." The fire is stoked even higher.

"That's been a good stock; look at the chart," Jerry offers from his chair.

"Look at the chart? Uh, that is such a dead patient. Mortal Kombat 2—what was the launch to peak sales of that product?"

"Four weeks?"

"Three weeks. Blockbuster product of that year. Three weeks!"

Jerry likes the rising emotion of the conversation, and knowing there is little the three of them can do in the next ninety minutes to change the direction of the U.S. stock market, he continues with his own line of questioning. "What's the worst stock? The one you hate the most? The one that's given you the most aggravation?"

"Autodog. Autodesk." Jeff bites immediately, then settles on a different company, "DSC. I had a triple in it before I got handed my head."

"Telco Systems. Perspective Biosystems," Jerry says.

"Critical Care America." Almost before Marshall has the company name entirely out of his mouth, Jeff has launched into a tirade about how he was out to dinner at the exact moment the company blew up, or at least at the moment the news was released that would send the stock reeling. It seemed to be one of those John Kennedy, John Hinckley, or John Lennon sort of events.

"September 1992," Marshall raises his voice, matching Jeff's enthusiasm for the story, if not the memory. "Because we were having a fabulous quarter—it was just days before the end of the quarter. This thing made Hiroshima look like a cherry bomb. . . . The guy got on the phone for the conference call and said, 'We're missing the quarter. That's all I'm going to say,' and then he slammed the phone down."

"There's a lot of 'em, when you do small companies, that are absolute frauds," Jerry says.

"Where's the market now?"

"You don't want to know." Jerry leans in to get a closer look at his screen and the market. "Dow down 40. Nasdaq down 35."

"Veritas?"

"You don't want to know. Twenty."

"Down."

"Legato?"

"Down."

"Net Apps?" Shorthand for Network Appliance, just one of the many entries in Jeff's personal techno lexicon.

"Up a half."

Marshall rejoins the tech pair here, cupping his hands like a megaphone and whispering, "Sell it." Like the voice of reason, or the devil's advocate, tempting them to take the profits where they can and run.

Jerry's phone rings, breaking up the trip down memory lane and the detour to the land of the Dow.

Marshall is back in Jerry's office within the hour, pursuing the flip side of historical disasters—those they rolled out from in front of the truck just in time, rather than those stocks they got run over by. "Look up N-F-O," he directs, and waits for Jerry to type in the ticker. "Do you want to see a stock we used to own a boatload of before I got here and you can thank me for selling it?"

"Should I thank you now or after?" Jerry asks and continues to look for the stock on his screen.

Jerry has given up looking for Marshall's stock, but instead takes its mention as a challenge. "What's the symbol for Phillips?"

"P-S-E? P-S-B? I don't know."

"Guess where that's trading?" Jerry looks up triumphantly.

"One and a quarter?"

"Less. We owned a million shares of it. A million shares. And I sold out of all of it. It's at five-eighths."

"Where did you sell it?"

"Higher than five-eighths, I know that!" Jerry laughs. "Sold it in the elevens or tens—all over the place. Had to get rid of a million shares. Do I get any credit for that sale?"

Another of the countless conversations and lessons between coach and player, mentor and student, boss and employee and partner. But again, Jerry makes sure that with the doling out of the lesson comes one more invisible hash mark. Another point for Jerry Frey.

The market has just opened, and Jeff is in Jerry's office.

"Did you see Dell traded 100 million shares yesterday?" Jeff says.

It was four times the number of Dell shares usually traded in a day, and Dell was just the beginning. Wednesday had been one of the busiest days ever recorded on Wall

October 8, 1998		
	Year-to-Date Performance	Rank
Aggressive Growth	-19.4%	45
Trend	-25.8%	25
Delcap	-23.3%	63
Dow	-2.2%	
S&P 500	0.1%	
Nasdaq	-9.6%	

Street. First came frantic selling, signaling that investors expected the woes of the fall and October to continue. A global recession might be afoot, the hedge fund business was under fire, and the dollar was falling. The Dow was down nearly 300 points by noon. And then the market changed its mind. Maybe the Federal Reserve Board would lower interest rates, the financial stocks were down so low they were cheap, and a Goldman Sachs strategist said she expected stocks to hit new highs by the end of the year. The Dow ended the day down just under 10 points.

No one rang a bell, no news item blipped on the screen, and no warning flashed on the tape. But the bear market scare of 1998 had ended. Those who weren't prepared—who hadn't drilled, kept alert, and had the courage and conviction to act—were quickly left behind. Historical research has shown countless times that all kinds of investors can lose money together over a long period of time in the stock market, yet the most remarkable gains are made very quickly— in a matter of days, within years-long stretches. And no one who opted to sit on the sidelines is allowed to participate.

For Jerry, yesterday's remarkable reversal in the stock market was the event he'd been preparing his team for—for weeks, if not months. The lesson was repeated weekly, and often daily. "You've got to execute. You can't get so apoplectic and caught up in what's going on day to day on the screen. You've got to keep doing things. You've got to buy and sell on the margins, consolidate around your best positions, keep talking to companies, keep looking at your companies. If you don't want to buy or sell and you freeze up, the fundamentals behind them may deteriorate without you knowing it. The stocks can go down, and then when there's a rally they don't participate. Make sure we're in the stocks that are going to participate."

Jerry has been brandishing that kind of conviction and passion to play since childhood.

In the fall of his senior year in high school, Jerry was treated to a hotel suite in downtown Scranton, the swankest hotel the seventeen-year-old had seen. The athletic director from Notre Dame had made the trip from South Bend, Indiana, to look at and talk to Jerry and two other Pennsylvania high school football players. For a small town Pennsylvania boy who grew up sleeping many nights with his football tucked under his arm, it was a visit from Knute Rockne himself.

The Irish athletic director, Moose Krause, and two assistant coaches sat questioning the three boys in a circle. What's the most important thing a player can bring to the game? Why do you play football? Why Notre Dame?

When Moose and the coaches turned to Jerry, the smallest of the three players by several neck sizes, they posed a simple question. A giveaway for most interviewees, a chance to shine and wow the coaches with the patriotism and collegiate allegiance that had been rehearsed since age nine in the local Pop Warner football league.

"Would you like to come and play football for Notre Dame?"

Perhaps Jerry shifted in his seat, crossed his arms over his chest, or looked around at the other players, who were assuredly salivating at the mere mention of such a fantasy. "No."

"No?"

"No. I'd rather go somewhere where I can play."

Sitting in a hotel room in Scranton, Pennsylvania, in 1963, Jerry knew his limitations. He knew his strengths and attributes, but he also understood his weaknesses. He was not the biggest player on his team. He hadn't broken any national or even local records. He wasn't selected for the all-star teams that competed in regional and state all-star games. But he was fast and he was smart. He was smart enough to recognize that he had to be playing the game in order to have a chance to win.

*   *   *

Jerry punches in a long-distance number from memory with perhaps no more thought than it takes for him to dial the four-digit number of the trading desk. "Bill Kane in? Bill? It's Jerry Frey. What kind of trucks you got out there? You got any F-150s? I need a super-cab. . . . What colors you got? . . . Green, hmm. I need a green car. What do you want for that? . . . Everything, huh? Dark green. . . . Would you take my pickup from me or would I have to pay you to take it? . . . 1990, 35,000 miles—the body's not in bad shape. It doesn't have any rust on it. Minor wear and tear and dings, but no major dents, no trees. . . . Can you have it fixed by today? Why don't you give me a call back; I'll drive up there today and get it."

The stock market has been open ten minutes, and Jerry is in the middle of the field, playing. His confidence and conviction—and yes, his cash—allow him to make a $20,000-plus purchase, by phone, in less than five minutes.

Moving up to bigger numbers, Jerry calls the trading desk. "Stu? Nice trade on that Gemstar. Yahoo! What do you think? . . . Yeah, maybe we'll hold on a little longer, see what happens. Got anything else on the desk on the sell side? . . . Well, I think, it's Friday so they'll mark 'em up and then it'll settle here for a while."

Then it's a call from a colleague Jerry used to work with in New York. "Yeah, Filenet just sort of puked on itself, so they took that down. . . . What about Clear Channel? I can't figure out what's going on there. . . . What do you think about these Internet things? Are they gonna have another life or are they totally dead? . . . Well, like American Online and Yahoo!, they're both down today. I'm just surprised, with a rally in the rest of the market here today, that they aren't doing anything. . . . I think they're still good ideas. The potential is that AT&T talked to American Online and offered them a big number. American Online and Yahoo! are the two leading players, so they've got that cachet going for them. But, the problem is that if the two top names don't react in a rally, then, in American Online's case, is it an 84-dollar stock or a 48-dollar stock? Who's to say? I mean, I could say each customer is worth this much and I could come up with a really big number, but I may as well be blowing smoke up someone's ass for all that's worth."

Jerry continues to curse October's roller coaster in the market. "Well, let me tell you, it sure hasn't been good for my sleep habits. . . . Oh, that comes with old age. That's why you should have young kids like I do, that way when you get up to go to the bathroom, you can go to the bathroom with your kids. . . . The risk is that everyone's done so well over the last three to four years that the hangover will be commensurate with the party. And it's been one rip-roaring party. We could be in for one hell of a disaster. . . . My best performing fund is down 20.9 percent for the year—and of that 20.9 percent, 21.6 percent of it was since October. So, going into October we were in positive territory. I went from first to worst so fast it'd make your head spin—and I didn't even do anything wrong. What did I do to deserve this? What am I being penalized for?"

But it is almost the weekend—two days for both Jerry and the stock market to catch their breath, relax, and prepare to move forward. Surveying his screen, the market, his performance sheets and holdings, and his own gut and conviction, Jerry now has the confidence to buy.

His computer, the Dow, and the market will grind away for the rest of the afternoon, but Jerry is out the door by lunchtime. He is on his way to a haircut, to pick up his two oldest sons early from school, and to make the three-hour drive to his hometown to pick up a brand-new forest green Ford F-150 with extended cab, CD player, and leather seats—the victor's prize Jerry has given himself for a contest he is now sure he can win.

CHAPTER 8

DO YOU HAVE
A BAND-AID?

Marshall stands just inside the door to Jerry's office and finishes chewing his bite of Danish from a morning-meeting pastry platter. "I'm a fool. I'm a fool," he says and rubs his thumb and two fingers out in front of him to shake off the excess sugar without dusting his navy pin-striped suit and polka-dot tie.

"What'd you do?" Jerry asks.

"I had been selling Aurora Foodservice and they were in here this morning, and I think it's gonna work. I've just got a little bit left, but I put that on hold."

"Well, just hold on and see how things settle. Hey, who dressed you today? You're looking quite dapper."

"I beg your pardon?" Marshall raises his eyebrows and tilts his chin forward to look down at Jerry sitting behind the desk. "I am always quite dapper."

"That's right. Actually, you are."

"This is my go-to-hell suit. I am going to hell. I'm heading up to New York."

Marshall leaves, and Jerry waits for the neon green message from Geri to appear on his phone, letting him know that his meeting is here before he walks up to the fortieth floor.

The balance of power and the upper hand between institutional investors like Jerry and the companies they invest in is constantly shifting. When a company is going public, the executives need investors' money, and they are nearly on their knees offering service and looking for attention. "My secretary can FedEx you those numbers this afternoon. Is that soon enough?" When a company's stock is riding high and has made money for institutional investors, and others are clamoring to get in, the company is the one looking down from above. Smiling, they survey the landscape below—peopled with investors controlling the millions and billions of dollars that let the slack out on their kite strings in the first place.

Shares of a software company, Bindview Development, shot up from $10 at the company's IPO to more than $20 in less than three months. Yesterday, the company presented to a standing-room-only crowd of investors at a technology conference in Baltimore. Somewhere between Baltimore and Philadelphia, and the roomful of salivating investors and Jerry's conference room, Bindview's CEO has cut his finger. Now, he sits calmly in a chair pushed back a casual distance from the table while he waits for $2-billion Jerry, whom he has asked to fetch him a Band-Aid for his cut. The CEO goes over scheduling details with the CFO and makes a call on his cellular phone. Using cellular phones to call from inside office buildings has become so ubiquitous in the past few years that the CEO probably doesn't even notice the available telephone in the conference room. He doesn't even think of asking to use one of the 60-plus phones in Delaware's surrounding offices that would surely be made available to him. Instead, the 35-year-old CEO of Bindview talks into the ever-shrinking ever-present power tool of the '90s. He alternates squeezing and inspecting his cut while Jerry roams the halls of Delaware's fortieth floor, asking various secretaries if they have any Band-Aids on hand.

Jerry returns unsuccessful in his quest, and the meeting begins. Jerry asks questions, the CEO and CFO alternate answering, and a balled-up Kleenex spotted with blood that sits between them slowly relaxes and expands as the discussion continues.

How about acquisitions? Competition? Microsoft? You looking at any UNIX platform companies? Distribution channels? What about recruiting new people? Sales, marketing, senior people?

"We have a great management team, but as we try to grow the company and expand, our bandwidth is going to get stretched."

As he listens to their answers, Jerry holds a pen slightly aloft in the air. He has brought no paper to the meeting. Only the custom-built English white oak table sits beneath his black ballpoint. He sat in Bindview's presentation in Baltimore yesterday, and a conference call discussing the company's quarterly earnings is preserved on a tape sitting somewhere in his office. This is not a fact-finding mission. Jerry is here to pick up on the nuances, to get what isn't said in formal presentations and SEC-monitored conference calls. He listens to learn more from *the way* things are said rather than from the things that are said. Jerry doesn't expect any market-moving insider information; the company is much too savvy for that. It's a relaxed meeting and Jerry lets the CEO and CFO do most of the talking. The more the executives talk, the more they reveal. Being public for three months isn't really that long.

"When did you guys close the quarter—the twenty-fifth or the thirtieth? Your receivables were so low it was like you closed it up five days early." Yes, it's an accounting joke, and both the executives smile.

The CEO takes the bait, "We didn't have to push it this quarter."

"Yeah, this quarter didn't need a push," the CFO offers the technical opinion.

"You guys had a pretty good run lately?"

"Yeah, for the last few quarters." The CEO pauses, as if daydreaming back to those rosy earnings-before-income tax-depreciation-and-amortization entries of three months, six months, and nine months ago. "For the last few years, we've had a good run."

"For the third and fourth quarter, we knocked the cover off the ball." The CFO helps fill the space Jerry has given them.

Having gotten them to display their confidence, Jerry moves in to question the commitment. Is it a confidence that believes that this is just the beginning, and things can only get better? Or is it a confidence that says, "I can't believe everything has gone so well, there's no way this can last forever."

"So, post-IPO, when does the lock-up open? When do the VCs want out—180 days? . . . Do you know where all this stands? . . . Any plans for a secondary?" Jerry asks.

The crude translation would be, "This whole song-and-dance is nice, but when are people gonna take their money and run?" Investment banks usually stipulate that company insiders—including the venture capitalists (VCs) who bought shares in the company, often for the proverbial pennies on the dollar before it went public—aren't allowed to sell their stock for six months. Their shares, their money, and their commitment are "locked up" for 180 days.

"Well, nobody wanted to sell out when the stock was 20," the CFO says. So, why the heck would they want to sell now when the stock has slipped back to $16 a share, is the unspoken corollary. It is likely that, at some point, as with many growth companies, this logic will hit the wall of diminishing returns. The stock price will have climbed so high that the question for many investors, and perhaps insiders, will be: "Why *wouldn't* I want to sell at these prices?" For many executives and entrepreneurs, it's a reasonable question, and selling some stock is a reasonable response. For years, they have been forgoing all but a minimal salary or bonus, in an effort to make the business fly. Once the company is flying high, it's usually time to sell a few shares, pay off the mortgage, and send a kid or two to college.

Jerry flips quickly through the black tri-fold presentation booklet the CEO has offered to help spur any remaining questions or issues he may be concerned with. Jerry closes the book and pushes it back across the table to the CEO. "What should I have asked you that I didn't ask?"

"Hey, you asked that at our last meeting. That must be your standard last question." And indeed, the CEO is right. Jerry concludes nearly all of his meetings with that question. Jerry, the investor who is always looking to keep a slight and silent edge for himself, has just been caught using the same pickup line at a bar.

With that, the meeting's tug-of-war rope has been pulled squarely onto the side of the company. The CFO takes it as an opening to pose a question, "If we unlocked early, what would you think of that?"

Almost assuredly unbeknownst to the inquiring CFO, the rope that has seesawed back and forth across the table during the past thirty-five minutes has just sprung back in Jerry's favor like a rubber band. With this one question, he knows that the company is considering getting special permission to sell more shares early. Yes, we are confident and committed, but would you and the investment community mind if we cashed in some of our shares just three months after presenting our company to you as the invest-ment of the future?

"Robertson Stephens says 'Nothing for 90 days,'" the CFO con-tinues. "November 1 will be 100 days."

They've surely been watching the calendar with an eye toward the countdown to Christmas. They won't hit the 180-day mark until late January, and that can feel like an eternity when your stock price is at $16, a 60 percent premium over your IPO price.

For Jerry, the CFO's question is both an admission and an oppor-tunity. He knows that, in almost all cases, more stock of a given com-pany coming into the market means the rest of the shares will come down in price. A few more sellers have entered the game, and perhaps no additional buyers. As a shrewd trader, Jerry knows he could sell out of the 116,000 shares he owns in Bindview now, for about a $400,000 profit, and miss the downturn to come. But he has decided that Bind-view is a company he knows and likes, and one he wants to own rather than trade. And as an institutional investor, one of Jerry's goals is to build positions in the companies he believes in, at the cheapest prices possible. If Bindview's executives or VCs want to sell out of large blocks of their own stock, they will ask their investment bank, Robert-son Stephens, to sell the shares, either quietly to a few large institu-tions or widely in another offering to the public. With a company like Bindview, which Jerry does actually believe in (after the meeting, and to himself, he gives them one of his highest endorsements, "They've got a pretty good little business, don't they?"), it is a chance for him to get more shares at perhaps a discounted price.

It is just the kind of opportunity Jerry, the investor, looks for. He constantly asks himself, "What advantages can I offer my share-holders through my knowledge of companies and the market?" And now this meeting has provided him with one more answer to that question.

* * *

For much of the rest of the morning, Jerry listens in on confer-ence calls of company executives delivering quarterly earnings to money managers listening in from around the country. He is also interviewed over the telephone by brokers sent his way by Delaware's sales department. On three different calls, he goes over his own employment record on Wall Street and gives the history of the market since the bear market of 1974. He talks market theories, he talks about a change in leadership, and he talks about dollar cost averaging. The listeners on each of these calls ask simple questions and want simple answers. What stocks are going higher? When will the market start going back up?

He is put on hold twice and is hung up on once, surely by accident.

"This is the craziest business, I tell you. Here you've got the fund managers." Excitedly, he starts to sketch a series of concentric circles on his notepad. "Then you've got all these brokers around them who don't know anything, selling to their clients who know even less. The fund managers have a reasonable understanding of what's going on, and then it gets out to all of these people who. . . . It's like a big party game, where you tell somebody something, and they tell somebody who tells somebody else."

Jerry tries to concentrate on his computer screen, but remembered bits of the conversations of the past hour keep interrupting and aggravating him. "People are gonna get their 401(k) statements soon, and they're gonna be negative for the first time. . . . People are gonna say, 'Stocks are down, what's wrong?' This woman says to me, 'They've been down for two months.' Two months! These people have been making money for five fucking years! They want to be told it's going to be going up by the end of the year. Marketing totally drives this. So these brokers have sold these funds to people at the tippy top of the market. Whose fault is that? What do they want *me* to tell them?"

He is exasperated. It is the constant reminder that only December 31 counts. People only like you when you're up. When you are up, the market must be doing well; when you are down, it must be your fault. For nearly nine months of the year, Jerry has managed one of the top-ranked growth funds in the country, and yet it seemed to him that no one wanted to talk to him or see him or sell his funds. During the first six trading days of October, the

Aggressive Growth Fund dropped 21.6 percent, and now everyone wants to talk with him, has suggestions to offer, has a bone to pick with him.

* * *

On a Thursday afternoon, Jerry is waiting in the Philadelphia Airport for a flight that has been delayed. John and Jeff are away at conferences, Marshall is in a meeting out of the office, and Lori has left for the day. Steve is the remaining member of the growth group in the office.

Steve doesn't mind being left as the keeper of the market today. The added role helps him fill the high-backed leather executive chair behind his desk. He takes the calls from the trading desk, and those from salespeople and companies trying to capture any of the growth team's ears. This afternoon, the market and the group's confidence climb higher with each successive call.

First, it is Stu from the trading desk. It's a courtesy call to the group to let them know that Alan Greenspan, the chairman of the Federal Reserve Board and the watcher of all things inflationary and recessionary in this country, just cut interest rates by a quarter of a point.

When the Fed determines that spending is tight and the economy could use a jolt, it lowers the interest rate it charges banks, which, in turn, usually lower the interest rates they charge customers. A drop in the interest rate can mean good news for consumers, and it can mean very good news for the stock market. First, stocks get a boost from the assumption that people will spend more—on cars, houses, and other big-ticket items. Second, companies will spend more freely on equipment, upgrades, and other improvements that may boost profits. Higher profits mean higher stock prices.

Today's move by the Fed is an unexpected rate cut. The Board wasn't scheduled to meet again for another four weeks. But concern over the economy was growing, and the group gathered to issue an emergency rate cut. It is welcome news to business and consumers, and a surprise gift to the stock market. Within minutes after the announcement, the Dow is up 250 points.

Ten minutes later, Marshall is on the phone from a meeting outside the office. He has already heard the effect of the rate cut on the overall market; he wants to know what Mr. Greenspan has done for the Delaware growth group.

"Up 8 percent, 7 percent, 7 percent, and 3 percent," Steve jokes in response to a succession of stocks Marshall asks about. "We don't own stocks that go down," he laughs. "It's against the discipline. . . . The market's going to close up 300. We'll see what happens."

Then John is on the line just after the market closes. Steve reads off the prices of more stocks, the conviction in his voice growing with each dollar and percentage mentioned. "Mellon Bank, who bought that for you? That's right, your analyst. . . . Some blockbusters today."

Jerry, the last to call in, asks for updates on the fewest stocks—one stock, to be exact. Before he left for the airport, Jerry put in an order with the trading desk to buy 600,000 shares of Chancellor Media Company. The Dow was up 102 points for the day, Chancellor was down a dollar a share, and there was no little bird singing about an impending rate cut.

"You just put it all out there, don't you? That's pretty bold," Steve smiles broadly as he adjusts his headphone set on his ears and releases Jerry's call from speakerphone. "It's up four."

At the halfway mark in the most dreaded month, the Dow closes up 330 points for the day. The march toward December is gaining momentum, and it is finally starting to feel like it might be in the right direction.

*   *   *

Even though the stock market remains closed over the weekends, the business lessons don't stop for Jerry. His middle son had heard a rumor from some classmates that Mike's Cards, the neighborhood trading-card and comic-book store, had closed down. But, hearing the word from a five-year-old is not that different from getting an earnings estimate or a target stock price from a Wall Street analyst. Until further investigation, it is just a rumor. To see for themselves, Jerry drives his boys by the trading shop, which is next to the movie theater in town. Sure enough, the store is dark, and a sign lets passersby know it is indeed shuttered. For the boys, who had spent many an allowance inside the store, it was Armageddon.

"How could Mike do this?" Jonah, the five-year-old, asks.

His nine-year-old brother Sam is already picking up some of his father's instinct for a good business. "I bet he had to close because sometimes the store wasn't open when we wanted to go."

Jerry spends the rest of the drive around town explaining that running a business isn't as simple as it seems. There are other factors—details you'd never thought of, crises you hadn't expected. It's not as easy as selling a baseball card and collecting a dollar.

Jerry's meeting in Minneapolis on Friday had taught him just that. His business wasn't just buying a few stocks and collecting some checks. His business was also about trying to determine what other people wanted—and convincing them that you were the one that would deliver it. Friday's trip was another visit with Delaware's sales and marketing professionals, the people offering the growth group's services—for a fee, of course. The meeting was with executives responsible for deciding where a big block of a company's pension money would go. Jerry gave his best spiel, hoping that at least some of the block might be sent his way. From Jerry's perspective, the meeting was going well—the man on the other side of the conference table had been in the business for a while. He understood the market's cycles, the vagaries of a given investment style, the importance of committing to someone for the long term, and the achievement of logging some really stellar performance. Being able to put the usual marketing presentation booklet aside, Jerry saw an opening to try to offer something more—to take a risk, and try to be something a little bit different. Every other two-piece suit that comes into this guy's office is going to be able to explain the ups and downs of the market, and how his team hopes to get around the downs and ride the ups. Jerry had to offer him something else, something more.

He looked over the portfolio of stocks that the company owned as investments. Jerry noticed two names that he held in his mutual funds.

"Coulter Pharmaceutical? Do you know what they do?"

Well, no, not exactly.

It was Jerry's opening. He explained some specifics about what the pharmaceutical company did and what drugs it was working on, but, more importantly, he told them that Coulter was likely working on an acquisition. Was this inside information? they wanted to know. They hadn't seen it in the news, they said. No, it was just something Jerry learned from his routine meetings and conversations with company executives. It had come as an answer to Jerry's loosely but directly worded question, "Where do you expect the growth to come from?" The response: "We'd probably be looking at some acquisitions." Simple. He had asked and they had told him. This was a guy who would ask the obvious questions and give straight answers. Jerry's knowledge, forwardness, and simple nature helped drive the wedge pushing the Delaware growth team up the list a little further. He was sure he'd be hearing back from the company by the end of the year.

On Monday morning, Jerry is back at his desk, inspecting the daily performance sheets from Friday. He pauses to look at each number for his funds, and lets his rollerball pen rest next to each index that is outperforming him for the year. This is the sign that Jerry has looked at the

October 16, 1998	Year-to-Date Performance	Rank
Aggressive Growth	-4.2%	46
Trend	-15.4%	28
Delcap	-11.2%	63
Dow	6.4%	
S&P 500	10.2%	
Nasdaq	3.2%	

numbers, the sign that his rank has registered in his mind at the start of the trading day. Next to the performances he is trailing, he leaves black dots on the white page filled with numbers. They can be seen on the surface, and their impressions can be felt faintly through the other side of the paper. Jerry feels those numbers much more deeply.

"It's just like January, when you spend the next few weeks digging out of the hole you melted into in the first week of the year." He shakes his head slowly at the sheet and actually growls quietly.

He moves on to the list of phone messages Geri has already typed up for him this morning. A salesman from Soundview, a technology-focused investment bank, called to wish him a "Happy Anniversary."

Jerry checks the date on his watch. He calls Geri to check her calendar. "Oh God, did I miss my anniversary?" It does not occur to him that this Wall Street salesman would not likely know or care about Jerry's anniversary. On the other hand, it did not occur to this salesman that Jerry did not know or care that today was the eleventh anniversary of the last stock market crash, October 19, 1987.

So they'd done it. Analysts, traders, fund managers, and the market had made it past the date of the last Crash with no signs of tragedy in sight. (Sure, there was 1929, but that was too long ago; and 1997—well, that was too short-lived.) Now there were only ten trading days left in the month, and then the curse of October would be behind them. They could look ahead to December, and the end of the year, without looking over their shoulder for the damage October might wreak on their portfolios and performance.

By the time the group gets together for the weekly meeting at two o'clock, the Dow is up 86 points.

"All I know is that the small-cap rally started within one hour of when I told PaineWebber small caps were due to rally," Steve jokes.

"Next thing you know, you'll be doing commercials with Peter Lynch," Jerry says, and then looks down at the performance sheets for the past week. "Don't panic too severely."

"When you look at year-to-date, the quarter-to-date, the month-to-date, the numbers are trending downward," Steve says.

Marshall translates the observation into English, while his eyes shift back and forth between this week's and last week's peer group printouts. "It looks like we're getting worse. We dropped a notch in the peer rankings."

"If you've got anything on the sell side, get it done," Jerry says, and he lets a stack of research drop on the table—advice, charts, and statistics for the taking, which the group decides are mostly for the leaving.

"It may look totally different at the end of the month, so I wouldn't go into a total panic," Jerry says, the voice of encouragement when things are down, the cold drip from the wet blanket when the group and numbers are exuberant. "In Aggressive Growth, I still feel we have too many names."

"I say, if you look at the top ten names, we don't have enough there. The concentration still isn't high enough," Marshall says. When the big names move, we want to be in them big. The more evenly the investments are spread out, the more even performance will be. They do not want to be even. They are aggressive growth. When the market jumps, they want to jump higher.

"How about our weighting in financials?" Steve asks. Do we have too much money invested there, or too little?

"We brought it up last week, so it's a little more in line with the market's weighting. But is it something we really want to be making a bet on?" Jerry looks around the table.

"But if there's a rally, it will ride on the back of the financials," Jeff says.

Lori jumps in, "But people will turn on a dime. Last week, everyone's downgrading companies, then we have one good week and everyone's upgrading."

"Yeah, but I wouldn't chase it," cautions Jerry.

"If you're right, you're a genius. If you're wrong, it's disastrous. That's the problem with macrocalls," Marshall says.

Again, it's back to one of the group's frequent debates. Do we want to try to predict the market overall or just stick to what we know—following companies and investing in individual stocks?

"Marketing is saying they can't sell our fund because there's gonna be a gain. They say it's done too well—people don't want to buy it and then be hit with a capital gain. It's ridiculous. 'We can't sell your fund when your performance is down, but now we can't sell your fund because you've done too well.'"

Taxes again. When mutual funds make money in the stock market, the government wants its cut. It's usually in November or December that a fund company pays out its gains and lets investors know how much they need to pay taxes on for the past year. Knowing this, many investors will avoid buying funds that have done well during the last few months of the year. They don't want to owe taxes on something they owned only for a few weeks.

In addition, taxes and mutual funds often provide an extra wrinkle to the market in late fall—increased volatility. Just like individuals, a fund manager can use losses to offset gains for tax considerations. So, before fund companies calculate and distribute those gains for the year, there is often a flurry of fund managers' selling losing positions in an effort to offset gains and avoid giving shareholders a big tax responsibility. All the maneuvering must be done by the last day of October—just one more variable in an already highly variable season in the market.

* * *

With just over a week to go in October, Jerry stands at the head of the thirty-eighth-floor conference room, addressing a group of besuited men and women. Every few months—or whenever the firm hires enough new brokers to fill a conference table—the fund managers speak to the newcomers. It is a chance for the brokers to listen to the stories of each of the different funds, ask their questions, and formulate their sales pitches. Jerry faces the group like a coach speaking before a game—his feet are firmly aligned with the width of his shoulders, and he either holds his arms across his chest, or he lets them fall and slips his hands into his pockets.

"Aggressive Growth. It's a vertical slice of the market. We look at growth across all market caps." He looks around to see whether this has sunk in. Most simply, a company's value in the stock market is the number of shares that exist in the company, multiplied by the shares' stock price: market capitalization. That's how investors and finance reporters are able to bandy about such phrases as "Microsoft is bigger than GE . . . Amazon is bigger than ten Barnes & Nobles . . . AOL is almost twice the size of Disney. . . ." It has nothing to do with size, or sales, or number of employees. Some investors—like managers of small-cap funds—may only look at companies with market caps under $1 billion. Large-cap funds may only invest in companies over $10 billion in market value. Jerry's Aggressive Growth Fund can buy stocks of any size; that's one of the most basic tenets of the Fund. The team can buy Microsoft with a market cap of close to $300 billion, or they can buy shares of a tiny IPO that may be worth just $20 million in the market (of course, they will buy it with hopes that the deal will be not so tiny in a tiny amount of time).

Jerry moves on to how the team chooses stocks, what kind of growth rates they look for, cash flows, and other financial ratios in which the brokers gathered around the table have no interest.

One of the new brokers stops Jerry with a question about the Trend Fund. "The Trend Fund. Is that because it's supposed to be focused on new trends?" No, not necessarily. All the funds are looking for growing companies taking advantage of new trends or changes afoot, but the Trend Fund looks at small-cap companies, DelCap looks at mid-cap companies, and Aggressive can invest in companies of all sizes. Clearly, this crowd will pick up phones and sell the funds using different tactics and data than Jerry would.

The brokers are not interested in average annual earnings growth rates, or return on assets, or positive cash flows. They want to talk stocks. When they leave this conference room, these brokers will call other brokers and they will all talk to friends, colleagues, and individual investors about the markets. Give us some good stories. What names do you like out there? What are you looking at? What's gonna be the next hot stock? Or, if not the next one, tell me you've at least been in one recently, and my client might have the chance to join you in the next one you see.

Jerry gives it to them. "Restoration Hardware." He uses the stock as a way to illustrate what drives the group's decision process when buying a stock. A woman at the table quickly writes down the name and sets her pen back down on her notebook. The bottle of Poland Spring water sitting in front of her is half full.

There are more names. Star Telecom. Pacific Gateway. The group's sell discipline. When and why do they sell stocks. Ah, and then the slide of opportunities pops up on the screen: what the next Staples, Cisco, or Dell can really mean to a fund.

"Staples. We owned it early and we owned it big. . . . There are some big tax advantages to being able to hold things longer. We put more emphasis on buying small companies that will become big companies." Taxes. This time Jerry's got them working for the fund rather than against it. Because the group doesn't have to sell companies when they reach a particular size, he can hold on to them for longer periods. That way, the profits not only continue to grow (ide-ally), but the gains can cross the line from short-term to long-term, which puts them in a lower tax category.

Then, it is time to talk about what all this analysis, discipline, and emphasis can do for your performance. "As of March 30, we were number two of all the equity funds in Lipper. Our one-year perfor-mance was 101 percent." He nearly swallows the number and looks up at the screen rather than the crowd around the table. He states these facts with no emotion nor any of the exclamation they deserve. The better the numbers, the more reserved Jerry is. "At June 30, our one-year returns were 60.8 percent, and we were ranked number two of 884 Lipper growth funds."

One of the new employees sitting at the opposite end of the conference table leans in, as if to get a closer look at Jerry and the numbers on the screen. "What? Are you kidding me?" He nearly whispers it.

Jerry brushes the awe aside with a story of a 60-year-old general contractor whose broker put his entire savings in some very aggres-sive funds. That's not who this is for, and it's not a game to be played. "In reality, it's not a straight road to heaven." He tells them that his own wife brought home her 401(k) mailing last quarter from a different fund company. It was a major shock to her that she had lost money in the market. How could Jerry let this happen?

Having dissolved into homespun stories and warnings about the risks of stock market investing, the presentation is officially over. The broker from the end of the table calls out, like the reporter trying to get the last question in, "So is the Dow going to 6400?" The Dow has been hovering around 8500, and this guy wants to know if it's going down. Really down. He waits intently for an answer, a gold Cross stick pen clipped neatly to the breast pocket of his starched white button-down. It is like a group of adoring fans or sports reporters, just the other side of the fence—so who's going to the Series this year? Who do you think will take it? Can the Yankees do it again? We won't hold you to it. Just give us something—anything we can hold onto. You're down there on the field, we're back here in the stands.

"I haven't got a clue." Jerry folds his arms firmly across his chest again. "You know it's gonna do one of two things. It's gonna go up or down."

* * *

With just days to go in October, Jerry sits reading the paper and sipping a cup of coffee fifteen minutes before the market opens. He reads over a one-column summary of the news of the day, and then lets himself linger over *The New York Times* sports pages. He laughs as he reads an article on Kenny Anderson, the 28-year-old point guard for the Boston Celtics, and his money troubles. The bills keep mounting every week and every month, but with the National Basketball League still in a lockout, there's no paycheck to pay those bills. "Somehow in this list he has his priorities screwed up—on the top are his agents and lawyers, and on the bottom is his mom's house."

Jerry visits his own mother as often as he can and speaks with her on the telephone regularly. Some of his mail still gets delivered to her house, and she lets him know when he's received anything. When his brokerage statements from the investment bank Smith Barney come, she calls to tell him, "Barney Smith sent you something." They rarely talk about Jerry's job, and they speak of the stock market even less frequently. After a few down days in the market, she will often call to check on him. "She's worried I'll lose my job and come back home with my laundry," Jerry laughs.

He shakes his head as he looks over the thousands of dollars Kenny Anderson owes every month. "Yes, portfolio managers are overpaid. It's hard to make the argument that they're not. But basketball players? Give me a break. The guys that'll be really hurt in this strike are the guys that are being paid $150,000 and can do nothing else. Jordan and those guys, they'll be fine. It's all the rest of them that will really suffer."

It's a frequent tirade. Professional athletes being paid too much money, owners just buying up talent to win the pennant or the cup at the end of the year, players going wherever the most money is dangled. There is little loyalty between players and teams and between owners and players. To Jerry, professional sports have lost the spirit, the passion, the competitive drive to win for the sake of winning. Now, it's all money.

He gets up from his table and moves to his desk. The stock market is open for business.

Just after eleven o'clock, the group gathers for its weekly meeting.

John comes in carrying two cans of Coke and sets one down in front of Steve. "Anyone else want a Coke?"

"Oh, so you finally found the free Coke machine downstairs?" Jerry smiles at John's generosity. "They talked about that Coke machine at the annual budget review. They said they were spending thousands on that Coke machine. But all the top guys—Wayne, Jeff, and Dick—said they couldn't kill it." Sure, Kenny Anderson and the hot shots of the NBA get their free Nike gear, their cars, houses, and pools. In the trillion-dollar mutual fund industry, the perks are only slightly less glamorous. At Delaware, it's the free Coke machine. No need to spend the 65 cents yourself. It's on us.

Everyone is seated; Jerry turns to business. "Well, we've started to dig ourselves out of the hole we got into at the beginning of the month. So, I'd say if we had another couple of weeks, we could pull ourselves out of this." He looks around the table. He knows they are all experts in their fields and working their hardest, so he resorts to a rhetorical challenge. "So, if anyone has a good investment—like a takeout—make it a 4-to-5 percent position at the top and run it up, 'cause I'm sick of looking at these numbers." Be bold. Find something that's going to make a lot of money, fast. Find me a sure thing—a company that's going to be bought out for a big premium—and buy every share you can. Let's get out of this hole and into some positive numbers.

They nod and laugh knowingly. There are no sure things.

"Hanley was here last week from William O'Neil, going over some new screens and things. So, you all heard him and can decide if you want to use anything." Jerry has been trying to get the group to use the database more, to set up more screens to search for new companies—to try to do things a little bit differently, to try to get there first.

"That system, you could get lost in there for days," Jeff says.

"Oh yeah. We'll never come close to using the potential of that system," Jerry agrees. But even if we use it just a little more, one more screen, one more search each week, maybe for that one last idea, that could be our edge. "Hanley liked utilities."

"And he liked restaurants, too," Lori offers.

"I'm there. I am *so* there. You're preaching to the choir." Marshall leans back in his chair.

"All of that is indicative of a bear market—utilities, health care, restaurants—stocks that have been beaten down and are domestic based. So, I think there are still some mixed signals as to where things are going," Jerry says.

There are only two months left in the year, and investors are waffling. The future of the market is still uncertain.

*   *   *

On his morning drives into the office, during the hours he lies awake unable to sleep, and in the minutes he stands in line waiting for his muffin, Jerry has begun to think about the future. He's been formulating a plan. Mapping out a strategy. He has let the market be in control for too long. There are just over two months left, and Jerry's going to have to take charge if he wants to make a difference. For Jerry, it's late in the fourth quarter, and the game will end in a tie or a loss if he doesn't take action. He's got to stop playing defense. He's going to have to start taking some risks, making some bets, laying more than a little on the line.

He has studied his position sheets and trading screens until he has them nearly memorized. He only glances briefly, in disgust, at the peer-group rankings that are brought to his office every Monday. It is so much easier to look at such data and feign surprise—"Oh, I'm still number one"—than it is to see your name slip further down the pack with every printing. He no longer waits for the mutual fund performance postings at the end of the day to calculate and compare the top competitors. This late in the race, it is almost useless to look at how many laps separate the leaders from the middle of the pack.

He's now flat for the year, after having been up as much as 24 percent in July. Jerry's world has changed so much since those balmy days of summer. Back then, there was hardly an index he couldn't beat, a growth fund he wasn't ahead of. Now, when he looks at the daily performance runs that are delivered as he eats his breakfast, he has to look more closely than he has all year to find a number he is ahead of. He is behind the Dow by 5 percent, and the S&P 500 and the Nasdaq both left him behind 10 percentage points ago. On paper, the small computer-generated numbers look like mere digits. But in investing and the stock market, those five- and ten-percentage-point differences can feel like a chasm. Many managers spend the entire year working to achieve a double-digit return—and very often, even twelve months of research and investing don't get them there. Jerry has nine weeks.

"God! I hate talking to you. You give me all these goddamned cockamamy ideas. Your inventory becomes my investment," Jerry tells Bob, one of the few salesmen he speaks with every morning. He hardly sets the receiver down on his telephone before he picks it up to dial the four-digit extension of the trading desk.

"Stu? Vinny? Stu. American Online. They may open it down here a little bit. They may. I want to buy 20,000 for Aggressive Growth." It's a big order for Jerry, especially with AOL's shares selling for $120 apiece. Within the brief moments it will take for Stu to execute the trade, Jerry will have invested just under $2.5 million. The stock market will be open for business in ten minutes.

With that one order, Jerry upgrades America Online to the most important stock in the Aggressive Growth Fund. He will own 29,000 shares, and at just over 4 percent of the Fund, the stock will be his biggest holding. With one phone call, he slides a big stack of chips over to the AOL square on the roulette wheel. Sure, there are smaller stacks on 49 other squares in the Aggressive Growth Fund, waiting to collect minor payouts. But the AOL stack teeters above all others. Jerry and his gut have decided, "This is where I'm going to hit it big." And at 4 percent of the fund, he has bet just about as much as he can on it. Most mutual funds—Jerry's included—are not allowed to let any one stock account for more than 5 percent of a fund, so as not to let one stock recklessly skew the performance. Especially on the downside.

But America Online is a company Jerry is willing to make a big bet on. He has followed the company and the stock for years, and he likes the fundamentals. He says it's the strongest Internet name, he understands the business model, and he doesn't mind the extra kick the stock gets from being a well-known name among individual investors.

Lately, Jerry's been "hearing" a lot about America Online. He's been in and out of the stock many times already this year, and has kept a steady position in it for six weeks now. He's been hearing about a possible deal America Online may make with one of the phone companies or maybe another big technology company. "Could be AT&T . . . could be Sun Microsystems . . . maybe Bell Atlantic. . . . What about Netscape? . . . Can't tell right now, but looks like it could be something major. . . . It's definitely going to get the stock moving."

Even if there's no deal right away, or no deal at all, there are other rumors to keep the stock moving and keep investors guessing. This morning's call to Jerry mentioned AOL being put in the S&P 500 Index in the next four to six weeks . . . definitely by the end of the year. Sure, at this point, nine weeks before the end of the year and before an announcement of any kind, it's all rumor. Even in a game of telephone with a few links, this is a message with even fewer words to get lost along the way: AOL, S&P 500.

If the call proves to be more than rumor and America Online is put into the S&P 500 Index, it will indeed be good news for the stock. It means that every index fund out there that has as its goal "to match or mirror" the S&P 500 would have to buy AOL. Because that's what index funds do—they own the exact stocks that make up the index, and they buy and sell them when the index moves them in and out. It's an effort to match the fund's performance with that of a given index as closely as possible. Of all the indexes out there, the S&P 500 has the biggest following among index funds—more than $800 billion in mutual fund money was going to do whatever the S&P 500 did. And that meant a lot of money managers would be chasing shares of AOL if S&P said they had to.

But that's AOL the rumor. Then, of course, there's AOL the movie. Opening in theaters everywhere in seven weeks is *You've Got Mail,* starring Meg Ryan, Tom Hanks, and AOL.

"That's sure to be worth five points in the stock," Jerry says and smiles every time the subject of the movie about online romance comes up. Sure. Tom Hanks, Meg Ryan, schmaltz. If the movie does give the stock a five-point bounce, that schmaltz could be worth an easy $145,000 to Jerry and his fund.

Sure, days and weeks of research and analysis go into some stock investments; but for others, there's the schmaltz factor—the gut reaction, the sizzle. Ben & Jerry's stock soared several points when cookie-dough ice cream became the must-have nosh. Coca-Cola could've attributed a jump in its stock price to women television viewers' delight with a hunky and shirtless male model named "Lucky" featured in Diet Coke commercials. Victoria's Secret would follow this same strategy when it simulcast a live lingerie fashion show on the Internet, helping to send the stock of its parent company up nearly 10 percent in a single day. So, why not a sure-fire hit movie featuring your company as best supporting actor and actress?

Just after the opening bell, Jerry calls the trading desk again. "Vinny? How much of that Clear Channel did we get? Twenty-five?" It's only important to speak in thousands when placing orders to buy or sell. When listening to reports from Vinny or Stu, a simple "ten" or "twenty-five" is understood to mean thousands of shares or millions of dollars. Why waste a breath on words that are already innately understood and felt?

Jerry watches the numbers on his screen blink the movements of the market's opening. Three minutes pass. "Vinny? It's me again. Discreet Logic. The stock is at 10½. The company is gonna announce earnings tomorrow. Buy me 25,000 in Aggressive Growth. Start buying it a little at a time. After they announce, the stock's gonna go up. Why don't you start buying me 50,000 in Trend."

Jerry refocuses on his screen to gauge who is ahead so early in the morning. Who knows more at this point in time, Jerry and the salesmen and traders he's just checked in with, or the stock market?

Who's winning twenty minutes after the opening? Daily, hourly, and often minute-by-minute, Jerry types in the symbols of companies, indexes, and other mutual funds. It is his way of staring into the screen and asking the great central processor of the U.S. stock market, "Mirror, mirror on the wall, who's the fairest of them all?"

Tucked under the swivel base of the monitor are the four lottery tickets Jerry bought yesterday while he was out getting a grilled cheese sandwich and potato chips for lunch. "It's up to $40 million now," he says with infectious exuberance. While he doesn't regularly buy lottery tickets or gamble, he admits, "Every once in a while I'll walk by the stands and say, 'Hey, there's 40 million bucks. Why don't I give 'em a buck and see what happens?'"

Jerry picks up the phone to return a call from Jon, one of his regular salesmen. They talk about eBay, the latest wonder-IPO to turn heads on Wall Street and make investors across the country salivate. "That was sure a hot one, wasn't it? God, I played that one wrong. . . . You know what their top items are? Beanie Babies. That made me a little nervous. How you gonna build a business on that? Whew, I sure read that wrong."

Jerry started hearing the buzz on the Internet auction site over the summer, and the company was in his office just last month presenting him with countless reasons why he should invest in the IPO. Jerry listened to the company's pitch, he asked questions, and he took notes. Who else does this? Your relationship with AOL? National advertising? Competitive barriers to entry? Your business model? By the end of the meeting, he had small but definitive checkmarks next to every issue. His concerns were addressed and he was willing to buy.

At the initial offering, Jerry bought 15,500 shares at $18 apiece. The IPO was spinning heads all around, and investors were oohing and aahing up and down Wall Street. One of the most influential analysts in the business issued her official recommendation for the shares even before they began trading—an almost unheard-of move on Wall Street. And the recommendation was to buy, buy, buy. On the first day, the shares jumped 162 percent to close at over $47 apiece. But Jerry decided eBay was something he'd like to trade rather than own, so he sold the shares two days later for $45, a profit of just under half a million dollars. Silently, he congratulated himself for his discipline in taking the fast buck and not staying around long enough to lose it all. Now, just four weeks later, the stock was trading at over $150 a share. Jerry's 15,500 shares would have been worth over $2 million. But, sometimes IPOs are like the lottery: Here's a buck and let's see what happens.

As Jerry packs his black canvas briefcase before leaving for meetings in New York, Jeff walks in waving a sheet of paper in his hand. "Now here's one of the most honest pieces of research you'll see." He holds the paper in front of him like a palace decree and reads to Jerry, "eBay. Our twelve-month target price on the stock is $100. Why? Because we say it is." The report was written long before the stock even flirted with prices like $100 a share.

Jerry takes the paper and reads over the three-sentence assessment for himself. "See, this is just stupid. This is one of those things where I bought it, it got to what? Forty or fifty?—which was then a ridiculous valuation—so I was stupid to own it even there. So why not hold on and see if it gets even more ridiculous? But then I did another stupid thing and sold it. It's all relative. If you're stupid enough to own it at 50, why aren't you stupid enough to hold on 'til 100?"

He thrusts the paper back at Jeff, zips up his bag, and is out the door.

Still buried under the papers on Jerry's desk is the giveaway, or the "deal toy" that the eBay executives left behind at the end of their presentation, as a memento of the company for Jerry to keep. eBay didn't make anything, or really sell anything except Internet space, so it wasn't as if they could give away their product. And T-shirts, pens, and tote bags are so redundant. Instead, eBay gave out something its investors could really use: a shiny money clip with the company's logo dancing across it in bright red, purple, yellow, and green. Especially green.

CHAPTER 9

THE HANGOVER IS COMMENSURATE WITH THE PARTY

It is a warm day in late October, the kind of day that encourages weatherpeople to talk about Indian summers. It has encouraged Jerry to take the day off and enjoy the sunshine. He often finds that a day away from the office can be more productive than a day in the office. Sure, he travels to conferences, company meetings, and marketing pitches. But time by himself, away from the click-clicking of the computer and the tick-ticking of the Dow, is different. As Jerry has progressed in his career, he has felt more comfortable taking such days for himself, truly believing that a break in the routine, a jolt to his thinking, can be what's best for all.

Like a tickle in the throat presaging the oncoming cold, Jerry usually feels the day off coming for a few weeks. Seeing ample white space on a calendar day, he starts declining meetings and luncheon invitations. He tries to avoid Geri's requests to make any commitments for that random Tuesday or Thursday. When the day finally approaches, and Jerry has been successful in rescheduling or putting off any pertinent work for the slot, he lets Geri know, "I may be out that day." She has worked with Jerry since his arrival in Philadelphia and she understands implicitly. It is not, "I'll be in Chicago on Wednesday for marketing" or "I'm heading to New York for a conference on Friday." No, when Jerry's phone rings on the allotted day, and company executives peer in to his office to chat, Geri's only explanation will be, "He's not in the office today."

To say that he's playing hooky or taking a mental health day wouldn't be right. No, it is indeed a workday. He's thinking. He's strategizing. He'll ponder the past; he'll plan for the future. He will ask himself the question, "What's it going to take?" and he must answer, "Do I have it?" It is a chance to look within, in an industry that often seems so without. Really, it is a chance to play golf.

Jerry drives the three hours up to his cottage in the Pennsylvania mountains, picks up the mail, and is at the golf course in time to enjoy a bowl of soup for lunch. He plays about 12 holes in the afternoon, shooting a 48 on the first nine. Not a record-breaking round, but admirable. A few long drives and some challenging putts. Jerry knows he doesn't spend enough time playing or practicing golf to really bemoan his play. Nonetheless, he knows he is a good athlete and has the confidence and the concentration to be good. He could be a player.

Later in the day, as the pro-shop caddy carries Jerry's clubs from the course to his car, Jerry catches up with one of his salesmen on his cellular phone. Throughout his play, he alternated holes with phone calls to the trading desk, to Geri, and to other salesmen, from the protection of his golf cart. This one is just the kind of call you would expect to see a $2-billion money manager make from a golf course on a quiet Thursday. "Things are that good, huh? . . . Maybe a deal with a technology company in Texas, huh? Hmm, interesting. Yes, and you have a nice weekend too."

Checking his pocket for a tip for the caddy's work of carrying the bags the dozen or so paces to the car, Jerry finds only a $20 bill.

"How much change have you got?" Jerry asks.

In a combination of bills, the caddy pulls out $8.

"Keep the change," Jerry says, swapping his $20 for the $8. As he takes a step toward his car, the caddy is quick to seize the moment.

"Mr. Frey. . . ."

Jerry is sure he has never met the caddy before, but figures the club must require its employees to be familiar with the guests.

And then there's the question. "You got any good stock ideas?"

It is the unavoidable request of money managers, stockbrokers, financial planners, and business reporters in the 1990s. It is asked by the dry cleaner, the nursery school teacher, the neighbor, and the sports store clerk. It is the question that says, "It's all a game, everybody's playing, everybody's winning, why can't I?"

And now the caddy wants an answer. Jerry has spent the day thinking about risk, calculating variables, thinking about his options, weighing conservative play versus aggressive. It's just a job, it's just the stock market, it's other people's money. But he has a family, shareholders, responsibilities. He's spent the day telling himself, "It's not that easy." And now this kid, who Jerry thinks can be no older than 19, is telling him, "Yes, it is that easy. I just gave you eight dollars and you gave me twenty. I know how the stock market works."

For a moment, Jerry considers not answering, or giving one of many accessible self-deprecating remarks about doing the opposite of anything Jerry does in the market. But he doesn't. The sun is shining, the Dow is up 123 points, and the idea is fresh. And so is this kid.

"Aware. The stock is at 12 and it should keep going up. Just don't forget to sell it."

Rather than scurrying to the phone to call his broker, or his computer to log in to his own trading account, the caddy ups the ante. He lets Jerry know he is willing to go further, to risk it. That's nice that the stock will be going up, but straight stock investing is for my grandmother, I'm looking for something a little more complex and turbocharged.

"Is it optionable?"

The line would become a mantra for Jerry throughout the rest of the year. Sometimes he would repeat it when he wanted to remind himself of the level of greed the rising market has driven people to. Other times he would recite the phrase to point out the overconfidence people have in the market—stocks were such a sure thing, there's got to be some other tool I can bet on to make even more money.

In his office, Jerry checks his screen. In the two days since he left to

October 30, 1998	Year-to-Date Performance	Rank
Aggressive Growth	7.8%	28
Trend	-3.7%	22
Delcap	-1.5%	53
Dow	8.7%	
S&P 500	14.6%	
Nasdaq	12.8%	

play golf and debate the world with himself, the market had climbed 220 points.

"I should stay away more often." He then makes the rounds of the group's offices, gathering the team for the weekly meeting.

"Performance. Obviously, it's sparked. I'm not so sure it's the end of the bear market. There are still some issues out there, but I think we've got the right stocks."

"It looks like consumer's gonna have a really good day," Lori says, as she picks raisins one by one from a red Sun-Maid box, a remnant of the weekend's Halloween candy.

Jerry jumps topics and even years, already trying to turn the group's thoughts and sights to next year. "In January, you just don't know if the same thing'll happen that did this year, where the whole market just flopped over and died."

"Who cares?" Marshall asks rhetorically, voicing the opinion of most of the group if not most of the market. It's this year that counts. Next year is still two months and one bonus check away.

"China is behind us, the hedge funds are behind us, the Fed might cut rates again in November, maybe December too." Jerry catalogs the market's most recent crises in an effort to gain footing. "I don't have a good answer. Is it over and things are gonna move up from here? Or do we think it's gonna go down and we need to raise cash? 'Cause if it goes down, we've seen the numbers. We are gonna get slammed."

"Unless you're going to, like, 35 percent cash, it's not worth it. If you're going from 5 to 10 percent cash, what's the point?" John says.

Cash it in, lock it up, book it. That's the conservative move to keep some of the gains you've already made in the market. If you're up 60 percent in July, the only way to make sure you're up 60 percent in December is to sell everything, go to cash. Risk losing nothing. But then the risk becomes not gaining more. Going to cash is a bold move, but it can also be seen as chicken shit. It is saying either the market isn't going to do any better, or I can't do any better than the market. I'm cashing in my chips and going home. Well, what about cashing in just *some* of your chips? Sending some of that money back to the room with your husband or wife for safe-keeping.

But the more you send back, the less you have to play with, to make some real bets that could have real payoffs. You've got to decide. Do you have what it takes to make those big bets? Do you have the confidence in yourself? Do you think your luck won't run out—because it's not luck? Or, do you count your lucky stars and your dollar bills, or your millions of them, as you cash in and secure your standing, or at least part of it, in the year-end rankings?

For most mutual funds, going to all cash isn't actually an option. Shareholders send in their checks to be invested in the market, to be out there working, not to be held in cash. Even though the growth team can't really sell the funds and go to cash, it doesn't stop them from talking about strategies to guarantee some of their gains.

"What about the Aggressive Growth Fund, should we think about having any sort of hedges there on the downside?" Jerry looks around the table at his team. He's asking them the question he's been asking himself for the past few weeks. What are you made of? Do you have It?

There is a pause in this group that is rarely short of an opinion, a joke, an insult, or praise.

"I just hate to give it all back," John says, endorsing the conservative view. Maybe cash in some.

"Well, I'd look into it," Marshall agrees.

Jerry knows where the group stands, at least for now. None of them is willing to sprint to the top; they want the harnesses and the net—or at least a few safety ropes—on their way up. Jerry will have the final say on the next move. There are two months left. Do they slow themselves down with protection, and hedges, and a large cash position? Or do they position the peak in their sights and strive, knowing that a fall from such heights, this late in the year, could prove irreparable?

They move on to talk about retail stocks, the health care industry, stock selection.

"I was reading *The Economist* over the weekend. Some sort of end-of-the-world scenario piece," Jerry offers. "God, you finish one of those and you really get depressed."

"Yeah, if those guys knew what was going on, they'd be running money instead of writing bad news articles," says John. It was writing, more than math, that actually brought John to Wall Street. He first worked as an analyst, researching and writing reports on companies, before discovering that he, too, would prefer investing in companies to writing about them.

Then Jerry tests the group again. He tells the story of a manager whose performance was going down quickly and whose shareholders were pulling their money out even faster.

"So they just said, 'Screw it,' and went 100 percent short for August, and they got it exactly right," he says. They took their money out of the market just in time for the Dow to drop 1,300 points.

"Oh, that's ridiculous. That is way too Vegas," John says. "I'd never give anybody like that money. It's like winning the lottery and then saying you're a good money manager. It's like throwing the Hail Mary pass."

"And somebody caught it," Jerry says. It is more of the dialogue inviting the team to take a bold stance. Are you conservative, are you aggressive, or are you mediocre?

After the meeting, Jerry is back at his desk, making calculations on his notepad and checking stock prices on his screen. "The market's fading a little. You know, sometimes stocks just get tired. They just go and go and go, and then they fade." His eyes continue to move over the rows and columns of companies and prices. "Amazon.com. 130. God. American Online. I bought that the other day. Up 7."

He leans back in his chair, getting a broader view of his screen and the market. "It's such a shitty business. You're never just right. You're never invested exactly right, in the right stocks, at the right time, fully invested. Part of me wants to get it just right, if only academically." Again, he is debating with himself whether to play it safe or to go for it. Put some in cash, hedge a little, or bet it all? "But for me, it's best just to go with the market, to take signals from the market as to the direction it's going, rather than make huge bets on the market."

For today, Jerry will let the market lead and he will follow.

*   *   *

"Oh, don't tell me you've got a deal for me," Jerry says to a sales-man. "The thing that'll end this rally is deals. Things are back on track here, but people still aren't ready for deals yet. That'll kill it."

They talk about their weekends and the market's October swoon, and they talk about stocks.

"Yeah, I see it's up, like, four points. You guys out there hyping it? . . . I have a hard time believing they'll make any money, to tell you the truth. . . . All right, well, I guess I'd better put away my prej-udices and think more clearly. The valuation still has me a little wor-ried—although from what I heard, the quarter coming up is gonna be huge. They beat the revenue number by something big. So would I short it? No."

"Someone pointed out something interesting to me. Barnes & Noble bought Ingram, the book distributor. Bertelsman, who's Ran-dom House's publisher, made an investment in Barnes & Noble. So there, they've got control all along the distribution chain. That's the kind of thing that attracts the government."

"Because Amazon is held retail, it is not an institutional name. You talk to the guy on the street that owns Amazon, you tell him, 'Barnes & Noble bought Ingram.' He's gonna say, 'Who?' So no, I don't think it's gonna slow Amazon down. That being said, I don't own the stock." .

He has owned it, wishes he had held on, and would like to own it again. As Jerry speaks to the salesman, the shares of Amazon.com are pulsing on his screen, climbing higher with nearly every blink of the ticker.

"The S&P is up 19 percent. It's another 20 percent year. It's been 20 percent, 20 percent, 20 percent. It's unbelievable. The conven-tional wisdom is: The hangover is commensurate with the party. . . . We got hammered in early October. We've bounced back here, actu-ally really well. But I'm just concerned that this rally is a sucker's rally and we're gonna get sucked in here. . . .

"Well, heading into next year, I think the rhetoric around mid-year is going to be Year 2000. A lot of companies may delay spending on computers for three to four months. GM might say, 'Well, let's see if these work first. We'll just hold off on buying for a few months.' To GM, that's nothing. But if you're a little company on the receiving end or anywhere along the food chain of that order, it's the end of the world." Jerry knows that many of the stocks in his portfolios are the links along that food chain. They are the companies that make the switches, the chips, the nodes, and the diodes. They are the companies for which a missed order can mean the end of the world. And the end of the world for a company means the end of the climb for a stock.

"I'm worried what I'm gonna do when it heads back down. Owning small growth, those are the names that are gonna get hit. . . . So, I'm looking into some tools for protection on the downside." Jerry continues his search for guidance on a stand to take.

"In 73–74, there was a huge rally, right before the shit hit the fan. If you don't believe me, ask Bob; he told me. There was a big rally and then it all just ended." Could history repeat itself? Am I getting sucked in before the shit hits the fan? I've been warned, I can see the signs. Do I listen to other people? Do I heed the calls? Or do I trust myself?

"When this thing starts going down, it doesn't make one bit of difference. It only matters what you own on the upside. Because you can underperform on the downside, but if you lag on the upside, you can probably just pack it in." He waffles again. Maybe he won't hedge. Maybe it's best just to hold steady, follow the market. Own what you trust, trust it to go up. He's repeating to himself the lesson he so often gives others. Don't panic, buy more when you can. Get in position to participate on the upside. That's where you want to differentiate yourself. Being down 5 percent or 20 percent, there's little difference—no one cares about you. Being up 5 percent or 20 percent, there's a huge difference, and people tend to care a lot— with their money.

* * *

It's one week later and the group is still debating cash. Should we go to cash? Who has cash? What are they doing with it? How much is enough?

"For what it's worth, Keith says all of Boston's at 10 percent cash and it's all gonna come charging back into the market." Lori opens up the weekly meeting with a tip she heard from an analyst. Whether "all of Boston" means just Fidelity and its $500-plus billion in mutual funds or an even larger pool encompassing all Boston-area money managers, it's a lot of money. Cash is good, and cash being put to work in the market is better. The more buying there is, the more likely that demand for stocks will increase, pushing the prices up and pulling fund portfolios along with them. "It's probably already come in during the last week, but there's enough to sustain these levels 'til the end of the year."

Lori has meant this as good news for the growth team, but Jerry is still stuck on how other people are strategizing and how to protect himself from getting caught. "But if you have 10 percent in cash in a portfolio, that doesn't do much for you. You've got to either have 35 percent or 0 percent."

"Yeah, and it's not like people are gonna put that whole 10 percent to work. They may use 3 percent or 4 percent of it," Marshall says.

"Everyone seen the peer group performance sheets?" Jerry asks, picking up his own printouts that show the Aggressive Growth Fund ranked twenty-seventh for the year.

"These are our bibles," Lori says, incredulous that Jerry could even ask such a question. "There's nothing we care about more than when these lists come out."

It is true. The sheets serve as a scorecard against the competition, and they are a worksheet for calculating what the numbers on the bonus check at the end of the year will be. But, few save the printouts longer than a day or two. The performance is past, and there are new numbers that will be valid for only the 65½ hours between the market's close on Friday and its opening on Monday. It's as if the numbers are written with the knobs of a child's Etch-A-Sketch toy. Jiggle it and the numbers disappear.

"We've made up some ground," Jerry continues. "DelCap keeps edging its way up. It keeps poking its head into the money."

"Are those lists the best way to look at this?" Marshall asks. He wants to know, "Isn't there some other way we can be paid? We're working hard, and it doesn't say so on this printout."

In the profession of managing money, or the game of the stock market, nothing is definitive, nothing is permanent, nothing is *yours* until the last day of the year. It's not like salespeople who log in such good numbers during the first half of the year that they can coast through the last six months. No, in the stock market, it's almost as if those great numbers or your successes are on loan to you— a loan that can be withdrawn at any time. Those same stocks that are up 40 percent mid-year could be down 10 percent or 20 percent by December. All those runs you rack up on the scoreboard early in the game can be taken away from you in the ninth inning.

Jerry pushes a stack of research on the table toward the group. He usually brings a handful of reports, charts, printouts, and data from research analysts and strategists, or from stock screens he's run. Every time, he hopes that his team will take some of the material, will read it, and think a little differently than they do within their own office walls. Most weeks, it is left behind. Shuffled and reordered on the table, but, like so many cold peas on a plate, left behind.

"One worry coming up is on the deal side—there are a lot of IPOs coming out. . . . Another is if rates don't come down between now and the end of the year. When is the Fed meeting? This week, or is it next week? If rates don't come down, how will the market react to that? Probably not well. Earnings season is almost over, so I think we did well there. So our concerns are really external at this point." It is Jerry's market recap and setting of the stage. "My concern is that we start to go down again. If we have another January or beginning of October—when the market really went down—it's gonna go down fast and hard. We've seen how quickly something can go down 20 percent. It takes you forever to make it, and you can lose it in a matter of days."

The group nods in agreement. The first six trading days of October, they lost 24 percent. But that seems so long ago now. It's a full four weeks and 1,200 points ago. It's a new month and a new market, and bonus numbers are only six weeks away.

"I'm thinking about using some sort of hedges or collars to protect ourselves," Jerry says. A collar is just one more form of protection in the market. The idea behind a collar is to put a limit on how much a stock or a portfolio can lose. Jerry and the team might like to have a collar around the fund that keeps them from losing more than 5 percent. The problem is, just like a shirt or dog collar, this one goes all the way around. If they cap themselves at losing only 5 percent, they are capped at gaining only 5 percent as well.

Jerry continues, "It makes you ask yourself, 'How much do you think you can make between now and the end of the year? Should you just lock in some of the gains now?' But as John said, it's tough to run an aggressive growth portfolio with a collar around it," Jerry looks around. It is a continuing discussion among the group: Look at both sides, play the devil's advocate, rehash the same issues, and mine for new data and new opinions. "So, any thoughts, concerns, ideas? I'd be interested to hear."

"It's expensive."

"It changes your focus from stocks to hedging." Instead of looking for ways to keep climbing higher, they'd be looking at ways to stand still.

"We aren't market timers."

While he listens, Jerry turns the black binder clip that had been holding the research and strategy pages together. He bends the silver metal clasps in his hand. They easily push back and forth, offering little resistance in either direction. He pauses after listening to the group's opinions on protecting their gains or going for more. In just one week's time, they have reversed their outlook.

"Okay. I just wanted to get your thoughts on that." He snaps the clip together audibly and sets it back on the table.

Then he catalogs various marketing meetings scheduled for the group and its high-ranking performance. "We got a note from SEI . . . City of Nashville—they're doing a small-cap search, looking to place $25 million. Our numbers were submitted and we're in the finals, so I've got to make a presentation. Smith Barney, they've called with some interest. The Morgan Stanley wrap product, that's up and running. So, on the marketing side, things are looking like they are going well. These wrap fees—I tell you, they're charging 4 percent or 5 percent for these things," he scoffs. A wrap product is an investment for investors who fall in between the categories of average mutual fund shareholder and high-net-worth individual. Financial firms can offer investors asset allocation, a checking account, and other extra services as part of a wrap program. Of course, those extras come at a price.

"It's like retail. People pay that much for their mutual funds," Lori says.

"I never pay retail." Marshall turns to address Lori. "Those shoes I bought last week? I got him to throw in a tin of polish and a shoe tree."

"At the mall?"

"Yeah."

"I beat you there. I was at Sears and I bought my wife a new dishwasher." Jerry jumps in to join the competition for the deal.

Talk drifts back to performance and how the direction of the market and perhaps the fortunes of the group have changed so quickly.

"Yeah, some marketing guy came in and said, 'Hey, you're up 35 percent in the last four weeks. That's pretty good.' I said, 'Yeah, well don't forget that it can come down just as fast.'"

"Hey, but you want to sell to those guys," John says, interrupting Jerry's cautionary remarks. We sell ourselves to marketing. Marketing sells us to shareholders. "Get them out there selling hard. Bring in the cash so we have it when the market comes down."

"Yeah, that's right. You get some new cash, some of these stocks come back down, there's nothing against putting cash to work in your own names." Jerry nods, agreeing with John's suggestion. Collect the money when you can, when your numbers are good. Buy up the stocks the fund already owns and believes in. Any extra cash can be a little extra push. And in the end, that extra push may be just what we need. "You get to the last week of the year, buy up another 5,000 shares in some of your names and you can really drive 'em."

"And there's nothing against that," Marshall says emphatically.

CHAPTER 10

ALL I WANT
FOR CHRISTMAS IS
A DOT-COM IPO

Jerry is at his best when activity and opportunities swirl around him. Whether the market is up or down, Jerry is happiest when there are things to fix. He likes having "little projects" and "fires to put out." He likes helping people, and he likes being the guy people naturally want to call on. He may complain about it at the time, but only half as loudly as he would if he thought they were calling someone else to fix the same things.

Jerry says if he weren't a money manager, he might like to be a carpenter. He says he'd probably do some building—houses and furniture: starting from scratch, from nothing, and making something that will last. But he also likes finish carpentry: fixing things, putting the polish on, making his mark that will make something just right and will impress the careful observer. For just such projects, he has a garage full of tools, many of which he's never used. He set up a woodworking shop in his brother's garage because his wife wouldn't let him buy any more equipment. But he's ready—in case he gets the call or the inspiration. He's prepared to build and to fix.

This morning, he shuttles back and forth from his desk to the hallway and his table. He has a list of "little projects" for Steve— "None of which he'll like," Jerry says. In the past few days, he's had flights to marketing meetings canceled, and he's met with the wrong accounts. His babysitter is pregnant. The stock market just opened. And he spilled coffee on his tie this morning.

The coffee on his tie is almost good news to Jerry. It tells him that he is very present—clumsy, but present—in everything that is happening around him. It is a silent reminder that he does have some responsibility for things going right, as much as he does when they go wrong.

Jerry looks at his performance sheets. The group has made up some ground since the October losses but is still four percentage points behind the S&P and six behind the Nasdaq. He thinks to himself that beating the indexes is out of the question. The differences this late in the year are simply too great. He tries to content himself with performing well for the rest of the year, holding steady, giving the shareholders some profit, and simply giving it his best effort. But the Jiminy Cricket voice that he won't let speak aloud tells him, "Don't give up yet, you could do it."

November 11, 1998	Year-to-Date Performance	Rank
Aggressive Growth	13.1%	27
Trend	0.7%	22
Delcap	2.0%	49
Dow	11.6%	
S&P 500	17.0%	
Nasdaq	18.6%	

"The problem is, for us to beat the indexes, two things would have to happen," he tries to talk himself out of getting his hopes up. "Everything would have to go right for the Delaware Aggressive Growth Fund, and everything would have to go wrong for the indexes. But if things were bad at the major indexes, it'd be tough for Delaware Aggressive Growth to do well."

So the market has to do well for Jerry to do well. And Jerry has to do something to do better than the market. He looks at his screen to see what might make the difference for him.

"The Internet stocks are just unstoppable. American Online was down big yesterday, but it's up huge again today."

Just then, he asks a visitor in his office, "You win the lottery last night? Fifty million, you know. Some guy won it." He smiles and says the words with the same wonder his nine-year-old son had when he told him about the jackpot this morning. "Yeah, my kids love the lottery. I guess I'm teaching them gambling habits." He laughs and turns back to his screen to see where the market has moved.

After lunch, Jerry reads *The New York Times* at his conference table. "For a guy who dodged the draft, he sure does like shooting people." Jerry addresses a photograph of President Bill Clinton and an article about preparations to bomb Iraq. He pulls out the business section and lets his eyes scan the lead page. "To cut rates or not to cut rates?"

"That sounds like a guy who hasn't decided what he wants." Marshall strolls into Jerry's office sucking on a Dum Dum's rootbeer lollipop.

"I never knew P&G owned Hawaiian Punch." Jerry has moved on in the business section.

"I never knew you cared."

"I like Hawaiian Punch."

"So do I. But that makes us and about 12 million six-year-olds," Marshall rasps out the words and follows them with a series of hacking winter coughs. The lollipop's sweet rootbeer scent wafts through the room.

"You sound terrible," Jerry says, looking up from the paper for the first time since Marshall's entrance. "If I get sick—is that an STD you have?"

Marshall looks puzzled. (Clearly, neither of these two was in college in the '90s. Marshall doesn't know what Jerry's talking about, and Jerry thinks his newly acquired phrase is original.)

"Do you know what that is? Sexually Transmitted Disease," Jerry says, pleased with himself.

"I think the only way you could get what I have is if you stuck your tongue down my throat or I drooled on your desk. And I think there's an infinitesimally small chance of either of those happening."

Jerry stands up and carries the stack of newspapers to the trash. "I may kiss you, but it would be in more of a platonic manner."

"Yeah, you bet it would."

* * *

A week and a half until Thanksgiving, and Wall Street's deal calendar is starting to get crowded. There are IPOs of companies that want to sell their shares to the public for the first time, and offerings of companies coming around a second or third time. The calendar usually starts to slow down near the end of the year because investment bankers know that managers don't want to juggle their holidays and vacations around luncheons, breakfasts, and slide presentations. It's too easy for a company to get lost in the shuffle during the last two months of the year. One of the unwritten rules on Wall Street is: If you're gonna do your offering right, do it before November.

This year, the Dow, the hedge funds, the collapse of Russia's economy, and the President's extramarital affairs threw a wrench into that plan. The 1,300-point drop in the market in August spooked companies off the calendar for September, just in time for October to scare them again. But now it's the second week of November, the market has recovered, and stocks and investors are flying high. There is a full stable of companies panting at the public gates to be let out, and there's just as much investor demand waiting on the other side. And the success of the recent wave of Internet IPOs has left investors singing a chorus of "All I want for Christmas is a dot-com IPO."

Geri comes in to check Jerry's availability for an 8:30 meeting on the Monday after Thanksgiving.

"No."

"He knows you don't see companies before nine, but he was wondering. . . ."

"Bob is a good friend, but no." Jerry doesn't like anyone else dictating when he has to arrive at the office in the morning. Once he enters the building, his hours are someone else's and he lets schedules and meetings and others' needs rule his days. But no one gets to tell him what time he has to come to work. Most days, he is in the office before 8:30. He sits at his table and has his orange juice, coffee, and a corn or blueberry muffin. He pages through the paper and eats his breakfast. By himself. He rarely takes calls, and few people come to visit during this earliest interval of the day. When he stands to toss his muffin bag and coffee cup in the trash and washes one aspirin tablet down with his orange juice, his workday begins. He has clocked in and will now see clients, customers, companies, or colleagues.

So no, he won't take the 8:30 meeting with the executives from Bindview.

"Bindview?" Jerry looks up, repeating the name Geri has mentioned. "I just saw those guys, like, two weeks ago. I don't even need to see them at all. The only reason I need to see them is to remind them how they told me they weren't going to do an offering."

Indeed, the CEO and CFO had sat across from Jerry in the conference room on the fortieth floor exactly four weeks ago. And they told him they wouldn't be selling shares any time soon. They raved about their company's performance. And they assured Jerry they had no intention of selling any shares. They went on about their fabulous growth prospects. And they told Jerry no one wanted to sell any shares. They smiled over the remarkable growth the company had seen in the three months since going public. And then they asked Jerry if maybe it would be all right if they sold just a few shares.

Now they were making the rounds to money managers again, with 3 million shares up for sale, hoping to raise another $60 million for the company and its original investors.

*   *   *

Jerry walks up to the trading floor to check on the status of the latest Internet IPO—theglobe.com. He expects it to be a hot one. The deal was pulled off the calendar when the market fell apart in October, but with the 248 percent first-day success of Earthweb just two days ago, theglobe.com was revived. Now Jerry was hearing rumors that theglobe.com shares might begin trading as high as $50. Last night, he told the investment bank managing the deal he wanted as many shares as he could get at $9 apiece. There were a lot of investors in line for shares, so Jerry's funds got only 2,800. But a quick $41 profit a share would be over $100,000 the second the stock opened— if indeed it opened at the rumored and much fantasized-about $50 a share number.

"If this thing goes to $50 a share, it'll be a $500-million company," Jerry says as he shakes his head. "They have revenues of something like $10 million and losses of $6 million," he shakes his head again.

The arms of Vinny's butter-soft black leather jacket just sweep the floor as he leans back in his chair. It is Friday and the initial 9:30 opening bell flurry of the trading desk has passed. He is relaxed and waiting for the weekend. But first, he and Jerry will wait for theglobe.com to open.

"You know, with some of these hot IPOs, they come down after the opening and then they climb back up. So why don't you sell on the opening. Why don't you top-tick it? You can do that, can't you?" Jerry says and Vinny smiles. "Then, see if it comes down, and buy some more if it comes back down." Sell it to 'em twice. Scalp ours at the highest price to the first round of buyers. Then when the line and the prices slow down, buy some more, and we'll sell 'em as soon as they go up into the next round. This one could be hot enough to ring the bell twice.

Some days, Jerry's job is finding and researching core investments for the fund—building up the foundation that will last. On other days, it's getting in a quick IPO or a few trades in the margins—the finishing touches that add polish and gleam to the fund.

At 11:12, the number next to the stock market's newest ticker, "T-G-L-O," blinks green on Vinny's screen. Shares of theglobe.com are available to be scalped to the public: $90 a share. A ten-bagger on the opening trade. The stock immediately jumps to $97, and Vinny quickly sells Jerry's shares in chunks for $86 and $84 apiece. The field of buyers and sellers is crowded and the prices are heady. Vinny backs off from a second round of buying. By lunchtime, the stock has drifted down to $72.

*   *   *

Back at his desk, Jerry sorts through paperwork, research, and phone messages. He pauses to go through the daily William O'Neil printouts, detailing technical changes in any of the stocks he owns. Jerry reads aloud some of the highlights of today's fax, "Children's Place, new high; PMC-Sierra, new high; Staples, new high; Network Appliance, new high; Clarify, new high—that was a good idea." It is Jerry patting himself on the back, enjoying an afternoon of feeling that he has the right touch. A software company, Clarify, had been a hot stock, then cooled for several months along the familiar path of overpromising and underperforming in an early quarter. Investors had ignored the stock for months. At a technology conference last month, Clarify's presentation was scheduled for late in the day. Most investors had seen six or seven presentations by then, and many had retired to their hotel rooms, or at least to their cell phones, to catch up with their offices and trading desks. Jerry found himself to be one of the few in the ballroom who was listening to the executives' pleas for notice and a second chance. The story sounded good, the timing looked right, Jerry seemed to be at the front of the line. He knew the company and its dynamics well, and this looked like a good time to add it to the portfolio. A chance to add a position he liked at an attractive price. When he returned from the conference, he called Stu and Vinny to put in an order for 75,000 shares at $11 apiece. Now, three weeks later, the stock is dancing across Jerry's screen at $19 a share, a $600,000 profit for the fund.

* * *

As November progresses, the IPOs pick up more steam, and Jerry's quest for the hot ones gets more heated. It's starting to resemble the summer months, when Jerry's in-box teetered with prospectuses for new offerings, and he could've gone without buying lunch for several weeks with so many investment banks wanting to bring their companies and sandwiches through for a chance to meet Jerry and his $2 billion. "Over the summer, there were so many deals you couldn't see them all. I'd just tell Vinny and Stu, 'If it's hot, get me in it. You guys sort through them.' The salesmen would call and ask you if you want a one-on-one with the company. I'd say, 'Is it hot?' They say, 'Well, that's so crass.' I say, 'If it's hot, put me in it. Give me 10 percent of the deal. I don't need to see them.' The salesmen get very annoyed, they say, 'Hey, you're not playing by the rules.' "

So Jerry usually plays by the rules. He welcomes the executives to his conference room, lets them give their slide show, and leave their deal toys. And sometimes he will eat the sandwiches they've paid for and flip through the booklets they've brought. Leading up to the meeting, Jerry gets the buzz on the company and the offering from colleagues and competitors who are seeing the same presentation and eating the same turkey sandwiches at conference tables in New York, San Francisco, Baltimore, and points in between. The buzz is what's important, so Jerry will often wait until his phone lights up, letting him know that the executives have arrived and they are waiting in the lobby or the conference room before he turns to the facts.

In fifteen minutes, Jerry is due in the conference room at the end of the hall to meet with executives of E-Tek Dynamics, a telecommunications equipment company that is hoping to go public in a $40 million IPO—4 million shares at $10 apiece—in the next few weeks. He flips through the prospectus, getting his bearings on the company and its business. Everything is in order, he understands fiber optics, he knows the competition, he has invested in companies like this before. And then the familiar tune hits a scratch and starts skipping. He reads the section over and over, and works out the numbers in his head: Recapitalization—who's getting what for how much?

"The VCs came in and got a ton of shares at $4 a share, they gave the founders cash for some of their shares, now it's a year later, and they'll go public at $10 a share or so." His disgust increases with each statistic and accusation. "This is one of those deals that when the market is really hot, it's put together to make a lot of people rich." He continues to read, and the rest of the once comfortable and familiar melody unravels for him. "Let me tell you, this is bullshit. All their revenues come from, like, four or five customers, and their gross margins aren't very good."

Soon, he is reaching into his second desk drawer for a small stack of his own business cards to pass out to the executives waiting so eagerly for Jerry Frey and Wall Street to help make them rich.

He returns from the meeting with a sandwich on his plate and a bottle of water. His mood is much changed, whether it's the food's or the meeting's doing. Jerry often goes through such conversions during IPO presentations. He goes into the meetings focused on the money and the deal, and he comes out infected with the excitement of the product, the entrepreneurs, and the opportunity.

For most money managers, it's the best part of the job: meeting entrepreneurs, hearing new ideas, and seeing innovative products that may change the world. The growth group meets with hundreds of executives each year. And, although some days the free sandwiches or bagels seem to be the main attraction, the intelligent exchange of ideas keeps the group energized. Each group member has a different style and takes something different away from the meetings with companies, salespeople, and analysts. Universally, they have done their homework and are well prepared. Style differences aside, it is an experienced team that wants to learn and wants to win.

Marshall goes into meetings as polite as any Four Seasons concierge, but he doesn't mind bashing the company with robust enthusiasm once the elevator doors have closed behind the visitors. John, on the other hand, has the ability to be critical from start to end of a meeting, all the while having the party across the conference table like and respect him. Steve goes to meetings prepared with a list of pointed questions and financial minutiae, and he quizzes the company or analyst with them. Once the meeting begins, the stance softens, and he too conducts himself with respect for the companies and near reverence for the executives. "My greatest day was when I met with Wayne Huizenga. I could tell anybody about it and they knew who he was," Steve says. He keeps the business card of the founder of Blockbuster and executive of Republic Industries in his Rolodex, to show friends.

For Jeff, the ideal meetings are with technology engineers. "These people are in the sixth or seventh deviation of standard intelligence," he says. "You sit at a table with some of the people from Microsoft and you realize you're in the presence of white light." Lori immediately gets down to business in her meetings. Colleagues and salespeople say she can analyze a retail story better than almost any analyst. For Lori's part, she says she just always "got" business. Her best job was the summer between high school and college, when she worked at a Bloomingdale's on Long Island. That interest in retail, combined with her undergraduate degree from The University of Pennsylvania's Wharton School (basically getting an MBA education in college instead of waiting for grad school), squarely set Lori up to face off with most any retail stock—and win.

In his meetings, Jerry is polite, but he does like to run the show. He likes to hear about hard numbers, hard facts, and concrete products. Sure, he wants to know how the widget is made and how much the widget will sell for, but he also wants to know who makes the machines that make the widgets.

As Jerry sits at his conference table, looking out onto the smokestacks of Philadelphia's train station, his words turn contemplative. "I've got some respect for those guys. They're going to put together and build a business." This is the general, anonymous language Jerry uses to talk nostalgically about America and the way businesses are built and money created. This sort of talk imbues his job of staring at blinking numbers on a computer screen, with history, grace, and corporeal substance. "They have an actual product and they're going to produce it for as cheap as possible, and they're going to sell it and other companies can buy it."

His next words belie the true meaning behind his nostalgic romp into the ABCs of how American capitalism works. "It's tangible. It does something. It's admirable." Is it a silent condemnation of the wave of Internet IPOs that so many describe as producing nothing, owning nothing, and selling nothing? Is it Jerry's silent backlash against all of the hot deals that have made his funds money this year? He will put his order in for 26,000 E-Tek shares, alongside his orders for theglobe.com, Internet America, and every other World Wide Web deal he can get his hands on in the closing weeks of 1998. But, as he eats his sandwich and looks out over the industrial railyard of the train station, and the Franklin Field football stadium that was built for the University of Pennsylvania back in 1922, it is some small satisfaction to Jerry that some businesses are doing it "the old-fashioned way."

And, in the new-fashioned way of Wall Street, E-Tek will begin trading for $12 a share two weeks later, raising more than $48 million for the company and its founders. Jerry Frey's E-Tek shares jump more than $24 in one day and add $365,000 profit to his fund.

* * *

"Everybody got the numbers? So you're comfortable with those?" Jerry asks the group as they get settled around the table. "I'd say the rally has brought valuations pretty much back to where they were. So, it's just been a rearranging of deck chairs on the *Titanic*."

"How about just 'on the boat?'" Steve suggests.

"No, I think the *Titanic* is apt," says Marshall.

The group discusses the meeting of the Federal Reserve Board tomorrow morning and the effect on the stock market of the all-powerful words and actions of Alan Greenspan.

"You know what they say, 'Don't fight the Fed,'" Jerry says. "So, if you're thinking of buying something and you're not sure, you might want to wait 'til tomorrow." If you want it, buy it. If you're unsure, let's see what the Fed does first.

Most nod, and Lori continues to suck on a cherry-red Blowpop.

"Deals. If it's an Internet stock, do it. I don't care what it is, just put us in it."

"Did we do the one on Friday?" Marshall asks.

"theglobe?" Lori adds.

"Yeah, we did that one, but we didn't do the other one," Jerry says. It is late in the race, and Internet deals are simply "this one" and "that one." "Speaking of deals, Ticketmaster is coming out. It sounds like a pretty warm deal, and USA Networks may run off this, so don't be surprised if that takes off going into this."

"Yeah, we've got a big piece of USA Networks," Marshall says, letting the boss know that he's already done his homework, and if the deal flies, he's already halfway toward home plate.

"Dave Adams called me on Acxiom," Jerry says. Just one of hundreds of calls from a salesman on just one of hundreds of stocks.

"What did he say?"

"Oh, I don't know."

"He was probably calling to ask *you* a few questions on it."

"He was calling because he's looking out for his commissions. He used Acxiom as a way to get into your voicemail," offers John.

Jerry laughs at the suggestion. "Yeah, he's been paid $36,000 this year, and he was paid $469,000 last year." This year, the salesman's firm has been sent only a fraction of the trades Delaware sent them in the past, and now he'd like to get his name out there and get those cash registers ringing again.

"The only stock he's called me on this year was Action Performance," Marshall says.

"Little toy cars?" Jerry asks.

"Little toy cars," Marshall says, laying both hands open on the table for the group to see. The empty hands seem to ask, "Is this a stock tip worth $469,000?" The silent gesture says, "There is nothing more to say."

*   *   *

The next day, a few minutes before the market opens, Jerry is delivering some of the most critical words he has offered anyone in the office in months. He is addressing a piece of promotional literature written by the marketing department regarding the growth group.

"This is a selling document," Jerry says, holding the one-page printout in front of him, as he takes a "Let me explain your business to you" tone. The over-eager marketing guy stands next to Jerry silently. He keeps his eyes focused squarely on the page, and doesn't raise his gaze to meet Jerry's. He hardly blinks as he listens to the swelling lecture.

"This is a selling document," Jerry repeats. "And I can't find any reason in here to buy small caps."

To use the marketer's own words against him, Jerry reads the first paragraph of the sales pitch aloud, emphasizing those words that are decidedly less, well, salesy. ". . . worsened . . . difficulties . . . troubling . . . stumbling. . . ."

"You read this and you think the world's ending. Yes, on an absolute basis, things are down, but on a relative basis, we're doing really well." Jerry thrusts the paper back, like a disgusted parent or teacher reading a plagiarized encyclopedia entry. "So why don't you take this back and rework it into something a little more positive. This is a selling document. It's not your tombstone. It's not something written in stone you're gonna do a dirge for."

The marketing guy leaves Jerry's office without uttering a word.

Jerry has spoken and the scales have tipped. He wants to sell. He wants to win. There will be no hedging along the march to the end of the year. Real businesses are built by people making products and selling them. Real businesses are not built by hedging, using mathematical formulas, being conservative, and trying to outguess the next moves of an intangible and unpredictable stock market. The only way Jerry knows to do business is to follow his gut, do what he knows how to do, and succeed. To get in the game and play his hardest until the clock runs out. Then look up at the scoreboard, and see if it was enough.

* * *

On the day of the Fed's November meeting, the market opens down and continues to fall for much of the morning. The fog outside Jerry's window obscures his view up much of the Schuylkill River. It is a gray day, and he has turned the lights on before the market opens. This is a rare move; Jerry usually keeps his lights off until he can barely read his screen, even in winter.

"Stu thinks he's gonna cut rates," Jerry says, looking at the falling numbers on his screen. It is another of many debates he will start with himself as he sorts out the issues, discerns what is in his gut, and makes a decision. "But, if he doesn't cut it today, he'll have to cut it next time. If he doesn't cut it, he knows the market will react, and that's bad. If a bad stock market affects consumer psychology, that could be bad for the economy and spending—especially heading into the Christmas season. Plus, Al Gore does *not* want to run with a recession going on. A lot of this is driven by politics. If you look back, in the periods before an election, the Fed is pretty accommodating."

He pauses before making his assessment. "I think I'll get myself convinced he's gonna cut rates." Another pause, as the ramifications of such a conviction settle in. "Where's my shopping list?"

Jerry finds the listings of his funds' holdings, and goes through each one line by line, starting with the largest positions first. Where would he like to beef up a holding? Where does he think he might get a little extra movement in a rally? Where might some extra cushion in interest rates make a difference in profits? If interest rates go down, where might consumer confidence and spending pick up? Should the group try to play off Americans' buying new houses or cars? Or load up on restaurant stocks, counting on more people eating out? He pulls out a stack of research from his briefcase. As he flips through pages of charts, he clicks his keyboard and mouse before turning each page. Soon he reaches the bottom of the paper on his notepad. The page is filled with tickers on one side and corresponding share numbers to buy in a second column. The paper is marked off methodically into three sections by straight lines he has drawn, assigning the trades to the three funds. These notes are the blueprints for his funds—calculations on where to build, fix, and polish. With a last glance at the computer screen at 10:45, he lays his bets on a rate cut from Alan Greenspan at 2:15 this afternoon. He walks up to the trading desk to deliver his wish list.

At 2:14 the Dow is down 70 points. Many of the growth group's largest holdings are down for the day.

By 2:18, the market is back up. The Fed has made its announcement. Alan Greenspan and the Fed have agreed to a quarter-of-a-point cut in the interest rate. When the announcement is made, Jerry is sitting at his conference table listening to a medical device analyst from CS First Boston. He doesn't get up to check whether the news has come across his screen, nor has he asked Geri to let him know if it does. He has made his bet. The money is spent. It will either be the right thing to do or the wrong thing to do, and it matters none whether Jerry is there to watch it on the screen.

Nearly an hour after the news is released, the Dow is up 74 points and Jerry is basking in the glow of having made the right bet. He stands at Geri's desk eating dry popcorn from a plastic bag. He rarely partakes in the group's snacks that are stationed on the shelf in front of Geri's desk, even though Geri and Lea buy the $1 popcorn bags, Swedish Fish, peanut M&Ms, lollipops, and hard candies with cash Jerry has given them. But today he stands leaning against the desk, eating handful after handful of popcorn, and talking of Alan Greenspan to all who will listen.

"Greenspan always said that one of the real pockets of inflation is the stock market. So, why should he go and do the stock market a big favor, when he could just leave rates alone and cut them in January if he wants to? No matter what the last few months have felt like or where small caps are right now, the market is still up big. The S&P is still up nearly 20 percent—and that is *not* an insignificant number. So then I got myself convinced he wasn't going to cut rates. I was really waffling, thinking I shouldn't have gone ahead and bought all those shares. But then I looked in the paper, and I saw that the October manufacturing numbers were down for the fourth or fifth month in a row."

It was one more data point to help Jerry decide where his stocks, his strategies, and his gut fit into the overall market and the economy at large. So indeed, according to Jerry's logic, Greenspan's rate cut wouldn't be a favor to the stock market; it was a favor to big industry—they needed the boost. Alan Greenspan would give it to them, and Jerry Frey would be in line to collect any scraps that might fall.

* * *

The news of the day—splashed across the front page of *The New York Times* and *The Wall Street Journal*—is the passing of the first generation of the Internet: America Online is making a bid to buy Netscape. The wonder-IPO that started it all, the creation of the boy computer geek and the middle-aged entrepreneur, the American success story of the 1990s. It was now just another buyout candidate. After going public in the fall of 1995 in the most talked about IPO to date, Netscape the company and Netscape the myth were to be snuffed out by America Online.

Jerry looks through his morning telephone calls and starts checking tickers. "American Online, now it's up two. Netscape, up two. Sun, up three. It can't be good for Microsoft. Oh, it's up two. They're all up. And what stock benefits from all of this and does the best?" he calls out like a game show host as he continues typing in tickers, "Amazon.com, up 6 at 197."

The market continues to bounce with up days and down days as the calendar marches on. There are more deals announced and more pronouncements made about the difficult Christmas season. The Aggressive Growth Fund is up two days and then down a day, up another three and down two. It is still unclear whether pulling out all the stops and going for it is the right decision. There are five weeks left, and Jerry may yet need those hedges and collars and big cash positions that he tossed aside like so many burdensome safety nets, harnesses, and extra oxygen tanks on the climb to the top.

"The market is right back up to the peaks of July—but it didn't break through. So the question is, will it be a double top?" Jerry says to himself, as he looks at one of the many strategic printouts and historical charts that have crossed his desk in the past week. A straight line connects the two points where the market has peaked. The bold black line seems to ask, "Will the market break through this line and keep going higher, or will it fall back down, after peaking twice—creating a double top?"

"Certainly, it didn't seem that there was any reason for Monday to be an outsized day. I looked at my screen and thought, 'Good God, why is it up like this?' There was no reason for it to be up so big," Jerry says and shakes his head.

A lot of money managers are superstitious. They are constantly being bombarded with charts, historical research, predictions, estimates, new names for old phenomena, and boxed-in explanations for unexplainable forces. Some rely on mathematical formulas to predict the movement of the stock market; others turn to astrology, the winner of the Superbowl, or the length of women's skirts, to determine the direction of the Dow. It is no surprise to see a money manager show more concern on the upside than he or she does on the downside. There is little interest in explanation on the downside—losing money is enough. But on the upside, there had better be explanations for how that money is being made—or it is feared to be the quiet stillness masking the approach of a destructive storm.

* * *

It is the day before Thanksgiving, one of the last trading days of the month. Jerry is sorting through research and prospectuses on his bookshelf. Like the rest of Wall Street, he is trying to clear out some business before the holidays.

Jeff stops in to show him a fake $1 bill with a rendering of Bill Clinton in place of George Washington, and the words "In Monica

We Trust" printed across the front. "Oh, and did I tell you about this Xoom.com?" Jeff asks. "It's an Internet roll-up. They're going public so they can go out and buy up a bunch of little Internet businesses and build a business. Apparently the deal is white hot."

"Put us in it. If it's white hot, we want in," Jerry says, hardly looking up from his stack of mail. Sometimes you look for a concrete business. Sometimes white hot will do. The end of the year is just one month away. It is not a time for deep analysis.

Jeff protests. "This thing is such a piece of shit."

"That's okay. We don't have to hold it long."

CHAPTER **11**

YOU CAN MAKE
ONE MISTAKE, OR
YOU CAN MAKE
TWO MISTAKES

"So, everyone's seen the numbers? Anyone have any complaints about the numbers?" It is the first Monday in December, one of the last times the growth group will sit together around Jerry's conference table to strategize and talk about the numbers for 1998.

December 4, 1998		
	Year-to-Date	
	Performance	Rank
Aggressive Growth	23.6%	16
Trend	6.1%	20
Delcap	8.6%	43
Dow	14.0%	
S&P 500	23.0%	
Nasdaq	27.6%	

After eleven months and six days, the scorecard shows the Delaware Aggressive Growth Fund to be in sixteenth place for the year. The Trend Fund is also in the top 20 of its peer group. But the last of the funds, the DelCap Fund, the thorn in the group's side all year long, ended last week as number 43 out of 100 competing funds. Number 43 itself didn't sound all that stirring, but the fund had been number 77 and had moved up 34 spots during the year, an impressive gain in a competitive industry where every step up the ladder means pushing against hundreds of other funds.The team didn't necessarily expect it to be in the top 10, or even in the top 25; they simply felt that, during the year, they had worked harder on the fund than the numbers showed. And perhaps their work might not show up in the one number that counts: bonus.

If DelCap fell below the top 50 competitive funds on December 31, there would be no performance bonus for an entire year's work on the fund. Thanks for the effort, better luck next year.

"DelCap's had a nice couple of weeks here," Steve offers.

"I want DelCap to do worse, then I'd understand why I'm not getting paid," John says.

"You are getting paid. We're in the money on that one," Jerry points out.

"I want all the money on that one. We deserve it."

Jerry turns the meeting to talk about specific stocks and the importance of putting to work any new cash that comes into the funds over the next few weeks. He tells the group he'll be having lunch in the boardroom with the new CEO of Delaware, "Anything you guys want me to say? Anything you need?"

They look around at each other, shrugging a bit, until Steve breaks the pause with a smile. "Money! Am I allowed to say it?"

"Sure you're allowed to say it. I've got to find a way to slip it in— not quite as obvious as you."

The others join in asking for more marketing support—more salespeople focused on the growth funds. It's an oft-played complaint among Jerry and the rest of the group. They run the top-performing funds at the firm and have some of the best numbers in the industry, yet the group feels that Delaware's salesforce can't seem to get anyone interested in buying more.

"We're here. Sell our funds. Buy our funds. Somebody, please, buy our funds," Marshall implores.

Jerry knows that these pleas don't necessarily mean, "We need more money because there are so many great companies out there, I've got to get investing. Send us your checks, help us support corporate America." No, a closer translation would be, "We need more money, because the more money our funds bring into the firm, the more fees we can collect. Send us your checks, help us support ourselves."

So Jerry moves right back to the issue that is on the mind of every group member during the last month of the year. "I talked to Dick about the possibility of going to a straight revenue-sharing model. There are some big negatives to that. Some huge upside, but there are risks, too." Such a plan would mean that, instead of doling out higher bonuses to the growth group out of gratefulness or goodwill, the firm would be required to give the group a certain portion of all of the new checks and all the new fees it helped bring in. But, if the market had a difficult year and the funds didn't attract new money, there would be no new revenue to share.

"It's insulting to me that in a year we've done incredibly well, they're looking for a way to pay us less." The diatribe from the group continues. It's easy to be vehement, confident, and demanding sitting around the conference table. They are like the little dogs yipping behind the bully in a fight, "Yeah, hit 'em again. I wouldn't let 'em get away with that."

"Pretty soon we're gonna be bumping into Christmas here, but, before everyone takes off, we should get together for Geri and Lea." Jerry reminds the group not to get so busy worrying about their own bonuses that they forget gifts for the assistants. "I did succeed in beating human resources into getting bonuses for them."

"I looked into gift certificates and found out where they each shop," Lori suggests.

For the past two years, Jerry has written bonus checks for the assistants from his personal checkbook. He knows that a lot of things can't be covered with gift certificates, so he agrees to the certificates in addition to cash this year. "How about a holiday lunch? Does anybody want to do that? Is that any fun?"

"Well, Ebenezer, I don't know," John says.

"To do it, it's got to be a very *fine* restaurant, or it's not even worth it," says Marshall.

They toss out five-star restaurant suggestions and look for days that aren't already booked with lunch meetings.

"We got a load of deals coming this week, and there's a lot of talk out there that the calendar is loaded after the New Year. That's why we're just trying to get through this year and deal with next year next year."

"Ain't it the truth." Marshall whistles and picks up the performance sheet to read off the standings for their three funds.

"Number 10 for the last three months; number 28, three months; and number 30, three months."

"Don't remind me. I'll start thinking about bonuses again, and I just got over that."

"And revenue sharing is: You share your revenue with us," Marshall quips back.

"Yeah. What's yours is ours, and what's ours is still ours." Jerry smiles.

"Yeah. What's yours is ours, and what's ours is our wives'." When he looks around and sees Lori, Marshall adds, "and husbands'."

With that, the group disperses.

*   *   *

Others in the group are consumed with the immediate concerns of this year's bonus and the numbers that will appear on their checks in three weeks, but Jerry has moved on. His concern is the bonuses for next year. He knows that he can do little to control what numbers will appear on the checks, but he can have some sway over the potential of what those numbers can be. He has kept his calendar busy with marketing meetings and sales pitches criss-crossing the country. The more people, companies, and pension plans that sign checks over to the growth group, the more money he will have to manage. And, if the firm approves the revenue-sharing plan he is pushing, there will be a bigger pie from which to cut pieces for the team.

Just this morning, an officer of the retirement plan for the city of Nashville called to let Delaware know that Jerry's group didn't get the business he had come down to compete for last month. It was a close contest, but they decided to put their millions into somebody else's pie.

"Before I went into the meeting, I was thinking, Nashville's a little bit conservative. So I told them, 'We are fully diversified. We invest in technology, but we aren't loaded up in the Internet and only chasing high fliers." The performance numbers are printed in black and white on the page, as are the resumes of the group's members. But marketing is all in the couching, the phrasing; you've got to sell them what they want. You've got to make a bet on what they want and sell yourself as exactly that. "The guy that went in after us told

them exactly the opposite. 'We love the Internet. We're in every single one of them.' They won."

An hour before the market closes, Jerry calls the trading desk to
check in. "Vinny? Do you guys get this research from Triad? They
say there are 23 deals coming out this week. They say about seven of
them are good—AboveNet, ExchangeApps, Global Networks, Infinity, InfoSpace.com—that's H&Q, so I probably have an interest in
that one—Internet America, Xoom.com—someone says that looks like
it's really good. The only two I'm really interested in are ExchangeApps and Infinity. The others I just want to be in if I can get a
lot of stock and if it looks hot."

Maybe next time, Jerry will be able to look across a conference
table at a multimillion-dollar account that is dangling in front of his
fund and sell himself, "We love the Internet. We're in every single
one of them."

Still on with Vinny, Jerry gets more specific. "Infinity. What was
the pricing range on the prospectus?" He opens up his calculator and
punches in a few numbers. "Okay, get me 125,000 shares."

Having just given an order to spend a quick $2.6 million, Jerry
calls his buddy back home. "Stew? . . . No, I didn't go. I got a doe
permit, want to go with me? . . . It's easy, you get yourself some hot
chocolate, some cookies, you sit on a rock and wait for one to run by,
then you blast 'em."

It's a little, or a lot, like this season of Internet IPOs. You get
yourself in a hot deal, sit in front of your computer screen and wait
for it to run up, then call your trading desk and have 'em blast it out.

"Oh yeah, buck? Anybody get any? . . . Coach got one? . . . It
was probably somebody's dog with antlers. . . . Yeah, maybe I'll
come up on Friday and go out for the last day on Saturday."

* * *

On a Tuesday afternoon in late December, Jerry puts on his black
cashmere overcoat and walks the six blocks to Philadelphia's Ritz-
Carlton. The center of the lobby is adorned with a train and ginger-
bread house display for the holidays, and soothing music and the
scent of pine boughs and trees permeate the halls. Jerry loiters outside the double doors of Salon Three, one of the Ritz ballrooms,

which has been partitioned off to serve as a presentation room for the Winter Sales Conference of Delaware Investment's wholesale brokers. It's essentially a refresher course on the selling rules and regulations, a motivational seminar to get the brokers selling into 1999, and a pat-on-the-back trip to Philadelphia and the company Christmas party for about 95 salespeople.

The group meanders out in the hall during a break between meetings: They snack on soft pretzels, pastry selections, and the mini ten-ounce soft-drink bottles that seem to be manufactured for the sole purpose of being sold to hotels for conferences and meetings exactly like this one. The attendees joke casually with one another and make disparaging comments about each other—as a group of competitive, friendly salespeople who are spending a week together are wont to do. They will spend nine hours listening to explanations of new insurance channels, retirement services, and financial planner opportunities, and they will listen to seven hours of presentations on Delaware's new positioning and marketing campaign and compensation schedule. Interspersed with these required lectures and question-and-answer series are six hours of presentations by the managers of Delaware's mutual funds—the showcase for the products. They've been taught how to sell, how not to sell, and how they'll be paid for what they sell. And now, finally, a glimpse at *what* they are to sell—the jewels behind doors number one, two, and three.

For the fund managers, it's their semiannual chance to get up in front of the sales force and shine. To show off, strut, and demand some respect. In this industry, the product, the mutual funds, and, at the head of those, the mutual fund managers, give these companies—and their salespeople—their entire reason for existence. As many a fund manager is quick to point out—they are It. They often come to these events grudgingly, not wanting to squander their time on these peons; they will come late to prove their superiority and the demands on their time. Yet, once the microphone is turned on and the charts light up the big screen at the front of the ballroom, the managers succumb to the adoration and the opportunity to swagger. Usually, early on in these presentations, the manager displays a slide that shows his or her performance for the year, which is, of course, decidedly ahead of whatever competing fund or index is displayed on the same slide. Essentially, the slide lets a reserved professional unzip his Brooks Brothers fly to say, "See, mine's bigger than theirs." A manager will often linger longer on this slide than on most others. To be fair, it is also the slide that the voyeuristic audience is most interested in.

Jerry, after nearly twenty years in the investment business and on the verge of finishing the year with the number-one fund in all of Delaware Investments, is still uncomfortable at these presentations. He is early, and he spends the minutes milling about in the hallway, not drawing any attention to himself. He is like a substitute teacher called in to fascinate a roomful of students who would rather be somewhere else, and who answer to someone else. By 2:45, the students have been corralled back into the ballroom. As the hours and meetings have ticked by, the group has shifted from the front rows of long tables and straight-backed chairs to those nearer to the back of the room—and the door, and the free sodas, and the sugar-laden pastries, and the bowl of ever-present cellophane-wrapped, white-and-red-striped hotel mints.

The presentation begins when the first slide flashes onto the large white screen standing just under the shimmering Ritz-Carlton crystal chandelier. The slide is titled simply, "Growth Funds." Jerry begins his speech with what he would claim qualifies as a joke, "Why small companies?" The requisite dramatic pause. "As this has been my career for the last few years, I've wondered that myself." A handful of people laugh, but few loud enough for Jerry to hear from the podium. He'll have to win them another way.

Looking out over the crowd of brokers waiting for his pitch, he can hear the marketing department's pleas to enroll him in presentation school. In a commanding voice, he tries to punch out a few short statements to grab their attention. "It is not a sci-fi fund. We are not 100 percent Internet. We are not 90 percent biotech." He is speaking quickly, and his voice echoes throughout the room. In his freshman year of college, Jerry's fear of making just such presentations forced him to argue his way out of a required speech class. After pleading with the teacher that he hated public speaking, he wouldn't do it, and would surely fail the course if he took it, the instructor took heed. Jerry had to assure him he would not become a teacher—presumably, the only profession Jerry, a math major, could have considered that would have put him in front of a crowd. No, Jerry promised. He would go into accounting, or engineering, or economics, and not force anyone to listen to him stumble and stammer. Now, twenty-three years later, Jerry is trying to win over a crowd of essentially professional speakers—people who get paid to talk.

"August 1998. We can all remember back that far, can't we?" Only Dinah, one of the Delaware organizers of the event, laughs. At least she's sitting in the front row. Glasses clink with ice, and the hiss of carbonation bubbles rising to the surface can be heard between Jerry's words. People are flipping ahead in their bound presentation booklets, impatient for Jerry to answer the question, "Anything exciting to come?"

"Average P/E. I think this is an interesting chart. It shows that the implied earnings growth rates of the underlying securities. . . . " Even the public speaking course may not have helped.

With the flash of the slide titled "Aggressive Growth Fund," Jerry's confidence and delivery begin to improve. "Potentially, this is the single best asset within Delaware." He goes on to explain some of the basic statistics of the fund and then turns to the inherent riskiness of an aggressive growth fund. "Don't take your grandmother's last dollar and put it into this fund. In the first six trading days of October, we were down 20 percent." The crowd gasps, perhaps not so much at the sheer magnitude of this disastrous performance, but at the fact that he would actually admit it—draw attention to it in front of a crowd. "And in the last twenty trading days of October, we were up 30 percent." Another round of gasps.

"It is emerging growth, not submerging growth." This is exactly the kind of phrase salespeople look for, to take back and work into their pitch to customers. The crowd sits straighter in their chairs and leans in to catch more of the gems Jerry might accidentally roll down the center aisle of the Ritz ballroom. "The outlook for small caps remains strong for the rest of '98 and heading into '99—much more so than large caps. . . . The biggest near-term risk is earnings disappointment. . . . I think the potential for change in leadership to smaller-cap issues may just be wishful thinking on the part of small-cap managers. . . . We're putting a lot less emphasis on health care. It's not that I'm prejudiced against health care; I'm getting older along with everyone else."

Someone asks about the tax concerns with the fund. A salesman wants to know: Does aggressive growth mean aggressive trading? Are you constantly buying and selling stocks for quick profits for which, in the end, the government is going to be calling on the individual shareholders to foot the tax bill?

"Turnover in the Aggressive Growth Fund is about 150 percent." To most people in the crowd, this probably sounds like some fast trading. Most funds turn over—or trade all of their assets—closer to 100 percent, or one time a year, as opposed to Jerry and his team's 1½ times every year. "If someone gave me a rate of return of 30 percent, sure it'd be nice to have that in an IRA and keep all of it. But really, if someone's giving me 30 percent returns, I'll pay my taxes and walk away." You've got to pay to play, boys and girls.

As Jerry nears the end of his 45-minute presentation, a salesman raises his hand to ask the inevitable question in a gathering of stockbrokers. "How about any specific names in the fund?" We've listened patiently to your spiel, now give us the goods. Something we can take back to our branch offices, bandy about at cocktail parties, and offer up to clients over the phone.

They've been warming to him in the latter half of his presentation; Jerry can sense this from the podium, and he decides to clinch it. To claim the crowd as his. "Amazon.com. It's one of those stocks we did extremely right at the very beginning." Take that home with your complimentary Delaware sweatshirt and see how many brokers offering plain vanilla mutual funds can match it.

* * *

Later in the week, the group of brokers returns for the final hours of training, review, and inspiration. After the last presentation on the firm's new ad campaign, the event's planners get up to present awards to various groups of salespeople who competed in contests throughout the week. "We're moving from the gunslinger approach to the assassin model for sales this year." The theme of the week was "Get Smarter in 1999." The theme song to the old television show *Get Smart* plays while the planners hand out certificates to the blue group. In the back of the room, a slight blond man in a navy sweatsuit and running shoes stretches to the side of the audio-visual table. He is mostly hidden from view by a rolling cart stacked with three-inch-thick Delaware Investment three-ring binders. Although he is well under six feet tall, when he stretches, the man continually bumps his head on the crystal sconce attached to the wall behind him.

Within minutes, he is out from behind the rolling cart, out of his warm-up suit, and standing in tight white leggings and a tank top. He dusts his hands with chalk in the back of the room, as a video announces the week's motivational speaker: "The 1984 captain of the men's U.S. Gymnastics team, and one of the few people to score a 10 on the pommel horse . . . Peter Vidmar." The crowd claps enthusiastically as he bounds down the center aisle of the Ritz-Carlton ballroom.

The exterior gap between a gymnast in a navy tank top with one hand on a pommel horse and his eyes on Olympic gold, and a roomful of khaki and button-down clad brokers who usually have their hands on a telephone receiver and their eyes on the Dow Jones Industrial Average is obvious. Peter tries to bridge that gap with his very first statements. "A 9.4 is not gonna get you there. A 9.4 is gonna make you one of the crowd."

Quickly, Peter moves on to the main point of his talk, and couches it in a term that business folk and market watchers are most prepared to receive—an acronym. It is something they can file away with investment staples like ROI, EPS, GARP, PE, and EBIT. "It's what we call ROV. Risk, originality, virtuosity. These are the areas that can raise you from a 9.4 to a 10."

First, he addresses the component that the brokers are most conversant in: risk. "Taking risks in my sport involves mistakes. Risk says I have to take chances. You know there's always someone else who's willing to take chances. If you just do it clean, that's not good enough. Without risk, you can only get to a 9.8. Without risk, you can't go all the way."

Peter cites examples, in recent Olympics, of the margins of making it and not. In one of the women's cycling competitions, after 50 miles of pedaling, the race was decided at the finish line. The difference between winning the gold and not was one inch. In a men's swimming event, the difference that meant a silver medal instead of a gold for Matt Biondi was one-one-hundredth of a second. Or, perhaps, Peter points out, the difference between Matt Biondi's clipping his fingernails the night before and not.

Peter interrupts his speech to demonstrate his points more dramatically with the help of his gold-medal-winning prop, the pommel horse, which has been positioned at the front of the ballroom. The crowd stares intently as he spins his lower body faster and faster, remembering to lift and alternate his arms, allowing every sweep of his legs to pass through. It is a program that, in total, is choreographed to show originality, virtuosity, and, of course, risk. Ultimately, it is a demonstration for which Delaware has paid $7,500 to *motivate*. For this purpose, Peter Vidmar is an excellent choice. Not only is he an Olympic gold medal winner, which, in its own right, has been enough to put many athletes on the endorsement and corporate speaking circuit, but Peter has also had professional training in selling, motivating, and changing the way people think about what they do. For five years, Peter taught seminars for Franklin Covey. To those not acquainted with Franklin Covey, it is seen as simply another day planner, a name-brand calendar and expensive organizer. To those who have taken the company's courses and implemented the "Franklin Covey system" into their lives, it can be almost a religion. For those who have invested in the stock, the company has meant a successful IPO in 1992 at $15.50 a share, and a jump to $24 a share when the company merged with Stephen Covey and his best-selling book, *7 Habits of Highly Successful People,* five years later. Sure, there's risk, originality, and virtuosity. But there's also the market.

"In gymnastics, the power-to-weight ratio is very important. . . . Someone that can make themselves look bigger than they are—that's the key to a good artist," Vidmar instructs. "In gymnastics, you need fast twitch explosive muscle response. . . . You can't have both. You can't have endurance and you can't be quick and explosive at the same time."

*   *   *

In Jerry's funds, he needs to try to have both. He needs a stable of core stocks to help him keep up with the market and contribute to enduring, long-term performance. But he also needs an explosive burst or two to push him past the competition. He needs a few IPOs, a couple of takeouts, and just one Amazon.com.

Within minutes of the market's opening bell this December morning, shares of Amazon traded up $45 a share. For most stocks, such a move would make for a stellar year. But in Amazon.com, it's often just a few minutes' ride, and it spins fewer heads than it used to. The stock is trading at $275 a share now, and Jerry's eyes are focused squarely on his screen.

A Wall Street analyst covering Amazon had released a report predicting a price target of $400 a share for the stock. The report sent the shares into such a wild trading frenzy that the analyst had to issue follow-up comments just a few hours later: "Our new target of $400 is a one-year price target, not a near-term price target."

With two weeks to go until the end of the year, Jerry is concerned with the near term. "Vinny? Buy me another 1,000 shares of Amazon."

"Oh man, that takes balls. To sell it and then come back and buy it up 100 points. That takes balls."

"Well, you can make one mistake, or you can make two mistakes. You can sell it and never buy it back, or you can admit you were wrong and buy it back up. Most people would never buy it back after they've sold out and watched it get away from them." The coach's lesson for the day imparted, Jerry ends his call to Vinny with a challenge, "Oh, and Vinny, bottom-tick it."

"It's up already," Vinny says in a high voice and laughs—you're crazy if you think I'm gonna get the low price of the day. You just gave me the order and it's already up.

"Well then, get in there." And Jerry's receiver goes back into its carriage.

Just before noon, he calls to see if Vinny got in there. Stu reports that the trade was made. Jerry bought 1,000 shares at $281. Not exactly bottom-ticking it, but the stock is already up to $293. That's $12,000 in just two hours. Time for a lunch break.

*　*　*

Jerry and the growth group walk together to Susanna Foo, an upscale Asian restaurant that is high on the list of Philadelphia's expense-account lunch and dinner spots. It's a Christmas lunch that Jerry wanted to take the group to—whether it got cleared on his expense account or not. As they seat themselves around a large rectangular table in a private room at the back of the restaurant, Jerry puts Marshall in charge of ordering the wine.

"Yes, I find food is often a nice accompaniment to wine," Marshall quips.

Once the orders for hors d'oeuvres, main courses, and drinks have been placed, Jerry pulls a piece of notepaper from his jacket pocket. He smoothes out the tri-folded lined paper and announces that he has "some little projects for everyone to work on. Things to keep in mind for next year. Things to improve on." A few of the team look at each other. They are unsure what to expect. Work at lunch?

"Geri, you've got to relax a little more. Don't be so uptight." They laugh a little. It's still not entirely clear whether this is a joke. Maybe Jerry couldn't think of a real project for the assistants, but he didn't want to leave them out? But, then again, Geri has her job, the group, and the office so under control that she relaxes easily.

"Lea, when Geri's out, don't be so blasé about things. There's a lot going on. Things that have to get done. You've got to start taking this job seriously." Now they know it's a joke. Lea is the kind of conscientious employee who lets you know when she's going to get a drink from the water fountain.

"Steve, you've got to, at any chance you get, attack Marshall."

"Marshall, any chance *you* get, attack Steve."

"Lori, you need to learn the difference between Tapas and top-less." They all laugh and Lori defends her confusion over a broker's suggesting a Tapas restaurant for dinner last week.

"John, you need to get room-darkening shades for your office so that when you and Steve want to have meetings behind closed doors, people can *really* wonder what goes on."

"Jeff, you've got to be a little more excited about some of your stocks. And you've got to start talking about them to anyone who will listen."

The group is enjoying itself and its success. The wine has been poured and the holidays are just days away. The team is the top in the firm and has a chance to be one of the finest in the field. They have all given their best during the year, and their coach has just acknowledged their contributions and accomplishments in the most sincere way he knows how. Jerry is enjoying his position in the middle of the table. He is confident, he is funny, he is well-liked—everything he was *not*, at yesterday's presentation to the brokers.

Banter remains light and upbeat. They continue teasing each other and knocking other fund managers. John mentions a competitor who trades her fund by the estimates on Whispernumber.com.

"Yeah, that's why she's banging the numbers like a sailor," Marshall says.

While eating his plate of prawns, Jerry brings up the subject of summer jobs. "I delivered milk one summer."

John offers that he worked in an orange juice factory.

Jerry lobs back, "I worked in an artificial insemination lab."

"And your role was?" John asks. The group breaks up laughing. "Inducement specialist?"

"You ever say things you wish you could just take back?"

"Inducement engineer?" asks Marshall.

"Yep, if you could just reel those words back in."

*　*　*

Back at his desk Jerry checks his computer screen. "American Online, up 4½."

Just after 2:30, Marshall comes in, snapping his fingers, "Jack Henry Associates."

John follows just behind, "That makes up for Snyder Communications."

"Snyder's down again?" Jerry asks and types the ticker into the computer.

John tells him that he's buying more. It's his way of letting Jerry know that he's been listening all these months. He's learning the lessons. If you believe in it, use the dips to buy more. Strengthen your position. If it's not a buy, it's a sell.

"Why don't you wait for a block to come up," Jerry says. Yes, I see you've been listening. But there's still more to learn. I think I'll sit in this corner office a little while longer.

Marshall says he wants to buy more Jack Henry, "It's doing well. Should I put it in Aggressive or Trend?"

"It all goes into Aggressive." Jerry is careful to alternate fairly among the group's three growth funds as to which one gets the hot stocks, the IPOs, or the stocks they know are doing well. DelCap and Trend have had their turns, now it's time for Aggressive Growth. Besides, the Aggressive Growth Fund could use the extra ammunition right now. There are less than two weeks to go in the year, and the fund has been struggling to keep its position in the ranking charts. It could use the push just to keep up. If it gets a big enough push and keeps rolling, the next two weeks could move the fund back up to the spot where it has spent most of the year: number one.

"299¼." Jerry looks up from his screen. Marshall pauses, not knowing which direction Jerry's mind and computer screen have turned.

"Amazon.com. God, that stock's amazing."

Marshall exits, leaving the position in front of Jerry's desk open for Steve to take up ten minutes later.

Just as Steve is about to speak, Jerry looks up from his screen, taps his pen on his teeth, and says, "301."

Steve pauses.

Jerry squints at him and taps his teeth a few more times, waiting for the answer to his *Jeopardy*-style riddle, "And the stock is?"

"301? Amazon.com?"

"Up 58."

"And most importantly, we own it, right?"

* * *

On the Friday before Christmas, Jerry is going over the printouts of all of the stock holdings in the funds. He stumbles over the price of Network Solutions. On the sheet, it's listed as $12, and the fund's purchase price is listed as $110 a share. It doesn't exactly appear to be one of the group's most stellar investments. But Jerry knows that, in reality, the stock closed last night at $112 instead of $12. Rather than just write it off as a computer mistake that will likely correct itself by tomorrow's printout, with no one else noticing, Jerry is concerned.

He's not worried that the mistake underestimates his own performance numbers for the day. He figures those dollars and the extra performance points will catch up with him. He worries about the people those extra performance numbers may not catch up with—individual shareholders who may have sold the funds yesterday and been paid less for their shares than they were actually worth. Rather than taking the goodbye, good riddance approach to anyone who would even think of selling out of his funds, Jerry thinks, "Thanks so much for playing—did we get you all of your change?" Jerry, who still spends much of his leisure hours with people who follow the doe and buck seasons more closely than they do the fiscal calendar, sees it as his responsibility to look out for the people. They are never classified as "the little people," they are simply people. Investors. Shareholders. They hold a share in this fund, and they have a share in everything he does, every day.

At the group's holiday luncheon, Jerry had left the fortune from his chocolate-dipped cookie sitting on the table: "The will of the people is the best law." This is not something of which he needs to be reminded.

* * *

There are two-and-a-half trading days until Christmas, and some members of the growth group have already left town on vacation.

Jerry is at his mountain cottage, where he has cut down and dragged home the holiday tree he picked out the previous weekend. Geri is out for the day, and Lori is considering not coming in the rest of the week. The office is quiet and relaxed, except for Marshall.

"Oh my goodness, it's opening down, oh my goodness, it's opening down." He rolls the introduction to the stock market's opening minutes of trading like he's announcing a horse race, his voice keeping pace with the thoroughbreds as they round the track. "Oh my stars, it's opening down." He stares at his screen for the 90 seconds it takes for the race to be reversed, "Yeah, go baby. Go baby. Good gracious."

He shuffles down the hall in stocking-feet to Steve's office. "I want to show you a stock. Acxiom."

Steve types the ticker into his computer. "Up nine-sixteenths. And you are so excited you can't stand it?"

"The trend is your friend." With that, he shuffles back down the hall to see what other Christmas goodies await him on his computer screen.

∗   ∗   ∗

While Jerry is away with his family, he gets an early Christmas present at work on December 22. Just before five o'clock on the Tuesday before Christmas, Standard & Poor's makes, what is for them, a routine announcement. The company wants clients, news agencies, and stock market officials to know that it will be making a few changes to its most followed and most famous index, the S&P 500.

Although the index is made up of only 500 stocks, Standard & Poor's continually monitors and analyzes thousands of stocks in an effort to choose the very best companies for the index. Throughout the year, it announces those names to be removed and those to be added—those companies that will be snared by the stagehand's net and those that will be put under the spotlight. Of course, being a public company in America has its own standing. But the top 5 percent get to represent everyone else in the S&P 500. And now, five-and-a-half trading days before the final votes are to be counted at the end of the year, the S&P is announcing a change in its voting lineup.

The announcement is a simple and straightforward list of the changes: "Standard & Poor's Financial Information Services will make the following changes . . . America Online (AOL) will replace Venator Group, Inc. (Z) in the S&P 500 Index."

Within minutes, even though the New York Stock Exchange is already closed for business, shares of AOL jump more than $15 in venues where the stock can still be traded. Sure, the announcement that the S&P wants the Internet company to help represent the rest of corporate America is a nice vote of confidence in America Online the company, but the investment community hears a different message. The message is that every fund manager of an S&P Index fund will be doing a lot of buying and selling to keep up with the index. With S&P's announcement, investors know that there will immediately be a very long line of people wanting to buy shares of AOL—specifically, 21 million shares, or $2.9 billion worth of shares of America Online. And the line starts here, at $138 a share.

Jerry and the Aggressive Growth Fund are standing happily on the other side of those red velvet stanchions, holding 48,000 shares of AOL that cost them about $57 apiece. That meant the fund had made $720,000 profit in one day, thanks to the S&P announcement. Note to Jerry Frey and Aggressive Growth Fund team: Put S&P on Christmas card list.

*   *   *

It is the first day back after the Christmas holiday, a weeklong vacation for Jerry. He sits at his desk wearing a plaid wind-resistant golf pullover. He types a few keys just before the market opens, "God, I forgot how to use this thing."

He dials Geri's number for help. "Yeah. I broke my computer. . . . They changed the password? They change it, like, every goddamned ten minutes. You'd think this was the CIA here. All I'm looking at is a bunch of quotes."

Flogged by technology, Jerry pulls a ruler from his desk drawer and uses it to inspect the daily performance sheet, line by line. The task completed, Jerry moves on to cleaning off his bookshelves and his desk. He picks up piles of research, faxes, and prospectuses by the armful. He stands above a small square of open space behind his desk and drops books of research reports with a thud, after he has glanced at the cover page. There is a pile for "keep," "maybe," and "trash." But, given that it is just days before the final bell of 1998, the "maybe" pile will become a "never," and the "keep" will become a "perhaps."

He pulls this week's *Barron's* newspaper from the stack and holds the cover back to take it all in, "Ah! Mary Meeker. Queen of the Net. Is She Too Optimistic?" A picture of Morgan Stanley's Internet research guru stares back at Jerry from the newspaper's cover. "No way," Jerry replies and sets the paper down on his desk. It is not a "maybe" and it is not a "perhaps." The paper will stare back at him from his desk, front and center, just inches from the mouse with which Jerry tries to control his small piece of the stock market.

There are two trading days left in the year. Is he too optimistic?

CHAPTER 12

STAR LIGHT,
STAR BRIGHT

It is the last day of the year. Thursday, December 31, 1998. As on every other trading day, the stock market opens at 9:30 and will not close until 4:00. As on any other weekday, Jerry drives into the office well before the market opens, to get his bearings on his day, his team, his stocks, and the world at large. The winter cold that seems to have taken up long-term residence in the back of Jerry's throat has now laid claim to his stomach, taking most of his appetite from him. For the first time in months, he skips his ritual breakfast of muffin, coffee, and orange juice. Even the thought of a cup of coffee makes his insides hurt. December 31 is no day to be saddled with heartburn. This morning, Jerry dines simply on a bottle of water and one aspirin tablet.

As the last two weeks of the year ticked by, Marshall and Jeff asked for the peer group rankings to be run daily rather than weekly. They do not want to wait seven days to see whether they have moved ahead of or behind the competition. Each morning, before the market even opens,

December 30, 1998		
	Year-to-Date	
	Performance	Rank
Aggressive Growth	33.9%	15
Trend	11.1%	25
Delcap	14.8%	49
Dow	17.3%	
S&P 500	28.9%	
Nasdaq	38.0%	

they want to know where they stand and what challenges lie ahead.

While he waits for the last six-and-a-half hours of trading to begin, Jerry takes another look at his performance sheets—as if by this point he does not know nearly every number on the page to two decimal places. "33.89. That's not a bad number." No, it's not a bad

254

number. In fact, it is a number that is better than the performance numbers of nearly 6,000 other mutual funds. It is 17 percentage points better than the Dow, and five percentage points ahead of the S&P 500. When asked to reflect on the number and his performance for the year, Jerry would say he is satisfied or pleased. He might even go so far as to say he feels "pretty good." But truly proud and thrilled, no. He will admit that, relatively, it's a great number. But, relatively means caveats, conditionals, and comparisons: "It was a really difficult year in the market . . . especially for small caps . . . compared with other growth funds . . . considering how far we've come since October. . . ." Jerry does not want to be great in context. Jerry wants to be great.

Like a sprinter grasping the starting block for push-off at the opening gunshot, Jerry is poised at his mouse and keyboard when 9:30 strikes. He immediately types in several stock tickers one after the other. At each one, he calls up the screen that shows him how many buyers and sellers there are, how many shares they want or do not want, and at what prices. He can get the current prices of all the stocks he owns, and even the current level of the major stock market indexes and indicators, just by watching his main screen, but the lists of buyers and sellers tell him what's behind the main screen. It's a little like skipping over the headlines and turning straight to the box scores. He has little use for the bigger picture at 9:30 in the morning on the last day of the year. This is a day when the details, the shares, and the pennies count. When counted, they add up to a lot.

Jeff comes in to give Jerry his first read on the day, just fifteen minutes into it. "Well, they tried to mark them up on the opening, so we'll see if they stick."

Jerry glances from Jeff back to his screen. So much can change in the time it takes a fleet-footed Jeff to walk the 16 paces from his desk to Jerry's. "They didn't stick."

Already, the Dow and Nasdaq are both down.

Jerry heads up to the trading desk to get a better read on the market's direction.

Vinny is leaning back in his chair with a foot up on the desk. When he needs to check a stock or pickup a call, he lets his leg fall to the floor and the chair springs forward. His business done, he raises his foot back up and the chair angles back.

Stu stands between his own desk and the television set where CNBC will be shown until it is turned off at the end of the day and the end of the year. Stu tosses a small toy made to look like a soccer ball. It's another giveaway from a salesman, or a trader, or some information service courting the business of Delaware's trading desk. It's a squeezable foam ball that's supposed to be used for reducing stress. Stu simply tosses the ball up and down in the air, seemingly for the sheer enjoyment of it.

The two traders will spend much of the day, as they have most other trading days of the year, replaying these same motions. Back and forth, up and down, back and forth, up and down.

"So, anything going on? You think these Internet stocks'll hold? They gonna mark 'em up today?" Jerry asks, as he leans against the filing cabinets that run along the windows behind Stu and Vinny.

"Yeah, I think they're gonna mark 'em up," Stu stops tossing the ball to answer. "I'd be afraid—some of these stocks, up like 200 percent in a year. I mean they've just had phenomenal years."

"What's AOL doing?" Jerry asks, speaking of companies that are up more than 550 percent in a year.

Stu leans over his desk to read the current price off his screen. "Down 3¾." The toy ball floats mindlessly up into the air as Stu goes back to his tossing. Up down, up down. He glances at the television screen, where Jerry is watching a report on a communications company.

"Peter Allmen owns a ton of that. He owns a ton of all these little junk $2 stocks," Stu says, referring to one of Delaware's senior executives. "And he has a ton of money—like $100 million. If you had that much money, why wouldn't you buy Cisco or Dell?"

"If I had that much money, I wouldn't be here," Vinny fires back.

"What's the matter? Don't you like our company?" Jerry asks.

"I do. But not *that* much. I'd be golfing in the Caribbean."

"Yeah? Maybe I oughta try that."

Now the executive face bouncing across the CNBC screen is talking about selling some of his shares. Insider selling always gets

Jerry's attention, "Yeah, it'll be interesting to see the numbers coming out on these executives cashing out their options. . . ."

"Yeah, they had this CEO on CNBC yesterday. His options were supposed to expire in July—he had, like, 2 million at $4. The stock was at $2 back in July but they extended the options to December 31. Last week, they announced an Internet site. The shares went from $2 to $48. So, he cashed in a bunch of his options."

They all shake their heads and look back up at the screen.

"I wish Lincoln would change its name to Lincoln.com," Stu says. If an Internet site can give a 2,300 percent boost in just a few days, then surely adding dot-com to Delaware's parent company would add at least a few points to the stock.

"Yeah. Why don't you put that one in the suggestion box," Jerry smiles.

* * *

By 12:45, some of the larger holdings in the group's funds have started to turn.

"Go baby! Whew." Marshall announces to no one in particular from behind his desk.

By 1:15, the confidence has changed from "Will stocks end positive?" to "How positive?"

"Sweet," Marshall narrates.

Jerry watches the letters and numbers blinking on his screen. As the minutes tick by, the pace of that blinking and the jumping stock prices quickens. The game of marking up stocks has officially begun, and Jerry and the group will be interested spectators for the next three hours.

The practice is a little like the seemingly inordinate number of police ticketing speeders on the last day of the month, just to make a quota. In the stock market, it's called "marking up your portfolio." Managers want the stocks they already own to close the day at the highest price they possibly can. It's the last day of the year, and all of those closing prices at 4:00 will go into calculating the most important number of the year: performance as of December 31. It leads many on Wall Street to think, "If we can juice it a little, why not?"

So, if a stock is trading around $50 all day, and no one seems to be that interested, a manager might go in and place an order—or two, or three. Sure, I'd like to buy some of that stock (I know it's a great company because I already own 2 million shares). Yeah, I'd like to buy 300 more shares, and, you know what, I'll pay you $55 apiece. Within seconds, the trade can be made, a red ticker on the screen turns to green, and the $50 jumps to $55. It's a great deal for the seller—a $5 profit per share, a quick $1,500 on an easy trade. For a fund manager just looking for a little boost before the closing bell, that buy order not only adds another 300 shares to the portfolio, it also improves the original 2 million shares by $5 apiece. Or $10 million.

The game of marking up stocks and marking up portfolios will only become more heated as the hours tick by. As more managers step in with orders to buy at higher prices, other managers of hedge funds—those who want to bet that a stock will go down—will come in with their sell orders, hoping to make the stocks close down for the day. In the very last minutes of the year, the stock market is little different from the schoolyard game of alternating grips on a baseball bat with an opponent, to see who has the last grasp when there is no wood left. In the market, the hands are changed to orders changing hands, and at four o'clock one player will be holding the last order. Time will be up. The game will be over.

* * *

"Working today is a waste of electricity," says Lea as she sits at her desk outside Marshall's office.

By 2:00 in the afternoon, Jerry has taken only three calls—from the three salesmen whom he speaks with almost every day, whether he is in the office or not. There are no meetings, and the fax machines sit largely idle. Marshall and Steve are sitting in John's office with their feet up on his desk. Jerry sits in his office next door, watching his screen, almost casually. He seems to be putting more effort into swirling the ice cubes around in his paper cup before shaking one into his mouth. With the cube in his mouth, he looks back absently at the screen to see if anything has changed since the last time he looked. Jeff strolls into Jerry's office to ask about any New Year's Eve plans. The office is in slow motion, like that last half-day of school—just killing time until grades are posted.

With the fate of his 1998 just 90 minutes away, Jerry pages through an inch-thick research report from Goldman Sachs, touting its own "Top Picks for 1999." He alternates turning the pages with entering the tickers on his keyboard and inspecting the stocks for himself. "Millennium Pharmaceuticals. Twelve-month price target, $25." He laughs to himself as he leans in closer to his screen. Today, on the last day of 1998, the stock trades at $26 a share, already a dollar above the goal the firm has set for the stock for all of next year. With nothing better to do, he picks up his phone to call the research analyst behind this prescient—if conservative—call.

Ribbing aside, Jerry moves on to discuss the market and performance. "Pretty good. Not too bad. We made it all in the last quarter. We were up, then we lost it all, then we got it all back at the end of the year. . . . Yeah, we could've taken the first nine months off, or worked the first six months and then gone on vacation for the rest of the year." Then it's back to the firm's list of best investment ideas for 1999. "eBay? Yeah, when they were in here, I heard that the largest portion of their business was Beanie Babies. I had a hard time seeing it go anywhere. It used to be that a stock was up a half-a-point or a point and it was a good day."

Indeed, eBay has gone somewhere—from $18 to $252, up 1,300 percent in the three months since its IPO in September. But Jerry opted to hold the shares for only two days, only a 150 percent climb. He couldn't say he really believed in it, or that he trusted it. He just didn't buy it. Now it seemed, everyone was buying it.

"I'm having a conniption here." Marshall announces his arrival in Jerry's office before he realizes Jerry is on the telephone. He stands just inside the door until Jerry is off the phone. "Staples is acting like dog. . . ." He stumbles, likely deciding whether the moment calls for a quick, common expletive or a more original, pause-causing phrase from the stock of expressions he imported with him from Kentucky.

"Somebody's shorting the stock." Jerry examines his screen.
"I know."

"Down two." Jerry barely raises his gaze to glimpse Marshall's reaction.

"Two percent or two dollars?"

"Down three."

Marshall stands a moment in silence. "You are full of crap!" he says loudly and then laughs that Jerry has gotten him again. "It's down a buck and I can guarantee it's not gonna be down at the end of the day."

"I think we got enough fire power in there." It's the boss's way of saying, without sounding like the boss, "We own enough already. Don't be stupid and go out there and try to support it."

"I'm gonna buy me some more."

"You can't buy any more."

"I can't buy any more in DelCap, but I can buy more in Trend." The group already owns nearly a 5 percent position of Staples in its DelCap Fund, the most its rules allow. But Marshall wants to buy, so he'll do it for another fund. His reasoning goes: If I've maxed out my Visa, I'll use my Mastercard.

"No, you can't. You can't buy any shares of an $18 billion company in Trend." Those damn rules again. The Trend fund is focused on small-cap companies under $2 billion. At $18 billion, Staples is slightly out of range. So, Staples is over his Mastercard's credit limit. He'll use his American Express.

"Well, then I'm gonna buy some in Aggressive Growth."

In the end, Marshall doesn't actually buy any shares of Staples. But, just maybe, his increased concentration on the issue will somehow convince other investors that they should buy instead of sell, and the stock will go up.

After Marshall leaves, Jerry shakes his head. "It's like pushing a wet noodle. There's nothing you can do to move Staples. There's not exactly 'hot' money in that stock." He looks back at his screen. "Citrix! I knew there was some hot money in that one. Up $4."

* * *

The end of the year is just over an hour away. The Dow Jones Industrial Average is down 85 points, the Nasdaq is up 11. Jerry's billions are bouncing around somewhere in between, and he is getting restless waiting for the bouncing to finally stop—for the year to end, the scores to be posted, the banners hung, and yes, the checks to be paid. While he watches over his shareholders' $2 billion on the screen, the superviser of Delaware's administrative assistants steps in to see Jerry. "I just wanted to check and see what time the girls could leave? Maybe 4:15 or 4:30?"

Jerry looks up. He simply stares at this petite woman, speaking in low tones so as not to let "the girls" sitting at the desks in the hallway hear of her generous offer of a half-hour early dismissal before the boss approves it. It takes him a moment to make the leap from his $22.4 million position in a networking software company to this new line of questioning. She wants and expects a reply.

"How about 4:00?" Geri and Lea would love to get home to their families early on New Year's Eve, and Jerry figures that five professional money managers can handle a few phone calls without "the girls." "How about now?"

Jerry listens intently as the woman explains, that, well, goodness no, she has to keep the girls until at least 4:00, and no other departments are letting assistants go until 4:15. Let's be generous but not frivolous.

As she leaves, he shakes his head and lets out a quiet snort of disbelief. It is an alternative response to his oft-used lament, "Donald Trump doesn't have to deal with this."

He goes back to his methodical clicking of the mouse and tapping of the keys. There are no calls to make or receive. Just watching and waiting for the bell to ring. For the boss—in this case, the market—to say, "You fought the good fight, you can go home now, boys." Over the rhythmic click and pause, Jerry can hear the banter bouncing between John and Marshall's offices.

"Down three-sixteenths."

"I called my wife. She said, 'Can't you come home early tonight?' I said, 'No, I'll probably be home late tonight. I've got to see how we did.'"

"Down one-sixteenth."

"There are only two reds on that whole screen. See—they knocked it down all day. Now look—one hundred, one hundred, one hundred."

"There it is. Up a quarter."

"Come on, baby. Come to papa."

Jerry shakes his head and laughs as the numbers on his screen continue to change. "It's amazing what a little greed'll do to a person."

"Fore Systems. Go baby."

Jerry takes the cue and looks up the stock himself. "Fore Systems, up $1^{17}/_{32}$."

On the other side of Jerry's office, Jeff stares at his screen. Until now, he has been an absent player in John and Marshall's duet. He slaps his hands together in satisfaction. Marshall scurries in, wearing no shoes. "Fore Systems," he announces, and then turns to hurry the twelve paces back to his own office. Jeff slaps his hands together again.

By 3:30, the dance of numbers and colors on Jerry's screen has advanced from a fluid waltz to the jitterbug. As the minutes tick down to 4:00, the breakdance seems the movement of choice. Many of the stocks that had been red all day are now trading up—and turning green.

The section of the screen where most of Jerry's Aggressive Growth Fund and Internet stocks are listed has the most persistent sprinkling of red. They are, of course, the stocks that investors—or at least traders—have debated most vociferously: Should they go up or down? They are the stocks that can move the farthest the fastest, changing the score of that debate with nearly every trade. Those who own the stocks obviously want them to go up, and those who are short the stocks want them to come down. Both sides are backed by a striking amount of conviction. But today, in the last minutes of the trading year, money counts for a lot more than conviction.

"Network Solutions. Up 8." Those who own it have it over those who are short as the clock ticks down to the last six minutes of the year. "Oh. Network Solutions. Up 11." It is of course a given, by the fact that Jerry is announcing these minute-by-minute improvements in the stock, that he is an owner. With victory nearly assured in this camp, Jerry moves on to closer contests elsewhere.

"Oh, it's a battle with the shorts over AOL."

The rest of the growth team has gone upstairs to watch the final five minutes of the year from the post of the trading desk. The Times Square ball that will be dropped eight hours later means nothing to this team. Four o'clock Eastern Standard Time means everything, and they intend to be standing on the sidelines ready to rush the field at the final buzzer.

Jerry, like a taciturn owner, stays in his office one floor below while the numbers change continuously on his screen. He hardly needs to use the mouse or his keyboard anymore. He is not looking for any one price or stock in particular. Each of the individual price-ticks of every single stock, and all of the trades, moves, ideas, and convictions Jerry has made or had over the last twelve months, are all blending into this final screen in the last minutes of the year. With all of the stocks he owns listed across the screen, and each of the major indexes that contain every tradable stock running down the first column, he can see it all. It is Jerry's entire year and the U.S. stock market metamorphosed into a single 17-inch computer screen plugged into an ordinary wall outlet.

Upstairs, Stu and Vinny man their trading posts while Marshall, Jeff, John, and George, another Delaware fund manager, stand or sit on the window sill shelf behind the trading desk. The television hanging from the ceiling in the corner shows CNBC's live coverage from the floor of the New York Stock Exchange. The Delaware growth team may have made it onto the sidelines for the final minutes; CNBC is actually on the field. A larger-than-usual countdown clock is shown in the corner of the screen, announcing to any viewers who may be brain-dead: "This is important."

The CNBC reporter is yelling into the microphone in order to be heard over the runners and specialists trading stocks at the Stock Exchange. Those in the crowd assembled around Stu and Vinny have raised their voices alongside the television's fever pitch. The most activity at the Delaware trading desk is the managers' reaching into one of the Christmas gift tins another trading desk sent over. Pretzel knots, twists, and nubs for everyone. Courtesy of PaineWebber. There are two minutes left in the year. Steve comes up to join the spectators, and even Geri makes a last appearance to deliver the official order tickets for the trades the growth group made throughout the final hours.

The television counts down the last ten seconds of the year with the numbers flashing large across the screen. George rings a bell that hangs from the ceiling in the corner of Delaware's trading room. CNBC's cameras have zoomed in on the chairman of the New York Stock Exchange ringing the bell from the balcony. It has tolled for the 1998 stock market.

Minutes later, Jerry exclaims his wonder at it all. "I don't believe it. American Online was down 3 at four o'clock. It prints after the close, up 2⁹/₁₆." So many trades were made in AOL in the last few minutes of the day that workers at the New York Stock Exchange are still entering those late trades into their system—making each successive "final" price less final.

Marshall and the others are all back in their offices trying to calculate the preliminary numbers. They want at least the exit polls before the final count is in.

"Did you see AOL now?" Jeff comes in to ask Jerry at 4:15.

"Up twelve." Jerry pushes his chair back from his desk and thrusts his arm into the air à la Tiger Woods after sinking a twenty-six-foot putt . . . uphill. "It's a hell of a business, isn't it? Beats pouring concrete in Sartell, Minnesota," he says to Jeff, and perhaps as a reminder to himself that it is because of just one conversation on a barstool that he is perched atop $2 billion of aggressive growth investments instead of working a job in construction.

"Fundamental research wins." Jeff says, drawing the conversation back to something he is more familiar with—Internet companies that go from $144 to $159 in a few minutes.

"Yeah, you gotta find one stock that everyone else wants to own. Now." Jerry laughs and looks back at his screen. He shakes his head in amazement. If the stock were up $3 or $4 for the day, that would be one thing—his investment acumen or his foresight into industry trends. But, to jump $15 in the last few minutes—well, that was something else altogether, pure luck, and Jerry wasn't ashamed to admit it, if only to himself. For the next 20 minutes, he would spontaneously shake his head and laugh quietly. He was all but expecting Glenda, the Good Witch, to arrive and tap his computer keyboard three times with her glittering wand while she joined him for a good laugh on the market.

At the end of the day, after the market closes, Jerry pauses to wax lyrical on his profession. "You move some over here, you add some here," he says and moves his open hands in the air, clearly liking where he's going with the metaphor. "You take away over here, shuffle it around. It's like painting a picture." He nods his head in contentment.

For this year, the painting is done and the brushes are put away. Now it is time to wait for the judges to inspect the picture. To see if Jerry moved the right things around, if he shuffled and added in the right direction. It is up to Jerry's bosses, and services like Morningstar, to decide whether his work will get the blue ribbon, the big bonus, or the five stars.

"Phew. I don't know if it was enough to keep us in the money: 2.55. I think that's enough." Marshall is in, the first to finish the preliminary calculations.

"What was it?" John appears in the doorway.

"2.55."

"DelCap? Wow, that's good."

"It might not be enough."

"Mid cap is up over 3," Jerry says, adding fact to Marshall's assertion that the fund may not have beaten the competition, but perhaps it has even fallen behind.

"Wow." It is possible that the group may have worked the entire year managing as much as $790 million in the DelCap Fund, only to slip into the bottom half of the competition on the last day. The difference between getting paid, or not, for a whole year's work on a fund could be hundredths of a point. The difference between clipping your fingernails or not. As Olympian Peter Vidmar told the crowd two weeks ago, "A 9.4 is not gonna get you there. A 9.4 is gonna make you one of the crowd."

＊ ＊ ＊

Six minutes after the official close of the stock market, Jerry checks his screen again. "American Online. Looks like it's 154 now."

"I wanna see my wife, but I wanna see what happened." He knows who won the game, but does a true fan leave late in the fourth quarter just to beat the parking-lot traffic? He picks up the dark brown suede leather Nautica jacket his wife bought him when they lived in New York and goes back to his desk. He sits in front of his computer screen. Maybe he can watch just a little longer.

Just after 4:30, his salesman Jon stops by to make a last visit of the year. They talk over results, and the salesman laughs that Jerry can't seem to figure out the closing price of one of his largest holdings. Maybe $2 billion in assets and one of the top growth performances of the entire year aren't enough to separate Jerry from the average investors with 401(k) plans and a few mutual funds and far more information than they know what to do with. The salesman gives Jerry three courtesy tickets for Disney's show, *Little Mermaid on Ice*, and takes his leave.

As Jerry makes his way down the hallway to head home, he sees John at his desk and figures he should say something. The team has worked hard, the final bell has rung—surely the occasion calls for some words. Jerry leans his head into John's office, "John, Happy New Year. Looks like we made a couple of bucks." With that, he is off to the elevator bank and another Thursday evening commute home. For today, and for this year, the climb is over. Jerry and his group can stand still, survey the competition, and admire their view on the last day of the year. And in three days, or 89½ hours, it will start all over. They will be standing at the bottom with thousands of other mutual funds. And they will have zeros next to their names.

＊ ＊ ＊

Standing in the hallway, Marshall announces to no one in particular. "I wanna see the competition."

"Half-an-hour 'til they post the numbers, and I can catch my train," John offers as he steps out of his office.

Jeff makes it a trio, "Should we have a few beers before we look at the numbers?"

"Oh man, I shoulda brought some in."

"We could get some." This is a group who knows a lot about buying things. A lot about supply and demand.

At 4:48, just twelve minutes before the final scores are posted, John and Jeff are back, toting a brown paper bag holding three 40-ounce bottles of Bud Light. As the only three members of the growth group left in the office, they clink their opened bottles and rise to match Jerry's eloquence on such occasions, "Cheers."

"Mike Garrison's up 99 beeps." Marshall offers up the performance of a competitor to the fraternal drinking atmosphere.

"Today?"

"Ninety-nine beeps today. He's up 7.83 for the year."

"He's a wuss."

"He sucks."

Having fully harmonized their banter to the 40-ounce bottles in their hands, they walk into Jerry's office and settle themselves for the wait. Marshall and Jeff sit down at the conference table and position their chairs so that they face Jerry's picture window looking out onto West Philadelphia.

"Beer and chocolate. My favorite combination," Marshall says as he spots the reflection in the window of John entering the office carrying one of the last remaining Christmas goody boxes from any number of brokers, salespeople, companies, or analysts.

John takes a chocolate and sets the box in the center of the table. He heads over to sit at Jerry's desk in front of the computer screen. For all the others, he will be on watch.

When the mutual fund performance numbers are posted on the screen, they will show that the DelCap Fund was up 2.55 percent for the day, enough to move the fund to the forty-eighth spot for the year. The Trend Fund closed the year up 14 percent and twenty-sixth out of 100 funds. Jerry and his team have locked in the bonus for every fund they run.

The Aggressive Growth Fund gained over 36 percent for the year, more than double the return for the Dow, nearly 10 percentage points ahead of the S&P, and just three points behind the Nasdaq. The Fund ranks eleventh in its peer group for the year, and for the year-and-a-half Jerry and the team have managed the Fund, it is number one. Of nearly 3,600 stock mutual funds in existence for more than three years, the Fund is number thirteen. Jerry, the group, and the Fund have bested more than 99.5 percent of the competition for the past three years.

When the Nasdaq Stock Market, the New York Stock Exchange, and every other trading venue tally their orders, America Online will be declared the most successful stock of the day. It is up 4 percent for the day and 586 percent for the year. The stock is the Aggressive Growth Fund's largest position, with 38,000 shares on the last day of the year. This once, Jerry got what he wanted. He was exactly right—in exactly the right stock at exactly the right time.

When Morningstar runs its calculations and analysis of over 10,000 funds at the end of the year, the Delaware Aggressive Growth Fund is anointed with the superlative five stars.

While John, Marshall, and Jeff wait for the magic numbers to appear on the screen, they talk sporadically. Mostly, there is the sound of the computer's central processor unit buzzing and its fan whirring while it calculates, compiles, tallies, ranks, and orders. Someone has won this game of high-risk, high-growth, and high-tech profits, and it is a computer's job to declare the victor. There is more spinning, clicking, and whirring.

Silently, the December sun sets on the stock market of 1998.

EPILOGUE

Four days later, it started all over for Jerry Frey and the growth group. Although their stellar performance numbers didn't carry over from December to January, their momentum, focus, and commitment did. For the full year 1998, the Delaware Aggressive Growth fund was the best-performing fund in the firm, and one of the top stock funds in the country. The firm took notice, the media took notice, and competing money managers took notice.

Jerry was happy with the performance, and others were pleased for him. It was like the time, not long ago, when Jerry returned to his hometown and stopped in to see his buddies gathered in the local bar on a Saturday morning. They were all putting their bets together to call in to a bookie in Wilkes-Barre, and Jerry wanted in on the action. After giving his picks, he inspected the sheet to see who had bet what on whom. Everyone was listed by various nicknames and acronyms. There was A.D., Duke, Moose, and others. "Who's LBMG?" he asked. "Oh, that's you," a friend replied. "Local Boy Makes Good."

It had been his year. Jerry was pleased with himself and his team. Just after the New Year holiday, he walked the eight blocks from his office to Tiffany's Philadelphia showroom and bought his wife the diamond.

The year gave Jerry the opportunity to do whatever he wanted. Calls came in from Chicago, San Francisco, New York, Boston, Philadelphia, and elsewhere. The offers were vast: bring your whole team; come yourself; start your own firm; run our firm; run a firm we start; be my partner; bring your own partners. For months he listened, he ran numbers, and he thought about it. All the while, he kept sitting in front of the computer screen on his desk or across the conference table from executives and enjoying his job.

He had done what he had set out to do. He beat the competition, he made money for his shareholders, he beat the indexes, and he made money for the firm. Delaware approved his revenue-sharing plan, and now the growth group gets credit and cash for the new business it helps bring in. So far, it's brought in a lot. The Aggressive Growth Fund, subsequently renamed Delaware Select Growth Fund, has grown from $147 million at the end of 1998 to $1.15 billion at the end of 1999. The Trend Fund has grown from $596 million to $1.04 billion, and DelCap, from $798 million to $1.01 billion. Delaware's management and shareholders have been so eager for more from the growth group that the firm has started three more mutual funds to be run by Jerry and his team: Delaware Large Cap Growth Fund, Delaware Technology and Innovation Fund, and Delaware American Services Fund.

The funds' performance during 1999 was just as spectacular as 1998—if not more so. Aggressive Growth (Select Growth) was up 78.2 percent, DelCap 64.7 percent, and Trend 60.5 percent for the year, while the Dow gained 25.2 percent, S&P500 21.0 percent, and Nasdaq 85.6 percent. For the year, the funds ranked tenth, twenty-first, and twenty-fifth, respectively, within their peer groups. For the two-and-a-half years since Jerry and the team took over the Aggressive Growth Fund, it was ranked number two. Among all stock funds that have been around for three years, the Fund was in the top one percent. And Morningstar still awarded the fund its highest mark: five stars.

Like the lottery, Jerry wonders if there's one more year out there with his name on it.

7357 4500 0973 8828
12/31/2021